MASARYK'S DEMOCRACY

MASARYK'S DEMOCRACY

A Philosophy of Scientific and
Moral Culture

⋙·⋘

BY W. PRESTON WARREN

CHAPEL HILL

19　41

THE UNIVERSITY OF NORTH CAROLINA PRESS

Copyright, 1941, by
THE UNIVERSITY OF NORTH CAROLINA PRESS

DESIGNED BY STEFAN SALTER

Dedicated to Social Justice and International Stability:
"Security without slavery, freedom without poverty, progress without violence."

—*Geoffrey Crowther*

Introduction

By HERBERT ADOLPHUS MILLER
Chairman of the Masaryk Institute

THERE IS NO WAY that the unusual political accomplishments of President Masaryk can be understood except through a knowledge of his philosophy. Professor Warren has made this knowledge available in English, and has done it so well that Czech students of Masaryk pronounce it excellent.

Since Masaryk was both a philosopher and a statesman, this book is of important value to historians and political scientists, as well as to students of philosophy and ethics.

Masaryk was an idealist who called himself a realist. One time in Washington he said to me: "I have always believed idealism is practical." It was the consistent application of this belief that made the Czechoslovak Republic for twenty years the only place in Central Europe where a free spirit could breathe. Its overthrow does not lessen the eternal validity of the Masaryk faith in truth.

This book makes clear the synthesis of learning, politics, morality and religion in the one statesman who has fulfilled Plato's ideal of the "philosopher-king." The treatment is profound and comprehensive. It presents the explanation of how Masaryk, unknown except to a narrow circle, and from a country to which statesmen were indifferent, could, starting at the age of sixty-four, establish in the world a conviction of the validity both of his character and of his political purposes.

Many years ago I asked Professor Masaryk what had impressed him most about Tolstoy. He replied with the one word "morality." There is one word that characterizes Masaryk: "integrity." This book shows how completely knowledge, experience, philosophy, morality, and faith in truth and goodness were merged into an integrated character.

My first knowledge of Masaryk came through Czechs who had been his students, whom I met in Chicago before the last war. They not only spoke with unstinted enthusiasm about him but, I soon noticed, they also had an outlook and feeling of responsibility that marked them off from others.

The Masaryk Institute, which was founded to promote cultural interchange between the Czechoslovak Republic and the United States, and now feels that its task is doubly important, very heartily sponsors this book by Professor Warren.

Bryn Mawr College

Preface

THE CONTRIBUTORS to this publication are notably numerous. My indebtedness begins with the General Education Board, New York City, through whose auspices I had a first-hand opportunity to build interest in and knowledge of Thomas G. Masaryk, the historic genius of these pages. This statesman, I very early discovered, answered to both a social and a philosophical ideal. In his breadth of concrete, scientifically cultural outlook, in his practicality and his abstract penetration, Masaryk presented in a single, fully integrated personality an amazing capacity for meeting and transforming almost every type of problem. Negatively, Masaryk appeared as a socio-personal symbol who was not in any sense one-sided, not remote from daily life, and not superficial. Positively, Masaryk symptomized an actively creative program for significant living, affording a system of solvents for surmounting both social and personal issues. My discoveries of these facts, and of the growing urgency of re-emphasizing Masaryk's outlook and methods in the mounting world-tangle, are the motives of this volume.

Particular acknowledgement is hereby made to the following English and American publishers for explicit permissions to quote sources which they publish: George Allen and Unwin, Ltd., London, publishers of six major sources quoted herein—sometimes at length; The Macmillan Company, New York, publishers of the American edition of Čapek's *Masaryk on Thought and Life;* Wm. Blackwood and Sons, Ltd., Edinburgh, publishers of Robert Flint's *Philosophy as Scientia Scientarum;* William Heinemann, Ltd., London, publishers of Wickham Steed's *Through Thirty Years;* and Eyre and Spottiswoode, Ltd., London, publishers of Masaryk's *New Europe* and the *Slavonic Review.* To all other authors, translators, and publishers, I make the acknowledgement of specific reference for all quoted, and other, data.

I am likewise indebted to a considerable number of persons who aided in obtaining materials from quite scattered sources. It is not expedient to list all of these here. I desire, none the less, to express my full appreciation to each of those who assisted me in any way in gaining these materials. My especial gratitude is due Dr. Vasil Škrach, President Masaryk's literary secretary. His patient attention to my inquiries and solicitations provided the groundwork of this study.

I wish, finally, to make a quite personal acknowledgement to Mr. Brackett Lewis, Executive Secretary of the Masaryk Institute. Mr. Lewis' suggestions and encouragement, assistance in communicating with persons whom I wished to consult and in a diversity of services—both in Czechoslovakia and in America —have been invaluable in preparing and publishing this work.

W. PRESTON WARREN

Greenville, S. C.
December 10, 1940

Contents

		PAGE
	Introduction by Professor Herbert A. Miller	vii
	Preface	ix
I.	A Review of Masaryk	1
II.	Democracy: Its Philosophy and Practice	32
III.	Sources of Social Effectiveness	63
IV.	Philosophies as Modes of Life	88
V.	The Logical Structure of Culture	112
VI.	Criticism: Its Philosophical Nature and Value	136
VII.	Constructive Realism: A Philosophy of Values	168
VIII.	Humanism: Moral Necessities in Values	189
IX.	Theistic Humanism: Masaryk's Philosophy of Religion	210
X.	Conclusion	227
	Bibliography	239
	Index	244

MASARYK'S DEMOCRACY

Truth Conquers

Pravda Vítězí

Chapter One

A Review of Masaryk

"WHO COULD BE THE PRESIDENT of a United States of Europe?" This question was asked some years ago by Emil Ludwig of that arch-critic Bernard Shaw. To this Shaw replied, "I know of only one man—that is Masaryk."[1] Masaryk had gained influence as the best informed, wisest, and also most courageous statesman of the World War era. His positive program and perspective, and high, selfless sense of justice held out hope for lasting peace.

Masaryk had indeed projected, before Wilson, Smuts, or even Balfour, a whole new Europe on a mutualist foundation. He started out December, 1914, to win the statesmen of the world to the need of reconstructing Europe's political, economic and even cultural order. He won them, furthermore, from sheer nationalisms to a broad, yet fundamental view of the issues of the future peace, paving the way in fact for that Wilsonian system of collaboration which centered in the League of Nations. This may have been abortive as a means to peace. Yet the notion of a mutualistic Europe in which each nation takes account of every other nation, in advancing its own interests, has not by any means been gainsaid. Rather, it has more insistently been shown to be the only possible condition for international stability or progress.

[1] Lev Sychrava, *T. G. Masaryk*, p. 5.

2 Masaryk's Democracy

Such thoughts may seem today to be outmoded. Can men any longer hope to cope with the chaos and the evils of our social ferment on grounds of truth and right? Masaryk insisted that they can, that these are the only actual bases of solution, that issues today are not different from the issues of the world of three decades ago; they are but exaggerated. The primary problem of mankind was then, if more clearly now, ideological: a conflict in men's viewpoints and thereby of their cultures; a conflict notably between aggressive absolutist systems which refused to take account of peoples' basic interests and those other social viewpoints which were universal in their comprehensions—implicitly at least—and clearly mutualistic. The moral welfare of mankind depended on the triumph of these interests and viewpoints. Their moral rightness gave them natural strength which only diabolical intrigue could surmount when coupled with sheer brute force. It is not without significance indeed that Masaryk's death, September, 1937, anteceded Hitlerism's bursting out in violent annexation of Austria, Czechoslovakia, and Poland. Not that Masaryk personally could have blocked the treacherous surging toward the East and West of mechanistic Nazi culture, especially at the age of eighty-seven; but he had gathered around himself the moral conscience of the world, and while he lived there was an enlightened, psychologic moral center for stability in Europe. It has been pointed out, in fact, that Hitler never ventured an attack on Masaryk. What he has done rather is take Masaryk's program for a new Europe and give it an extreme reversion.

Masaryk, in truth, was far more than a personality. He was an historically outstanding philosopher-statesman. As I. A. Bláha noted, "Masaryk conceived his whole personality philosophically."[2] For eighty-seven years he lived and worked for such high principles as honesty in thought; honor, justice and

[2] Jan Herben, Antonín Hartl, I. A. Bláha, *T. G. Masaryk, sa Vie, sa Politique, sa Philosophie*, p. 145.

A Review of Masaryk

statesmanship in human relations; and purity in religion. And these principles, in turn, were not just acquisitions from the air or ether. They grew out of living, and *living* grounded in a scientific philosophy of culture.

The time has come for a review of Masaryk; it has come upon us with compulsion. We had known of, and had honored him as a World War and a post-war statesman, whose high idealism and high courage were ending in eclipse and travesty. The story of his life has been familiar in large outlines and events. Yet his basic principles and conceptions, in so far as they have been known at all, have been considered as sheer sentiments. His concept of democracy has been confused with propagandist World War notions, while his idea of free peoples in a European society of unsubjugated nations has come to be considered as untimed and unrealistic. His motto, *Truth Conquers,* has been taken as a simple watchword or slogan, and its basis in Czech history and a critical philosophy of human relations has been ignored or misunderstood. It is time, indeed, that Masaryk's whole viewpoint and philosophy were known in their totality by at least the democratic world, and that open, constructive diplomacy were given scientific formulation on a soundly philosophic basis; that politics were grounded in a full philosophy of culture. This was the motif of Masaryk. Departures from this standpoint and method not just at Versailles, but by a thousand betrayals of sound thinking and practice—including confusions which have aimed at whitewashing aggressors—are all responsible for our present catastrophes. Our trouble is not merely with the encroachments of inhuman totalitarian systems, violent and disastrous as these are, but in the laxness and blindness of our own cultures which have afforded such systems their great opportunity. This, basically, is where Masaryk can be of great help to those who have the will to a positive outlook and purpose.

Born, 1850, in Hodonín, Moravia, just two years after the

battle for the freeing of the peasants and one year following the abolition of serfdom in Austria; two years after the manifesto of socialism in Germany and scarcely two years after Francis Palacký had cried in opposition to a pan-German council, "If Austria did not exist it would be necessary to create her," Masaryk spanned nearly a century of dramatic social events. And he was plunged from the first into an arena of ferment and conflicts. True, his family status afforded him no royal entree. His father was a coachman with the background of a serf; his mother was a former Austrian household servant. But his mother had resourcefulness and ambition, and her firstborn, Thomas, was vested with a continuously inquiring mind. By twelve, he had completed the *Realschule* and faced four years in which he would somehow have to fill in living before he could obtain a license to teach. His restless mind drove him from three posts in quite quick succession, gained him access to the German Academy in Brno, where in spite of "bread-and-butter" teaching, he launched out on studies of a free, broad, basic, cultural type. A literary, coupled with a philosophic interest, led him to the mastery of German, Latin, Greek, Russian, French, and English languages and literatures. Natural sciences appealed to him likewise, especially physiology, and brought him more directly to philosophy. By sixteen, he decided that he wished to be a philosopher, since as a commoner he could not be admitted to the study of diplomacy. Social motives quite especially governed his approach to and his outlook on philosophy, broadening its reach and importance, and guiding his interest towards a whole philosophy of culture. Plato drew him first, he said, "through his interest in religion, ethics, and politics and his extraordinary combination of theory and practice." In Plato, too, there was "that beautiful and astonishing synthesis of world opinions," stated with the artistry of a poet.[3]

[3] Karel Čapek, *President Masaryk Tells His Story*, p. 105.

A Review of Masaryk

Masaryk's own statement at twenty-five of these early events of his life discloses their personal side with an evolving achievement of wisdom. We include this autobiographic review here, since it has not been published elsewhere in English. "Pindar advises," Masaryk wrote in his *Curriculum Vitae* for the Ph.D. degree (Vienna, 1875), "that at the beginning of an undertaking one should do quite grandiosely, in order to win the favor of his judges on his first impression. Whether I shall succeed by a simple and unpretentious description of a short span of time, I cannot forecast; especially since this task which I now set myself is not wholly simple. What I shall recount of my youth is naturally portrayed in the light of present comprehensions; and much, perhaps quite incidental, has been forced into an artificially inclusive picture. There is missing, in fine, the genetic perspective which is essential for true judging of an individual as a special type and kind of man; though perhaps this very lack may be itself a means to valid judgment. I can, however, only offer the preliminary premises of my life; the conclusion (which time will in the future draw or perhaps some other better judge than I), I can not draw. Cellini rightly demands that an autobiography be written by a man who has reached forty. Will that of a younger person . . . be of any value? Finally: 'To the world belongs what thou thinkest; to thyself only, what thou feelest.'

"Born in a small provincial town of Moravia, March 7, 1850, I enjoyed in early youth a careful training and upbringing by my loving mother to whose devotion I owe everything; the sweet hours of homey affection and peace will always form my happiest memories. The love of my parents and my two brothers, in fact, was often my only, though rich, source of inner satisfaction. At six years of age, I came to the village, Čejkovice, where in the *Trivialklasse* I learned the first rudiments of wisdom. By good fortune, I became the comrade in instruction of the Count's son who enjoyed this privately, whereat also, I made good progress in German . . . With him I read the boys' stories of Nieritz and Schmidt. A detailed history of Bohemia and Hungary stirred me to affection for the past of my fatherland, which I learned to know accurately from a relatively good volume of statistics and a somewhat antiquated atlas. At that time, I invested in a register of all the cities of Austria and possessed myself in musing moments with the invention of a language which was to be equally intelligible to all; the alphabet consisted of numerals. The old knights, of whom I had read a great deal, excited us, my friend and me, to imitation. We each obtained a saddle and a burlesque uniform in which every Sunday, with our older chums as generals, we marched merrily as soldiers. When, in consequence of an accident, this play was forbidden, we entered an abandoned Jesuit convent as 'penitents' and amused ourselves by preaching, reading masses, and other churchly ceremonies.

"At nine, I lost my friend and fared forth once again to school. There, to the great joy of my parents, I became first 'pramiant.' In examination we had for our reading selection 'Uber den Sternen,' and I had to interpret it. The recollection of my recently deceased little sister forced tears copiously to my eyes and I could not continue my statement. The inspector, a Right Reverend Dean, was impressed with the matter. When the examination was over, he requested that my mother come to him and asked if she would not like to have me be school-reader. The outcome was that I went to the *Realschule* in Auspitz. . . .

"In the *Realschule*, since the teaching was in German, I had to learn almost everything by rote, which indeed, has not been without wholesome effect on my memory, as also for the cultivation of speech. In my first year, I already ranked second. During this whole time I maintained relationships with no one and kept myself from the baseness into which my school com-

A Review of Masaryk 7

rades had fallen. The [book on] Physiognomy [4] was my whole entertainment in the strange friendless world.

"After two years, I came back home to 'practice,' i.e., to study music with a school teacher and to instruct children. At that time, one could not be accepted in the course for teachers before his sixteenth year. I would have, therefore, to wait four years. What would remain of my knowledge? About that no one assuredly had troubled. I entered, accordingly, only to make my exit again in two months; I could not reconcile myself to the two squalling brats of the *gnädige Frau* who alternated all day long with '*zu praktizieren.*'

"Time passed on and I fell into a company of indolent ex-students. For a considerable time my thoughts were but centered on theater plays and other pastimes. . . . A certain indefinable shyness which I had acquired in Auspitz kept me remote, however, from the debauches which were the rule with young men at least there and then.

"Whether I would have succumbed without the sudden intervention of an energetic father, I cannot judge. I was, in any case, awakened by my father in the middle of the night, had to dress myself and—to Vienna it was for me. My dear mother went with me and brought me, on the recommendation of an acquaintance, to a locksmith; there I was to work four years, in order to become a journeyman. The commotion of a world-city, my relationships with my new 'comrades' soon became unbearable. My only satisfactions were the bookstores, to which I slipped away during the noon-hour . . . to read and reread the titles of the books and to speculate while at work about their probable contents. In the evenings, I read from my books or studied my *Stielerschen* Atlas, with the object of turning, in the end, to the page where my own homeland was . . . I determined to change my situation. Hopefully, I went to a book dealer, wishing to secure secretarial work or anything

[4] J. K. Lavater, *Physiognomy for Teachers.*

whatever, but I was rudely refused. Perhaps, if I had yielded to my lot, a little matter would not have completely discouraged me. A room-mate stole all of my books and sold them, even the *Physiognomy*. From that moment, I had no peace of mind. I saw clearly that just as for my mind I must have something, so for my emotions I also needed something. I did not reflect long but came home immediately. My father was beside himself over this disgrace which I, by this second 'change,' had brought upon him. On the advice of an expert barber, he gave me to the teaching of a master-smith to learn horse-shoeing, in order that I might in due time be admitted into the Institute of animal husbandry. I kept this secret for six months. Suffice it . . . that I was frequently boxed on the ears by the servants over whom my father had the supervision, when I drove in a hoof-nail poorly; therewith, I could feel what it means to be a 'runaway' student. The moral, 'shoemaker stick to your last,' both I and my father had to hear only too often from the envious and malicious rabble.

"One autumn morning, I brought as usual two buckets of water from the nearby spring. As I neared the smithy, I noticed that a man was looking at me intently; and as I looked at him, I recognized my piano teacher from the *Realschule*. Mechanically, the pails dropped from my hand; I went with bowed head away into the neighboring hills, to think over my lot . . .

"To be brief, I simply state that in a few days I was appointed assistant to the father of my former piano teacher; and that I, then, entered with the greatest zeal on my renewed calling—while in my earlier development I clearly saw the handwork of the Lord, who seemed to lead me by most varied ways toward an initially set goal." [5]

Such sense of happy destiny did not, however, last for long. Masaryk's was no ideal assistantship. He helped as best he

[5] Arthur Werner, *Th. G. Masaryk: Bild seines Lebens*, pp. 125-130.

could in teaching boys who were older than himself, received his room as his direct compensation, and "was allowed to pick up such scraps of information as fell in his way."[6] He obtained, besides, through Father Francis of Čejkovice, the post of organist in church and thereby gained a pittance toward the costs of living. The necessity of kissing hands both of the *alten Gnädigen* and the *jungen Fräulein* soon became an ordeal, and all in all, again his searching mind found itself in general dissatisfaction "in the daily repetition of instruction on one and the same thing. . . . I had," he said, "begun to teach natural science, geography, and such. This was forbidden me finally, however, because certain worried mothers had complained to Herr Dean that their children now had to learn such stupid history, 'which no intelligent man could need.' On the whole, however, the peasants were quite devoted to me and a deputation of them honored me with a visit that I might continue to teach much and that Čejkovice may some day know that from my pupils, 'right many corporals for the army were to develop.' . . .

"In the ritual of worship, I became conscious very soon of my lack of Latin. To this, too, there contributed another circumstance. In the half-ruined Jesuit library to which I had access, I found among other books a catechism from the 17th Century which spurred me to industry in study. There, in the thick-stomached volumes, were many teachings of the ancient philosophers scattered throughout; and since these were presented in the original, naturally I could not understand them. I could not at all read Greek. This disturbed me, and I conceived the possibility of learning the language. Confidently, I went to Father Satora, the chaplain of the place, who found my ambition very praiseworthy and readily promised me his help. Therewith he gave me an old lexicon which from that hour I learned by rote, in order then to trace about with

[6] C. J. C. Street, *President Masaryk*, p. 26.

vocable treasures in Latin citations and books. The aforesaid chaplain was not, however, an especially good person to speak to the school teacher, who was the representative of the German spiritual, yet national, party. I do not to this hour know one from the other. Through long conversation, however, I was won to the 'national' standpoint, in order in that same measure to be steeped in the favor of my chief.[7] In my enthusiasm, however, I had scant appreciation for his; and when I conceived the plan, in spite of his advanced age, I seized the first opportunity to be done with the Gymnasium and tendered my thanks to the schoolmaster. His wishes he sent with me on my way.

"I studied Latin, therefore, reported myself as a private student in Straschnitz, and took the examination with signal success. During that time, I concerned myself much with theological moot-questions and was particularly eager to devote myself to religious service. Father Satora did not lose this opportunity to make his protegé into a complete zealot, who even succeeded in converting a protestant, Mrs. Beneš of Čejkovice —originally from Mainz—to the Catholic faith. Since that time there has remained with me a certain sense of connection with the faith of my childhood and youth and a certain consciousness of cleavage with the stormy protestants and catholic pseudo-apostles. On this account, even the writings of Comte were to me later especially comforting, though we must not now anticipate.

"In vacation I went 'travelling' in the fashion of poor students, took my six gulden and went with my good mother to Brno to enroll. I entered the second class of the German *Gymnasium* with a cash total of seventy kreutzers in my pocket, which had

[7] Masaryk here inserted a note that through the study of Roman history and culture his view of "nationality" was modified so that, "I now share Cicero's views and agree substantially with Mill who in his *Logic*, Book VI, Ch. 10, states his position."

been left after I had procured the necessary books and other essentials. The first half-year I lived in inexpressible misery. At the end of that semester I was first in my class, and from that moment it went well with me, sometimes very well. On the recommendation of my mathematics professor, I went to the home of the chief of police in Brno, Le Monnier. To this noble man I owe the subsequent forming of my character. He was imbued with an inner love of sciences, and under his kind guidance my free time—and nearly all of my time was free—was devoted to extra-curricular studies. Little by little I made my way into the German classical writers of whom very soon Lessing was my favorite. Later, I passed on to the scientific authors. Humboldt, the older and the younger, gave me much wherewith to engross myself; and the natural sciences generally were my preferred studies.

"At that time I learned French, and busied myself, too, with study of the Slav languages. By translating from both French and Russian, I earned a little money with which to buy the most necessary books. In wholly free time, I wrote poetry, and especially in school during the teaching. I had, on one hand, the misfortune to have really poor teachers with the single exception of Father Mathias Procházka, from whose saintly procedure I gained a true picture of a good teacher. Our middle schools, unfortunately, do not amount to much; this means that the teachers are poor-thinking, bread-and-butter schoolmasters. I could not suppress my aversion to their methods and had accordingly much to endure. I was, therefore, 'gone with my hat' and learning diligently Greek and Latin grammar . . . The school soon became exceedingly taxing to me. Still I had to endure it as a means to my goal; so I threw myself all the more industriously into my favorite subjects. From interest in natural sciences I gradually came to philosophy. The then burning issue of Darwinism brought me right into the midst of the philosophical bustle. Without chart, without rudder, I sailed about on the open sea of meanings.

"In the year 1866 I joined several hotheads who were drawn into the battle for the Fatherland. In the dressing-station in Pressburg (Bratislava), I lay beside my friend Fojtik, the only comrade to whom I could then give my confidence. We talked all day about our futures. He decided to be a priest; I wished to become a philosopher—my friend is a priest. . . .

"In 1869 I went with my benefactor, who had in the meantime been transferred to Vienna where he then became director, and soon afterwards president, of the police. In Vienna, I continued my grammar-school studies and steeped myself still more in philosophical work. The university library I visited daily. I had then gone through the writings even of Lavater, Reichenbach, and many a dizzy mystic. The logic and psychology of the schools satisfied me not in the least. My favorite source was then a Bohemian translation of Lange's history of materialism, which I supplied with notes expressing my own unmeasured views. I then also read most of the Greek and Latin classicists in complete editions, whereas previously I could only use abridged school issues.

"Then, too, I learned English, since I rightly perceived that as a budding philosopher I could not do without the English master-writings.

"At the University I had myself enrolled in the Philological Department of the Philosophical Faculty, after my plan had failed whereby I hoped to be admitted to the Oriental Academy. I always wanted to be something other than a teacher: to be able freely, yet not really as a Faust, to philosophize. I had, however, to submit myself.

"In 1873, I lost by death my deeply loved brother. Since that time I have put my faith entirely in philosophy, sought in it consolation—and found it. The promise which I once made to myself will, with the help of God, be fulfilled. With the motto,

A Review of Masaryk 13

'nothing is great which is not true',[8] I shall go on through life, and on my way what can be bettered shall, within the limits of my strength, be improved."

There then follows a summary of Masaryk's extensive studies in language, literature, science, and philosophy, with attention above all to the greatest ancients. "The natural sciences," none the less, he added in conclusion, "and especially physiology, will find in me an industrious student."[9]

In a later *Curriculum Vitae* for habilitation, 1877, Masaryk added that his life-course led him more and more to sociology. "From 1873," he wrote, "I gave myself exclusively to philosophy, after I had assimilated the essential knowledge of the languages.... Zimmerman, Brentano, Brücke, Meynart, Langer, Stefan, Menger, Conze, von Eitelberger were my lecturers in Vienna. In 1876-1877, I was at the University in Leipzig. I there heard Drobisch, Zöllner, Wundt, Rascher, Curtius, Schuster, Ziller, and the theologians: Luthardt, Kanis, Fricke.... Concerning my philosophical tendency, I started from Plato and proceeded via Aristotle in the new empirical direction. Together with Plato and Aristotle, Hume, Comte, Mill were my teachers. This is all that I have to relate. Were I to speak still further, I would indeed make my wishes for the future. They form the conclusion to the premises of an early life full in experience, struggle, and work.[10]

The "conclusion" to these "premises" was fuller even than its antecedent life and work. Thirty-two years as a teacher of philosophy, almost all of which he spent in Prague. Editor of a

---

[8] This early motto gave place later to the more inclusive and still more positive *Truth Conquers* or *Truth Will Prevail*, derived from George of Podebrady, King of Bohemia, 1458-71, and first modern proponent of a European League of Nations. *Truth Conquers* became not merely Masaryk's motto but also that of his nation.

[9] Werner, *Th. G. Masaryk: Bild seines Lebens*, pp. 130-138.

[10] *Ibid.*, p. 140.

number of journals. Author of eighty-four books and brochures, including major philosophic studies, together with a thousand articles! Member of parliament, 1891–1893 and 1907–1914! Going abroad at the age of sixty-four to head the Czechoslovak program for independence and to uphold and clarify the cause of all small Central European nations in the World War crisis. Raising an army of Czechs and Slovaks abroad of over 100,000, and coming home, December 1918, as President of his country! Saying after four war years in which he scarcely slept well five consecutive nights, "Our work has just begun." [11] President of Czechoslovakia 1918–1936! Scant wonder he could say when in his eighties, "I am grateful to Providence for the fullness of my life." [12]

Yet the currents of his life did not flow smoothly or readily. Eighty-seven years against the current tells the actual story of his effort. Battles with the politicians over facts of Czech history! Battles with the laymen over superstitions of Jewish ritual murder! Battles with the clergy over forthright and informed religion! Battles with the Austrian diplomats over international intrigue! Battles with his own Czech leaders! None of these he sought himself. But he had the courage of his clear informed convictions, and took his stand upon two kindred mottoes. One of these he gained from Francis Bacon: "Knowledge is power." Around this he early organized a society. The other came from Huss and more directly, King George of Podebrady: "Truth Conquers." This was activistic in its implications, and fitted in with Masaryk's own active, yet philosophic temper. While other thinkers might not concern themselves particularly about the social violations of their sense of values, Masaryk was "up and doing with a heart for any fate." As soon as he was called upon, he lent his knowledge and his energies to an urgent cause.

[11] F. X. Šalda, *Masaryk, Staatsmann und Denker*, p. 21.
[12] Čapek, *op. cit.*, p. 177.

A Review of Masaryk

Despite his depth of philosophic interest and outlook, which led him into ethics, metaphysics, theology, theory of knowledge, and the philosophy of history, Masaryk, in fact, could no more avoid practical and political problems than he could escape philosophy and scientifically cultural scholarship. His whole conception of men's culture led him of necessity to politics. The very interests of mankind required the actualizing of sound social and cultural ideas, and politics performed a crucial role in organizing and adjusting men's relationships and interests. To politics indeed belonged the task of governing life in the best interests of all, and both science and philosophy were essential to its guidance. Every moral or social philosopher must accordingly take note of politics and be in fact a politician of a sanely cultural type.

Scarcely, therefore, had Masaryk become established as Professor of Philosophy in 1882 at the University of Prague, than he undertook to found the *Athenaeum*, a journal committed to the scientifically cultural education of the Czechs. Almost at once he was drawn into "the Battle of the Manuscripts." A philologist, Gebauer, asked Masaryk's permission to publish in the *Athenaeum* an exposé of the fabrication of two documents which had been "discovered" early in the nineteenth century, ostensibly proving the high culture of the Czech people in the Dark Ages, when their later German enemies wandered primitively through the woods of Europe.[18] The battle immediately

[18] Two manuscripts had, in fact, appeared, in 1817, in the church at Dvora Králova and castle of Hora Zelená respectively. These documents purported to be folklore of the thirteenth century, ascribing a notable level of culture to the Czechs of the seventh and ninth centuries, A.D. These "manuscripts" were discounted by the Czech authority Dobrovský with the discovery by the same man of the second document. Yet after Dobrovský's death, 1829, they were generally accepted. At different times, however, from 1855, their authenticity was thrown repeatedly in doubt, and in 1884 Masaryk joined with the philologist Gebauer in pushing the issue of the "genuiness" of these

was on. The politicians and their legions took the view that facts and scholarship be d——d; that the "Manuscripts" were instruments of action; that their truth or authenticity was irrelevant to issues of group consciousness and purpose. Masaryk replied that group life could not long stand when founded on a lie. This lie, furthermore, obscured the actual genius of Czech history and frustrated solidarity based on honest faith and sociological facts and principles. It was the duty of the recently re-established Czech University of Prague to discover and disclose the truth.

Masaryk, obviously, was no compartmentalist professor. He never wished to be a professor at all, he commonly maintained. He wished to be free to study and grow and to apply his scientifically philosophical findings to the affairs of his people and Europe. Yet the University and his professorship were the media of his approach to this work, and academic interests could not for him be severed from the wider interests of life. Nor could the practical interests of men be satisfactorily effected without agencies of sound culture. A university and community were interacting social groupings, and the university had a fundamentally social function which was no less deeply cultural because so definitely social.

Philosophy, moreover, was no purely theoretic matter. It had practical potentialities and outreaches. All philosophies, in fact, were modes of living as well as theories of reality, purporting to be valid; and he who would divorce philosophy from any of the aspects or levels of life, to that degree ignored essential philosophic data. Not that there was no value in or meaning to the purely theoretic phases of philosophy, but that philoso-

---

documents to a conclusive climax. Sentiment ran high, but the manuscripts were studied as to parchment, ink, anachronisms, sociological implications, and poetic merit. From every angle they were found to be forgeries of the late eighteenth or early nineteenth century, resultants of the mythological chauvinism of that period.

A Review of Masaryk 17

phies must square by implication and by human function with the facts and practicalities of daily life. And not that practicality was to be conceived in any mere immediacy of direct consequences; it spelled outcome over centuries of history—for nations past, present, and future. The net results in all human life were tests of real effectiveness.

The import of this view will be developed later. We cite it here to show that Masaryk's philosophic thinking led him of itself to politics, and that his professionally academic approach to these issues provided the ground for his studied conception of the goals and the methods of sound politics and culture.

It was his students, actually, who brought him into direct politics. He had taught them sociology and ethics, and related these concretely to the circumstances within which they lived. His students, therefore, set him in their vanguard not only as the teacher of a sane, penetrating, sound set of socio-political conceptions and methods, but as the actual leader of their post-university social programs.

They elected him to parliament in 1891, as a Realist in the Young Czech, quasi-liberal party.[14] His method of campaign-

[14] Masaryk's use of the term "realist" has a quite different meaning from that commonly accepted. For an adequate view of its meaning one must read several sections below (cf. index). It may be said, in brief, however, that by realism Masaryk meant especially moral realism but more accurately full realism, which takes account of ideals and principles along with concrete actualities of the moment. As H. Wickham Steed has written, Masaryk "taught that unlike the German notion of 'Realpolitik,' realism in politics consists not of a cynical disregard of principles but of a scrupulous reckoning with facts, moral and material; that honesty is not only the best policy but the only safe guide in public as in private life; and that character, not astuteness or trickery, is the first requisite in a statesman. Yet, in Masaryk's conception of 'realism,' honesty means more than ingenuousness; the honest man is, indeed, without guile, but is neither a simpleton nor a fool.

"Had Masaryk never been given the chance to put his theories to the proof, he might still be thought an unpractical moralist, an ethical dreamer, who would be no match for politicians skilled in the art of

ing has been described as follows: He called his meetings in cafes. On his first night, he read all evening from the New Testament, to the discomfiture of the members of the clerical party who made it their ecclesiastical business to oppose Old Czechs (conservatives) and Young Czechs alike. The next night, when this opposition commonly failed to appear, he addressed himself to economic and to social questions with an insistence on the constructive functions of politics.

His first impression when he arrived in parliament, he wrote, could be summed up in one word: *mill.* "When one visits a mill, he is stupified by the uproar of the multitudinous wheels —but one soon discovers that there is nothing to fear. Yet one does not feel [completely] reassured. He has meal on his vestments and face and finds it disagreeable to be so bespattered. Many a time in the Chamber, I studied the tumult; I reassembled the impressions which our popular chamber makes upon me, so agitated yet so little alive.

"No longer do I think just of a mill, but of a bourse and also a theatre.—And when my eyes discern behind the raised benches of the ministers and the president and functionaries of the Chamber, the grave row of ancient statues (one of them in the dress of a mediaeval duke disturbs my tableau), I evoke a church with its altar. This last image, however, is weaker than the others, has less vivacity, inasmuch as it is born of a theory of political science rather than of an impression of my senses. Mill—bourse—theatre—church: it is, how-

---

blackmailing governments, hoodwinking the crowd, and coining catchwords that signify in practice something different from their ostensible meaning. But in the course of his long life, he has proved that a fair fighter, master of his weapons, can be more than a match for the bravo who plays foul. As the leader of a new school of political thought and an advocate of new diplomatic methods, he beat the old school, again and again, on its own ground."—"Thomas G. Masaryk, The Man and the Teacher," *Slavonic Review* (March, 1930), p. 471.

A Review of Masaryk

ever, in this mill, in this bourse, in this theatre, in this church that the people sit and engage in politics."[15]

Masaryk reacted sharply from this unwholesomeness in Austro-Hungarian politics and resigned his mandates after just two years in parliament. The whole extant notion of politics oppressed him, and despite his more than forty years of studied living, he felt too unprepared to deal with such a problem. For seven years, he gave himself to the study of his people's history and to the issues of the organizing of society in their broadest aspects. *The Czech Question* and *The Social Question* were the outcomes of these studies, together with *Havlíček, Ideals of Humanity, The Modern Man and Religion,* and lectures on the national philosophies of England, France, Germany, Poland, and Russia. He returned then to politics with a clear consciousness of his political philosophy and program.

Politics was an issue of each nation's whole living, to be guided by cultural goals and a scientific realism. It was the business of politics to facilitate and to advance the whole nation's interests, by using all valid means of advancement, but most fundamentally by sound performance of small sociocultural tasks. Masaryk's political program, accordingly, was not just a political program in the usual party sense, but a scientifically critical movement toward reinforcing and socializing politics by methods of scientific and moral culture.[16] The concept of "unpolitical politics," which the Czech journalist Havlíček enunciated, became through Masaryk the standpoint of a politically constructive realism: self-sustaining, culturally consolidating, and progressive realism. From this viewpoint, politics could be neither a mere art nor a game, but scientifically elaborated and applied social ethics and philosophy of values. If this was not what politics really was, then this was what it should be—else a fundamentally essential social task was being

[15] *Les Problèmes de la Démocratie*, pp. 49-50.
[16] Čapek, *President Masaryk Tells His Story*, p. 202.

entirely neglected or, worse still, it was being anti-socially performed. The goal of true politics could be no mere momentary practicality or advantage, but the enduring interests of whole groups as individuals and nations. Realistic politics was, or in principle should be, concerned to adjust, facilitate, and advance the interests of all persons and nations. There was no place in national affairs for conscious isolationism. The Czech question Masaryk always conceived as a world problem. "Therefore," he wrote, "I constantly compared our history with that of Austria as a whole and of Europe. The object of all my journalistic writing and of my books was, so to speak, to fit our people into the structure of world-history and world-politics." [17] What, in fact, was "politics in the best sense of the word but the conscious forming of people?" [18] And all interacting factors and forces had to be fully considered.

It was 1900 when Masaryk returned actively to politics, and he was then fifty. And then it was that he founded his own Realist, later called the Progressive, Party. It was 1907 when he was re-elected to Parliament, but then began a series of events which was destined to make him leader of the political conscience of Europe. Offered the Speakership of the House in Vienna, he declined this office in the interests of the causes for which he had to take up and carry on his realistic fight. A famous address on behalf of free science and free moral faith set the tone of his whole efforts.[19] Then came the Zagreb trial in which involuntarily he gained the international arena.

Fifty-three Jugoslavs in Southern Austria-Hungary had been arrested, January, 1909, on trump charges of high treason. The Austrian government in driving to the East had just annexed the Balkan provinces of Bosnia and Herzegovina in violation

[17] *The Making of a State*, p. 320.
[18] Čapek, *op. cit.*, p. 224.
[19] *Freie Wissenschaftliche und Kirchlich gebundene Weltanschauung und Lebensauffassung.*

of the Treaty of Berlin. A pretext was essential, and this was fabricated as a Slav plot in the Austrian Empire. A group of South Slav citizens of Austria-Hungary were charged with secret organizing for treasonable activities. Several of Masaryk's own students were among those arrested. Under the realism of his teaching they had been working for Slav harmony within Austria-Hungary. But that, itself, was a state of affairs on which the government looked askance. Slav harmony meant solidarity of the overwhelming Austro-Hungarian "minorities," making it difficult for the government to maintain its tricky and oppressive absolutism. The government, in consequence, used its opportunity to deal with two problems by one piece of cunning. It charged the *harmonizers* with underhanded attempts to destroy the Empire, and prosecuted them without permitting them any defense. Thus was slain the cause of honest loyalty in the Empire! Thus was certified the need for some type of control in the Balkans!

The whole conduct of their trial was an artless travesty of justice. Evidence was forged from the start, and the judges, themselves, browbeat the accused. If any one of them attempted defense, he was remanded to prison. Next day the trial went on without him. Masaryk who had been drawn to the defence of his students, interpellated uncompromisingly in parliament, demanding that the government intervene to require justice. His "bold stand against the whole tendency of the trial marked him anew as the most publicly spirited man in Austria-Hungary and increased the moral ascendance which he had acquired throughout the Slav world." [20]

Masaryk, furthermore, carried the battle right into the camp of the forgers, catching them almost "red handed." He established the facts "that in February, 1909, when the annexation crisis was at its height, a secretary of the Austro-Hungarian Legation at Belgrade had engaged [a man named] Vasitch

[20] H. Wickham Steed, *Through Thirty Years*, I, 313.

as a 'tutor.' Vasitch's chief work as tutor was to put into good Serbian and carefully to copy out, in big handwriting on paper of large size, 'minutes' of the proceedings of the [supposedly secret society] 'Slovenski Jug' which had originally been fabricated in Croatian. Some of the sheets used were more than a yard long. When ready, they were affixed with drawing pins to the door of a Legation servant's room and reduced to reasonable proportions by photography, the photographs alone being sent to Vienna. Hundreds of 'documents' were produced in this way, and others were directly forged by a secretary of the Austro-Hungarian Legation." It was further shown by Masaryk "that Vasitch had been repeatedly consulted by the presiding judge in the Agram [Zagreb] High Treason Trial and that his forgeries had been known to the Court at Agram. Indeed, Professor Masaryk made it clear that Count Forgach, the Austro-Hungarian minister at Belgrade, if not the Austro-Hungarian Foreign Office itself, had connived at the fabrication of documents on the strength of which fifty-three innocent Austro-Hungarian Serbs would have been condemned to death, and Supilo and the leading members of the Serbo-Croat Coalition shot or hanged as traitors, if war between Austria-Hungary and Serbia had broken out in the spring of 1909." [21]

The episode of Dr. Friedjung followed on the Zagreb trial. Friedjung was the chief historian in Austria. His vindication of the documentary evidence used at Zagreb purported to be tantamount to proof. Given the fabricated data by the Austrian Foreign Office, he published part of it immediately at face value. His ignorance of Serbo-Croat and other Slav languages did not bother him at all. He had his evidence from too high a source, and resented any question of its authenticity. Yet when sued for libel by the Zagreb victims and confronted by Masaryk's discoveries and Vasitch's confession, Friedjung had to admit that he had been employed to perpetrate a gross intrigue.

[21] *Ibid.*, pp. 315-316.

It was then, though not until then, that Masaryk lost faith in Austria-Hungary. All his life he had upheld and worked for the hope that Austria-Hungary could be transformed into a morally just federation of its internal nations. Independence, he had pointed out, will not save a nation. The nation must preserve its independence by moral and by scientific culture.[22] But the "moral baseness" of Austria-Hungary was laid bare "by the diplomatic intrigues during Aehrenthal's chancellorship and by the Zagreb (Agram) and Friedjung trials." Austria "in all its substance, its history, geography, and ethnography," dynasty, and oppressive aristocracy, was "a denial of the modern state and nationality." [23]

Still Masaryk did not weaken his efforts. Charging Count Aehrenthal with complicity in the whole disreputable Zagreb affair—which the latter could but weakly and belatedly deny—Masaryk strove for accord in both internal and external relations. On Aehrenthal's retirement, in 1912, Masaryk undertook to work for rapprochement between Austria and Serbia. His visits to Belgrade were encouraging, but Count Berchthold, the new Austrian Chancellor, gave Masaryk to know that Austria-Hungary would have none of the matter.

Masaryk then essayed, in 1913, a scheme for Serbo-Bulgarian accord. This he succeeded in talking over with Bulgars and Serbs. Early in 1914 he had evolved a "complete plan" of agreement. A Serb friend in Prague was to take this to high officials in Belgrade, and following their acceptance—which had already been in principle forthcoming—Masaryk "was to have gone to Paris and London in order to get influential Western statesmen to put pressure on Belgrade and Sofia." [24] But events moved far too rapidly for this, and Masaryk's active program

[22] Jan Herben, *Thomas G. Masaryk*, p. 7.
[23] *The New Europe*, pp. 34, 35.
[24] *The Making of a State*, pp. 1-2.

took on a much larger vista: the creation of a largely new Europe from out of the old.

The World War, in fact, brought Masaryk to "the supreme crisis of his life" in which his whole moral realism was to be put to the ultimate test. What could be the course of the man who had become the acknowledged champion of the public right, with a common disregard of all costs to himself? Once more it was "characteristic of the man that he made no hasty decision, avoided all pronouncements and set himself to a thorough and intensive study of the forces engaged and of every factor that might affect the fate" of Europe and of his own people. "A full diagnosis could not be reached within the jurisdiction of the Austrian censor, and therefore before the close of 1914 he paid three visits abroad and pursued his inquiries in Holland, Germany, Italy, and Switzerland." [25] He dreaded the final decision which the war forced upon him, but his long studies of Austria, Europe, and world-culture led him to an irretrievable conclusion.

"Austria must be opposed in grim earnest, to the death"; it must be dismantled. "This the world-situation demanded." [26] The problem was not by any means just one of Czech freedom and interest. The Czech question itself was a world issue. Austria-Hungary as an empire blocked the course of European stability and of world progress. In its basic principles and constitution, Austria-Hungary was sum-totally decadent. Composed of nine national groupings, it was held together only through the absolutism of a degenerate dynasty reinforced by a kind of East India Company composed of two hundred families. The Austro-Hungarian government's policy was one of cultural suicide in subservience to clerical imperialism. Any comprehension of diplomacy which did not consist in tricky

[25] R. W. Seton-Watson, "President Masaryk," reprint from *Contemporary Review* (March, 1930), p. 7.
[26] *The Making of a State*, p. 4.

A Review of Masaryk

exploitation was beyond the Empire's statesmen. Czech claims to cultural and political autonomy, for example, were precisely on the same legal basis as those of the Hungarians. Louis Kossuth had pointed this out in 1871.[27] The Czechs had joined the Magyars and the Austrians in aiding them withstand the Turks in the sixteenth century. But the Czechs had been made the objects of Hapsburg Jesuitism in politics for their Hussite loyalties and activities, and no consideration of any rights of men or nations prevailed to uphold their legal status. Worse still were fortunes of the lesser and less individualistic groups of the Empire.

The true state of things became known in the war. Germany might weep about enemies within her boundaries. Austria-Hungary had them constitutionally. Racial purity had no place in Austria. "Sixty thousand executions and the assistance of Germany upheld the Habsburgs for a while," but the dissolution of Austria was a "natural and necessary historical process" which could not actually survive the war. Czechs and Slovaks, Jugoslavs, Poles, Ukrainians, Italians, and Rumanians in large groups refused obedience, and Austria collapsed from the weight of her own internal structure. She had no *raison d'être*.[28]

The question has frequently been raised: why could not Austria have been reconstituted as a federation? "There were economic reasons for such union of peoples." But whose national economy was this? Not Bohemia's or Moravia's! And not that of other internal groups! Masaryk's conclusion grew out of decades of experience supported by centuries of history. "Federation without freedom is impossible." [29] Union had been tried and was constantly betrayed. A new *psychology* was needed in which Czechs, Slovaks, and others would be treated as essential equals. When these had shown their cultural and political capacities, then federation might be voluntarily effected and sustained. But not in Austria alone! Rather, in a

[27] *The New Europe*, p. 48.   [28] *Ibid.*, pp. 35-36.   [29] *Ibid.*, p. 25.

United States of Europe, in which small nations would be constantly assured of their essential rights and ultimate autonomies. Austrians and Hungarians treated Czechs and Slovaks as subhuman serfs. The Hungarian dictum that "the Slovak is not a man" had no counterpart in the expressed attitudes of the Austrians toward the Czechs. Yet the same type of spirit showed itself in Austro-Hungarian and Czech relationships. There was no hope of reorganizing Austria on grounds of functioning equalities.

Not only, furthermore, did the Austrian Empire need dissolution in the interests of her peoples. Europe needed shaping up in structure and diplomacy. A whole new motivation was essential, and this could not begin to function without reorganizing from the bottom. Democracy must ultimately therefore become "the faith of all, a world view," government by all in the human interests of all. The issue was moral and ideological as well as political. "The political task of the democratic reconstruction of Europe," in fact, "must be attained and actually made possible by a moral re-education of the nations—either democracy or dynastic militarism, either Bismarckism or rational and honest politics, either force or humanity, either matter or spirit!" [30] These were the basic issues of the war (and peace). Democracy bespoke the cause of stability and wholesomeness in social relations.

As in Austria, moreover, group psychology made federation incapable of function, in Germany a philosophic national super-egoism left no grounds for considerateness toward non-Germans. There were many causal factors, certainly, making for the war and Germany was not by any means alone to blame. Austria was at least as guilty, if not guiltier. But the basic *motif* was Prussian or pan-German, and had its roots in German culture. Ignoring of this structural motif has been responsible for the failure of "historians" and others to concede the

[30] *Ibid.*, pp. 73, 74.

primary blame which belonged to Germany and Austria—as systems of sheer force and aggression. The motives of both Britain and France, with all of their imperialisms, were much different. The notion of a commonwealth of nations had no counterpart in Germany. Pan-German Titanism, rather, had swept the thinking of the German theologians and the politicians. The movement was not taken seriously abroad, anymore than Hitlerism had been taken seriously until 1939. But Masaryk had known German thinking first-hand, and he knew its consequences for politics and personal life. "The German nation of Thinkers and Philosophers" was a nation of subjectivists. Kant's "Pure Reason," in its serious attempt to transcend the chaos of empiricism, had in principle destroyed the outer world. Hegel, Feuerbach, Stirner, Nietzsche, and Bismarck carried this transcendental solipsism to its most fateful conclusions. A Faustian Super-Ego, then a Super-Nation, became a guiding motive within German thinking. The mind itself was all there was, and individual German minds were but parts of the Germanic super-consciousness. No other minds were "real" or mattered. Czechs and Poles were but ideas to be conquered, their skulls broken. Mommsen and Bismarck were agreed on this.[31] The German race of super-egoists were destined to be rulers of the world.

Extreme militarism was the natural outgrowth of this philosophical subjectivism, and intrinsic to post-Kantian philosophy and culture. "Modern militarism, especially Prussian militarism, is a scientific and philosophic system of objectivization, of compulsory escape from morbid subjectivity and suicidal mania.... In their spiritual isolation, the German philosophers and men of learning, historians and politicians, proclaimed German civilization and culture as the zenith of human development; and, in the name of this arrogant claim to superiority, Prussian pan-Germanism asserted its right to expansion and to

[31] *The Making of a State*, pp. 63, 337, etc.

the subjugation of others by sheer force. The Prussian State, its army and its fighting spirit became antidotes to morbid subjectivism. Prussian pan-Germanism is answerable for the world war, morally responsible for it, even if the Austro-Hungarian system shared its guilt and was, in a sense, still guiltier. The people of philosophers and thinkers, the people of Kant and Goethe, which claimed for itself the proud task of enlightening the world, was not entitled to seek in war a way out of the blind alley into which its one-sided, albeit highly refined, culture had led it. Nor could it honestly adopt and support the deceitful and short-sighted policy of the degenerate Hapsburgs. *Corruptio optimi pessima.*[32]

Masaryk's program, in consequence, demanded a new diplomacy based on a philosophically new cultural outlook with a new structure to Europe. Both structurally and philosophically, it was not by any means merely "the national future of the Czechoslovaks that was at stake but world progress. . . ." Czechoslovakia could not progress except on bases of world progress. World progress "depended on the favorable result of the great world struggle between two philosophical conceptions of the way in which world affairs should be directed."[33] As the German Emperor himself phrased it, it was a fight "between the Prussian idea and the American idea"; between "justice and violence," between "the Dark Ages and progress," between "the past and the future." One proclaimed unconditionally that "might creates right," the other believed "with Lincoln that right creates might."[34] The question at issue was that of

[32] *Ibid.,* pp. 348, 351.
[33] *The New Europe* (periodical), Dec. 21, 1916, pp. 304-305.
[34] Eduard Beneš, "The Political Activity and Philosophy of T. G. Masaryk," p. 5. "If I had to say which culture I considered to be the highest," Masaryk amplified in *The New Europe,* "I would answer the English, and American; at any rate, my stay in England during the war, and a very critical observation of English life convinced me that the English, as a whole, come nearest to the ideals of humanity."—p. 46.

the organization of life; whether life should be suppressed and coerced in the interests of a Superman or Super-state—by a theocratic-dictatorial-bureaucratic system—or whether it should be consolidated and mutually implemented in the interests of and through open efforts of all. It was an issue not just of "reshaping the map" but of the statesmanship of common good: informed releasing and empowering of men to live in positive and collaborative terms, giving stronger, broader, and more fertile bases to national and international life. "Europe's whole mentality must be changed. Her regeneration must be as much moral and spiritual as political. A policy *sub specie aeternitatis* is not merely possible but even necessary, but it can only be worked out on a purely democratic basis. Its foremost demand is true equality—alike in the inward and the outward sphere— an equality which extends to every citizen and to every nation." [35]

The war indeed was not a war "to make the world safe for democracy" as popular misconceptions phrased it. It was, none the less, and ought to have been, a war to renounce absolutism, test out and reformulate democracy and make it more effective in the world. Absolutism is subjectivism, democracy objectivism, as philosophical standpoints or theories. "The World War became a profound revolution which continued the great political change begun by the revolutions of the 18th century." Mankind joined together on behalf of men, in place of inhumanity in politics and institutions, striving for an ideology and program which would be adequate for life. "Everywhere was accelerated the transition from aristocratism and absolutist monarchism through constitutional monarchism to democratism. In a word: government by all takes the place of government by one individual." [36] That this struggle did not end with the

[35] *The New Europe*, p. 13.
[36] *Speech of T. G. Masaryk, . . . on the Tenth Anniversary of the Attainment of the Country's Independence, 28th October, 1928*, p. 14. Hereafter cited as *Speech on Tenth Anniversary*.

Treaty of Versailles was quite in keeping with the view of Masaryk for whom every gain must be consummated morally and consolidated educationally and practically. That the builders of the peace should have failed to recognize these facts shows the vital force of Masaryk's position, since the makers of the peace failed lamentably in building both toward its foundations and its superstructure. The very intensity of the recent counter-reactions is evidence of the far-reaching nature of the movement which Masaryk bespoke.

That Masaryk, furthermore, should have himself undertaken to direct this re-building of Europe placed him in the vanguard of human culture and right. And that he should have succeeded in winning politicians of the world to his highminded conception of the causes at issue marked him as a statesman of the most effective and constructive type. As Professor Charles Sarolea has written, "That an old teacher of philosophy, without money, without political influence, without any official following, should have imposed upon himself the duty and mission of challenging the Might and Majesty of the Habsburg Empire at the very moment when the armies of the Central Powers were carrying everything before them and seemed to be victorious on every front, that this old man should have conceived the plan of restoring the Bohemian State which had been wiped off the map of Europe, since the Battle of the White Mountain in 1620 and of further uniting that resurrected Bohemian State with Slovakian territories which, for a thousand years, had lived under Hungarian dominance, must have appeared to every sober-minded English politician, as a manifest proof of lunacy. And that this same old scholar, undeterred by the cynical scepticism of the wise and the indifference of the ignorant, should have proceeded to carry out his wild schemes, that he should have succeeded in converting to those schemes, the very statesmen and diplomats who had been most persistently hostile and that, in the fulness of time he should have made his fantastic dream into a living reality, will always appear to future generations as the most astounding miracle of modern political history."[37]

Yet Masaryk was more than the founder of a notable Republic in twentieth-century Europe. He was the primary effective proponent of a new European order. His writings, *The New Europe* and *The Making of a State*, were expressions of this program. The Czech question indeed was for him one part of a world question, and this world question was fundamentally one of morals and of education. Morals and education in turn were problems in marked measure of men's ideologies, or of conceptions and perspectives which are basically valid and thereby adequate to men's interests and needs. The issue was one, foremost, of a political science which would advance the common interests of nations, rise above the sordid battle for purely partisan causes, and coöperatively actualize the greatest good of all peoples. A "New Man, *homo Europoeus*," was, therefore, essential to Europe; and this new man was to be "the result not merely of external politics, but principally of internal." A program of honest, scientific "humanity" was the one motive-basis for all human relations, and this required achievement of an informed democratic perspective. History itself pointed to the present era as the time for achievement of this.[38] To such human attainment Masaryk was committed with the utter self-abandon and intelligent faith of a Socrates.

[37] "How Masaryk Converted the Anglo-Saxon World," *Central European Observer* (Prague), March 8, 1935, p. 67.

[38] *The New Europe*, p. 73 and whole concluding section.

Chapter Two

Democracy: Its Philosophy and Practice

MASARYK RANKS UNIQUELY as a statesman of democracy. Not merely is he to be credited with building up almost over night a distinctive democratic state in absolutist central Europe, but with a comprehension of the functional nature of a democratic system which stands out among the political philosophies of history. Assuredly neither Rousseau nor Kant had so clear an understanding of the *modus operandi* of democracy, whereas modern states like America and France had thought of it too simply. Democracy could not sustain itself as sheer experimentalism or yet as *laissez-faire*.

Masaryk's was no simple-minded view. Democracy was the most difficult of systems. While mankind generally and democratic politicians in particular misconceived democracy as a simple function of majority opinions, Masaryk discovered it to be a function of morality and science, and more profoundly of a whole philosophy of cultural history. "I come to this conclusion," Masaryk said in 1912, "that to be a conscientious democrat means to think philosophically, next to take in the teaching of history, to understand evolution—the philosophy of history. The problem is: how can the determinism of [groups in]

Philosophy and Practice

historical process be harmonized with the freedom of the individual."[1] History itself indeed points to self-determination of peoples as the essential direction of progress. The concepts of "individuality" and "nationality" are both resultants of this trend.[2] National democracy is the essential objective of government. Other systems violate human individuality and destroy their own foundations. The world has every right, in consequence, to look to every nation to move toward democratic government, and no pretense of incompatibility or lack of general interest can void their obligations to themselves and others to achieve the functions and the values of democracy. Yet a sense not just of individuality but of human mutuality is prerequisite to surmounting anarchy and incompetence within democratic government. And while such sense of mutuality is being brought to bear right now upon our "individualisms" and "collectivisms," democracy must be more and more deliberately directed toward the common, intertwined interests of all.

The prime question of democracy, in truth, as J. L. Stocks has later phrased it,[3] is that of the relationship of governing and governed. Democracy was well defined by Lincoln as government of the people, by the people, for the people. Yet Masaryk early pointed out that democracy cannot be in any modern state direct government by the people.[4] These must have a voice, sooner or later, in all matters of common concern, but how they may make themselves heard and how fruitful the hearing is a critical, functional problem. The way in which democracy functions, and continues to function in character, is the key to this issue.

There are, in fact, three quite different possibilities in rela-

[1] *Les Problèmes de la Démocratie*, p. 47.
[2] *The New Europe*, Part II; cf. *Ideals of Humanity*, Chap I.
[3] *Hibbert Journal*, July, 1936.
[4] *Les Problèmes de la Démocratie*, p. 52.

tionships of governments to people—not merely two.[5] There is that relation, first of all, in which people must obey the government with no hope of redress. This is absolutism, dictatorship, oligarchy, or some form of theocracy.[6] It is arbitrary and despotic, and, no matter how enlightened, it is repressive and inhuman. A second possibility is that in which the government shall and must obey the people. This in practice and discriminating functional theory is demagogy rather than democracy. Demagogy limits its science to the psychology of how to influence people. The motives of this influence, or goals of human government, are not carefully considered. Influence and control just for the sake of influence and control are the motif of demagogy; and this is much more clearly a dictatorship of the proletariat than the Russian system involves. Demagogy is the constant liability of a democracy, since it is a constant upshoot of parliamentarianism with its ready rendezvous for demagogues;[7] and parliamentarianism is the framework of any modern democratic government. "Democracy," Masaryk has commonly been quoted, "is discussion." Yet just as frequently he has insisted that it is not just discussion but "administration" of the affairs of all in the best interests of all.[8] And this involves a third mode of relationship: that of interaction between governing and governed, which allows for guidance from both

[5] This distinction is most clearly drawn by J. L. Stocks in the *Hibbert Journal* cited above. Masaryk was so intent upon the utter contrast of democracy and political absolutism that he did not make the three-fold grouping so directly. His common references to demagogy, however—as shown below—disclose that this three-fold distinction was implicit in his thought, yet that demagogy was bound up closely with "theocracy" in principle and was not really an independent, third type of political relation.

[6] *The Spirit of Russia*, Vol. II, Chap. 24; *The Making of a State*, pp. 449-454.

[7] Cf. especially Kamil Krofta, "Masaryk's Political Democracy," pp. 11, 12, 14-15; *Les Problèmes de la Démocratie*, p. 61.

[8] *The Spirit of Russia*, II, 507; *The New Europe*, p. 68.

Philosophy and Practice

sides with a constant revealing of interests and values. By this, the greatest good of the very greatest number may be actualized, and men can be, in a most significant degree, self-governing. This is actual, self-sustaining, constructive democracy.[9]

Democracy, in point of fact, is leadership as well as discussion. The issue of democracy is, in truth, the age-old issue stated by Plato twenty-three centuries ago, as the main problem of government.[10] There is, indeed, a significant parallel between Masaryk's democratic ideas and those of the reputedly undemocratic Plato. Democracy undertakes, and must undertake, an *interweaving of interests;* so must all politics, after some fashion. But democracy commits itself to that interweaving of interests in which the maximum consideration is given to the otherwise forgotten person. Its foremost goal is "true equality—alike in the inward and the outward sphere—which extends to every citizen and to every nation."[11] Democracy is the political expression of the morally humane ideal. It is the function of democratic politics, in principle at least, "to elucidate and realize ethical principles on behalf of and in the social whole." Democracy, however, is an effort not just at justice—though that itself is "the arithmetic of love"—but at the conjoint advancing of interests. It cannot be static or yet indifferent to the common good of all people. It is, fundamentally, a releasing and empowering of men, and consequent "organization of progress in all branches of human activity."[12] "Democracy consists in the unloosening of every energy," and is in consequence a "ceaseless search for union of all the vital forces in the nation."[13] "Democracy perforce desires to create the

[9] *The Making of a State,* pp. 436 ff; cf. also *Speech on Tenth Anniversary.*
[10] Plato, *The Statesman.*
[11] *The New Europe* (periodical), Dec. 21, 1916, p. 305.
[12] *The New Europe,* p. 68.
[13] *The Spirit of Russia,* II, 515; Krofta, "Masaryk's Political Democracy," p. 17.

new; theocratic aristocracy wishes to preserve the old."[14] Democracy, therefore, requires the very highest grade of leadership.

Democracy, by its very nature, is the most difficult of systems. It undertakes to give maximum freedom to men, give them an ultimate voice in all matters of mutual concern, and yet to sustain and facilitate their multiple interests. Other systems may effect their aims by simplified procedures. Democracy deals in paradoxes, in dealing both in individual freedom and in group-determination. Democracy thus can only gain its goals by interactions on the level of enlightened understanding. This means *leadership, critical thinking, science,* and *philosophy*. It means training both of leaders and masses, the elevation of men to higher levels of thinking and action. Yet democracy must somehow start to function on the levels of demagogy and uninformed opinion.

This is where Masaryk parted from Plato. He believed in equality to a much greater degree than Plato: not in absolute equality surely, but in the most tolerable degree of inequalities. His social ethics and politics demanded achievement of the maximum effective equality, and, above all, of the recognition of the Kantian principle that no man should treat another person solely or even largely as a means but always mainly as an end. The social possibilities of men are not by any means to be gainsaid. Yet the actualizing of these possibilities, as Plato held, is a function of full education, dependent on a social hierarchy rather than outright equality. Inequality, in fact, is the very nature of individualism. Hierarchy means organization, discipline, and order.[15] These are essentials of any forthright attempts at democracy. There "can be no government without obedience and discipline."[16]

---

[14] *The Spirit of Russia*, II, 515.
[15] Čapek, *President Masaryk Tells His Story*, pp. 180-181.
[16] "Masaryk's Philosophy of Life," *Slavonic Review*, March, 1930.

Masaryk, indeed, made a democrat of Plato in agreeing that government is a function especially of leading minds and more notably still of science and philosophy. "By its very nature," Masaryk maintained, "democracy counterposes science and philosophy to theology and scholasticism." Aristocracy and theocracy have no science, but "esotericism, mysteries, and prophecies." Demagogy, also, has recourse to myths and phantasies, the preconceptions and imaginings of the uninformed. Democracy, by contrast, is the social philosophy of science. "Knowledge, critical knowledge, is democracy . . . The practical import of the Kantian criticism is found above all in this, that criticism cuts at the root of mythological aristocracy. . . . Criticism, therefore, is a determinant, not of knowledge alone, but also of democratic equality and liberty. Without criticism and without publicity, there can be neither knowledge nor democracy." Modern science, aided and abetted by philosophical criticism, is the first principle of democratic thinking. It takes account of facts, wherever they are found, by constant "energetic observation," and "aims at universal agreement (of classes, peoples, humanity)." Yet this agreement is to be determined "solely by logical and educational methods," and not by any type of preconception. Science, therefore, in the sense of true and full science, is the very genius of democracy, since it affords to individualities the final voice in any issue. It is non-arbitrary in all of its methods.[17]

"Democracy works by scientific method, and its tactics are therefore inductive, realistic, and empirical; theocratic aristocracy is deductive, unrealist, fanciful, and scholastic."[18] Democracy is a rule of men in the light of the best knowledge available, in contrast to dictatorship and to absolute authority. "The most scientific policy depends upon experience and in-

[17] *The Spirit of Russia*, II, 510, 512.
[18] *Ibid.*, p. 515.

duction. It can claim no infallibility."[19] "Logic, mathematics, and some moral maxims may be absolute, that is to say, not relative as they would be if all countries, parties and individuals had a special morality, mathematics and logic of their own; but there is a difference between the [ultimate] epistemological absolutism of theory, and practical, political absolutism"[20] which denies to individuals their rightful individualities. The principle of individuality, in fact, on which democracy rests its theory and its practice, is a principle both of ethics and of fundamental science. Nowhere but in "concrete logic," with its factuality and order, could there be that justice to all individuals which democracy intends, and nowhere is there such occasion for each individual to be, in the whole complex order of nature, most totally himself. Other systems may gain order by imposition and suppression. Democracy attains its order by the arduous methods of honestly organized scientific effort. This indeed is the most difficult of procedures. It can take no short cuts. It must take cognizance of all the facts and individuals to be considered, and find their most natural posts and functions in the entire cultural system.

Yet science too depends on scientists, and they in turn are governed by philosophies of science (and of nature). These may be partial or substantially complete, humane or variously inhuman. Modern philosophy has tended toward "humanity" and a moral philosophy of culture. It has aimed at adequacies in life: "at the foundation of a new morality, at the elaboration of the new democratic political and administrative system, at democratic anthropocracy."[21] The spirit of modern philosophy may be summarized, in fact, in "three antitheses. Philosophy is absolutely opposed to theology, anthropism to theism; but this must not be taken to imply that theism is utterly false, or

[19] *The Making of a State*, p. 467.
[20] *Ibid.*
[21] *The Spirit of Russia*, II, 511.

Philosophy and Practice 39

that anthropism is atheistic, for all that is meant is that the anthropistic outlook and point of departure has come into its own in modern philosophy. At the same time, in the political sphere, democracy is counterposed to theocracy, to theocratic aristocracy, this signifying that democracy, likewise, possesses theoretic and philosophical importance. In ultimate analysis, modern philosophy has ceased to be the queen of the sciences. It does not occupy a higher plane than the special sciences, but ranks beside them." The relationships of science and philosophy are those of reciprocal dependence. "Antitheological philosophy is based upon the sciences, and its relationship to these scientific foundations is not aristocratic but democratic." It is "a relationship of equality and equivalence." [22] Science, in turn, as we shall see in Chapter V, is indebted to philosophy for its fundamental criticism, without which science could not even justify itself; and philosophic criticism notably is the archservant of democracy.[23] Philosophy of science, therefore, is not indifferent to democracy but is its actual counterpart in theoretic culture.

Democracy, in point of fact, is more than a social point of view or system. It is a whole philosophy: "a complete outlook on the world and life." It is "a special way of regarding the universe and life," [24] presupposing a metaphysic of socio-moral constructivity, based on an ethic of humanity and a philosophy of science. Democracy is a fight for a humanly free and unfolding world-order with no dictatorial and repressive prerogatives for any. Democracy, most obviously, is philosophic in its solution to the problem of authority. While aristocracy insists on special insights or on revelation and claims secret empowerment from on high, democracy finds its authorization in objec-

---

[22] *Ibid.*, I, 213; II, 510.
[23] *Ibid.*, II, 468 ff, 512.
[24] Krofta, "Masaryk's Political Democracy," p. 2; *The Spirit of Russia*, II, 514; *The Making of a State*, p. 458, etc.

tive evidence and standards. "Democracy likewise appeals to authority, appeals to the people, to humanity, to the masses, to civilization, progress, historical development, and so on. But these objective authorities must themselves be furnished with foundations," [25] and this is an achievement of scientifically critical thinking which may validate itself to all normal minds. Democratic authority is not private but public and discriminating.

This is then to say two things: (1) that democracy is not a simple but a complex system, and more sophisticated far than it seems in principle; it is an informed system—for nothing else can function as democracy—"democracy without thought is an impossibility"; [26] (2) that it is itself a philosophic outlook, and that philosophic outlook which keeps closest to the facts, i.e., to all the facts to be critically considered. It is the social phase, in fact, of a philosophically critical and constructive realism. Masaryk, indeed, "held 'realism,' as he conceived it, to be the true aim of politics no less than of thought and of life," [27] and, as we quoted Wickham Steed, Masaryk "taught that, unlike the German notion of 'Realpolitik,' realism in politics consists not of a cynical disregard of principles but of a scrupulous reckoning with facts, moral and material; that honesty is not only the best policy but the only safe guide in public as in private life; and that character, not astuteness or trickery, is the first requisite in a statesman." [28] Realism ought, in fact, to represent the disposition to face fairly and deal with full realities, and to have a sound and adequate conception of the world and life. Democracy does not deny to man the right to fulfil the world order but rather undertakes to facilitate this cosmic prerogative and

[25] *The Spirit of Russia*, II, 516.
[26] Krofta, "Masaryk's Political Democracy," p. 20.
[27] Steed, "Thomas Garrigue Masaryk," *Slavonic Review* (March, 1930), p. 471.
[28] *Ibid.*

Philosophy and Practice 41

moral necessity.[29] It is the business of democracy not to evade but to treat of reality.[30]

In all this, we have stated, Masaryk was in substantial agreement with Plato, who sought to maximize not just the State in abstract isolation, but likewise every individual in the State; and for whom any satisfactory government was a function of a scientific philosophy of existence and culture. Small wonder that Masaryk told his people that "democracy is truly a great task, a great problem" and that problems are solved "by people who think and possess knowledge"—not by those who are "merely elected." [31] Masaryk's difference from Plato lay in the "mutual concession of liberty and its constitutional observance" which Masaryk insisted is as fundamental to democracy as its "parliamentary and electoral technique." [32] Democracy combines, in fact, he pointed out (in his message to both chambers of the Czechoslovak Parliament, March 7, 1930), "the loyal recognition of civil personalities and the insurance of their cooperation." [33] This combination of the recognition of freedom with the insurance of wise and effective control presents, indeed, the basic paradox of democracy and makes democracy constantly a trusteeship of informed and competent leaders. "There is nothing which cannot be abused" either by leaders or their peoples. "Everything depends on whether people are decent and educated." [34] Yet this but makes the fiduciary phase of democracy that much more essential or functionally inherent. "'A truly democratic leader, cultured and critically minded,'" Kamil Krofta renders Masaryk, "will strive to com-

[29] Beneš, "The Political Activity and Philosophy of T. G. Masaryk," p. 15.
[30] *Les Problèmes de la Démocratie*, p. 48.
[31] *Speech on Tenth Anniversary*, p. 16.
[32] "Masaryk's Philosophy of Life," *Slavonic Review*, March, 1930.
[33] *Ibid.*
[34] Krofta, *op. cit.*, p. 27; cf. Čapek, *President Masaryk Tells His Story*, p. 204.

prehend the spiritual mutuality through which he has himself developed, and how much he has gained from his predecessors and his contemporaries; he will not forget the parallelism of views issuing from the same experience and from an observation of the same conditions, the same things and the same people; he will understand how these views of individuals coalesce, and how the so-called public opinion, the spirit of the age, the soul of the masses, or whatever one likes to call it, arises; a truly democratic leader who is scientifically minded must think and work with the masses for the masses, but he must do so consciously for morally political reasons and will not for one moment be other than certain that all social life in its historical development is the life of distinct individuals, more or less qualified, individuals responsible for their own conduct." [35] Individuals are the basic resources of nations and ultimate determiners of governments. It is for this reason that democracy must be the goal of all nations. Other systems cannot but defeat themselves through exploitation of those human entities on which they depend. Yet these very persons, important and resourceful as they are, need guidance in assumption of their responsibilities and, above all, in clarifying the issues of government (and life) within a democratic state.

This then is both the practical and theoretic paradox of democracy: the paradox of self-determination via enlightened and responsible leaders who are spokesmen of freedom governed by constraints of an honest, mutualist culture. Yet this is but its major paradox. Democracy is fraught through with paradoxes which while not so comprehensive are no less difficult and insistent. We shall consider three of these to which Masaryk gave particular consideration: the paradox of militarism in a democracy, the paradox of industrialism in an indi-

[35] "Masaryk's Political Philosophy," p. 12; cf. *Les Problèmes de la Démocratie*, pp. 103-104.

vidualistic culture, and the paradox of demagogy combined with bureaucracy.

The issue of militarism is the most acute problem with which democracy has to contend. Democracy is implictly non-militaristic since it is mutualistic in outlook and methods. Yet democracy has somehow to "protect itself against absolutism" [36] both from within and outside its constituted bounds. It cannot permit the violation of its human prerogatives without the sacrifice of its own principle and interests. The issue is an issue of preserving moral principles and values achieved through long-run history and so readily lost that no effort can be rationally spared to maintain these humanly essential gains. Not by any means is the question of military defense one just of the self-interests of a people at the moment. Nations must look to their future. The good of the majority includes those of the future. Democracy indeed is a dynamic, evolutionary motif for human relations. Its future depends on its present. Nations of men in this present are makers of lives for the future, and any humane achievement is not morally to be let drop at each threat of force.

Defense by force if necessary! This is prerequisite for maintaining democracy. Neither passivist nor yet pacifist surrender is realistic. Both are sentimentalisms, and sentimentalism is moral weakness: abandoning men to inhumanity and evil. Active, realistic, moral constructivity in outlook and effort deals in facts and situations of the moment; and not only does it anticipate but it prepares the future. This is the method of social advance. Democracy particularly cannot afford to be weak or to permit the taking away of its rights to self-government and freedom. A democratic nation must defend itself against enemies if or when these cannot be reasoned with or aligned in mutualist endeavor.[37] Democracy must achieve both a moral

[36] *Speech on Tenth Anniversary*, p. 19.
[37] *The Making of a State*, pp. 59 ff, 457.

and material readiness in its own defense, though its primary method must be that of conference and of frank discussion.[38]

Masaryk has been accused of a failure to appreciate the extreme pacifist position.[39] The answer is that pacifism fails to take account of actualities, assuming that the defender of a cause is the real aggressor and that there is no deliberate, misguided, and even diabolical evil, such as took advantage of the pacifist interest and spirit throughout the world, to abolish law-abiding human decency with total lack of conscience. In their unrealism, the pacifists are virtually responsible with Hitler for the present, successful outrages against the peace-loving nations. The extreme pacifists' ignorance of the actual malignant outlook and enterprise of the anti-democratic governments; their disposition to blame economics and imperialism (British and French especially) for the aggressive program of these deliberate foes of human law and values; their lack of comprehension of the basic difference between the motives of democracy, of which Britain, as well as Czechoslovakia, Switzerland, and the United States, is a notable example, and those of the authoritarian systems which Hitlerism especially epitomizes; the pacifists' failure to comprehend that war today is far more a matter of ideologies and their accompanying psychologies than of any of those other motives which they have picked upon; their belief that preparation for withstanding or surmounting aggression is itself the primary cause of war: all these miscomprehensions paved the way with golden nicety for Hitler's fifth columns and fomented collapses of defenses in democratic nations. As a reactionary movement, pacifism may serve a purpose, at times, in crystallizing sentiment and in securing appeasements between governments. But essentially, extreme pacifism is blind and weak-kneed in methods, and in-

[38] Krofta, "Masaryk's Political Democracy," pp. 19-20.
[39] *The Manchester Guardian*, July 24, 1936, review of Ludwig's *Defender of Democracy*.

volves the abandonment of moral good through non-resistance to evil. Extreme pacifism fails to comprehend the moral inviolability of nations and all normal groupings of persons. It fails to take cognizance of the fact that such groups are extensions themselves of the persons. Pacifists, indeed, would scarcely advocate the turning over of society to gangsters. Yet that there are gangster governments and gangster policies in nations was unmistakably apparent throughout Masaryk's lifetime and since. In point of fact, the same methods which are needed for dealing with a nation's arch criminals must be at hand for the arch crime of international lawlessness and aggression. There is no basic difference between group crime inside a nation and crime which is prepared by governments outside. The same necessity for protection and discipline exists, entailing, however, a much greater effort and program.

Masaryk spent days discussing this issue with Tolstoy in 1887 and in subsequent visits to Russia. "I held," he said, "that we must resist evil always and in everything, and maintained against him [Tolstoy] that the true humanitarian aim is to be ever on the alert, to overcome the old ideals of violence and heroic deeds and martyrdom, and to work with loving kindness and wholeheartedly even in small things—to work and to live. In extreme cases, violence and assault must be met with steel and beaten off so as to defend others against violence."[40] The idea of capitulating to force or aggression was for Masaryk undemocratic and unchristian.

Should Czechoslovakia have had an army and have been as much prepared for self-defense as was reasonably possible? To Masaryk this was obvious. The age-old danger of aggression had been accentuated by pan-Germanism of which Hitlerism has become the over-ripened fruit. The freedom of the Czechs and Slovaks, regained after three hundred and a thousand

[40] *The Making of a State*, p. 59; cf. Čapek, *President Masaryk Tells His Story*, p. 166.

years respectively of oppressive servitude, could be lost overnight—as in fact it was through British unpreparedness and pacifist efforts at appeasement. Negotiating strength lay in Czech preparedness for defense, if only this had been given opportunity to function. Czech soldiers served their purpose in the early days of peace, and they served a purpose later in making breach of peace more difficult. Not that they alone by any means could have kept the independence of their country, but they were a formidable factor for restraining and holding off enemies until or while other factors and forces joined in defense. That political intrigue and pressure broke down all plans for defense is not to be charged against Czechoslovakia or against Masaryk's philosophy, but against the lack of realism which engulfed the post-war world. The loss of Czech national culture and defenses soon proved, as anticipated, a sheer boomerang to human interests and values.

War, Masaryk maintained, is not the worst evil that can befall mankind, though it brings many other evils in its train.[41] The worst evil is that men should lose their sense of the moral principle of human individuality and be unready to stand up for the inviolability of persons and peoples. The principle of individuality, in fact, is the foremost principle of peace. Peace is not at all a separate end or value. Peace is but a state of constant interaction which is substantially wholesome and right. The loss of life by suicide and murder is greater actually in proportion in the times of "peace" than in times of war. War, in consequence, is only relatively a greater evil. Peace should be the function of the moral, cultural maximizing of humanity, affording positive expression to the social conception of justice. When peace is not established on this basis the world already is essentially at war. The major difference lies in the methods of war. Should those methods actually consist in sacrificing lives of people without permitting them any defense, the war

[41] *The Making of a State*, p. 61.

has features which are assuredly as bad as in overt fighting. Defense of *actual* peace, with mutual rights to culture as to self-determination, is a moral obligation of any nation—though war itself does not create peace but suffering. There is a great difference between defensive and aggressive fighting, ultrapacifists to the contrary; and the motives of these two can be readily distinguished.[42] The most that self-defense can do, indeed, is first of all to show the nation's will to live at almost any cost, and secondly to uphold its own integrity and right to manage its particular affairs. These are moral values, which can more readily be conserved than they can be regained, involving individualities of people.

It is from this realistic viewpoint, against the background of Masaryk's whole moral and social philosophy, that we must understand his insistence on the democratic necessity of self-defense and his strong advocacy of collective security as an essential of peace. Attempts to violate the individualities of nations are attempts to violate the personalities of the people who comprise them. Such attacks on human individuality as a first principle of moral life must be met by active resistance. But in so far as nations which are essentially moral in motives can organize to maintain order and advance human interests, the problem of defense can become much simpler and more hopeful.

It can, assuredly, be reasoned that democracy has no hope of vying with outright militarism in its own defense and that once it undertakes to offer competition it has sold out to militarism and aggression. Yet this is not a crucial issue. The history of the post-war democratic world is not that of any such direct selling-out to militarism but rather to unrealism and sentimentality. Whether militarism becomes a permanent state in any democratic country is a matter not of the acceptance of a strong militarist program to meet some emergency but of the

[42] *Ibid.*, pp. 59-60; cf. p. 457.

actual "democratic" spirit of the people themselves. They need not subscribe to militarism after the international crisis is past; and, in fact, in both Britain and America they reacted so strongly in the other direction after the first World War as to be incapable of dealing with realities. The problem is not to any high degree, in well-established democracies, that of surrender to militarism inside the nation, but rather that of realism and competence versus sentimentalism and sheer laissez-faire. That democracy, when fully alert to its task, can cope with militarism on the outside, is another matter. Here indeed is where the freedom and the genius of the human spirit has its incomparable advantage over purely mechanized and coerced efforts. Lord Tweedsmuir tells of how in the last desperate German drive in the Spring of 1918 there were thirty-seven divisions of the British Army to withstand seventy-five divisions of the Germans, and how in that moment when the British line had bent until it actually was quite broken: then every Britisher did what he had not been trained to do. He improvised, met the crisis with heroic insight and abandon, and saved the day for Western Europe. The Germans improvised too, and thereby they impaired the function of their plan.[43] None of their generals, Masaryk pointed out, showed great generalship: whether Hindenburg or Ludendorff or any of the others. "All the Hindenburgs and their like are good, painstaking, and conscientious generals, but they do not possess the slightest spark of genius. It cannot be otherwise; the Germans have . . . only the craftiness of a greedy aggressiveness."[44] Whether Hitler's diabolic genius could succeed under circumstances other than those which have paved his way to date is a fair question. Certainly there have been times when he could have been stopped. The readiness of people throughout the

[43] J. Buchan, *The King's Grace, 1910-1935* (Hodder and Stoughton, 1935), pp. 210-215.
[44] *The New Europe*, p. 41.

Philosophy and Practice 49

world, however, to take the pledges of this arch-liar at face value presents an added problem in his case, yet does not enhance his actual genius as a general. The human factor has, in any case, to be considered with regard to war, as in the furtherance of peace, and that ultimately is the stumbling block, if not the pit, of unconditioned militarism.

The test of any democratic state is the democratic spirit of its army. Masaryk was completely committed to a democratic army for a democratic state, and he had faith that this, with democratic union in a Society or League of Nations, could maintain and advance his nation and democracy throughout the world. "Our army must be democratic," he insisted. "The old barriers between civic life and the army must fall. There must be no distinction between the two spheres. We do not want to have an imperialistic army. Our soldier must know and be imbued with the principles of genuine humanity. None the less—indeed for that very reason—he must be a man of courage in accordance with the old tradition of: 'Every Czech a Captain!' Even in the instance of the army, ideal and spirit are the first consideration." [45]

"Our State arose out of war and through war," Masaryk said in an address to an army deputation on the fifth anniversary of the proclamation of the nation's independence; "but its actual rise we owe to our own determination, and that of all the nations of Europe and the world, to put down the system of violence that was based on the old militarism, to liberate the oppressed nations, and thus to strengthen and extend democracy. . . . I know that the opinion is still widespread, that an army must be always ready for attack, and that if it is designed in advance merely for purposes of defense it cannot be either properly trained in the military sense or feel confident of victory . . . I can only concede that an army which is genuinely democratic and thus purely defensive presupposes

[45] Krofta, "Masaryk's Political Democracy," p. 34.

a higher personal and civic morality [italics added], especially loftier views as to what is real character, valour, and heroism. It is the task of the military authorities to train up and consolidate the army in this loftier spirit. Even a democratic state demands sacrifice of its citizens and its soldiers—a readiness to sacrifice their lives should this be necessary. To demand from citizens the sacrifice of their lives, to demand that from citizens who are thoughtful and conscious of their responsibilities —this involves precisely the highest stage of personal and civic morality." [46]

Democracy produces, or can produce, the highest and the greatest type of soldier because democracy develops men. The human factor is its speciality. This is at once, indeed, its danger and its strength; for it permits untrained and inefficient people to have an equal voice in and even manage its affairs. Readjustments in a time of crisis, accordingly, are slow and difficult; and since almost every time is in some respect a time of crisis, democracy entails that men and nations are quite continuously getting into difficulties and spending an immense amount of their resources in trying to get out. A recompense, or consolation to be more exact, is that they do not commonly get as far into difficulty as non-democratic states, and can therefore get out at a far lower cost. But the dangers of unreadiness and inefficiency are great, so that democracy can only really be protected and advanced by unalloyed and informed work.

This brings us to the second paradox or problem of democracy: the paradox of industrialism in an individualistic culture. Here, again, however, Masaryk does not seem to have had the difficulty, which is rife in democracies, of confusing democracy with its purely political phases, and of failing to see that democracy is a principle of industry as well as of politics. Democracy, he maintained, is a system of work. Its foremost issue

[46] *Ibid.*

Philosophy and Practice 51

is the organization of labor. "Democracy demands that all shall work." Yet "democracy aims, not merely at work, but at the spirit of industry." The democrat triumphs by work, physical and mental, "over the aristocratic ideal of indolence and violence." The whole motive-force of democracy is the organization of socio-personal life for purposes not just of immediate advantage but conjoint progress. And since democracy is the most difficult of systems, democracy is largely work: "co-effort by all for the state as a whole." Democracy demands constant and positive work in detail.[47]

This does not mean, however, any necessary loss to human individualities, for this is the very ground on which individuality can express and maintain itself: i.e., on an industrial basis.[48] This is the condition for the preservation and advancement of all individualities with which democracy is in principle concerned. The exploitation of individuals and mechanizing of their lives is still another matter. This is not to be surmounted by the abolition of industrialism but by social morality and a truly democratic culture.

From Masaryk's standpoint, in fact, the concept of democracy was a principle neither just of politics nor of industrial life. It was, as we have emphasized, a whole philosophy of culture. "Genuine democracy," he stated, "will be economic and social as well as political."[49] Democracy, above all, must be moral and religiously spiritual in its character and program. This means that it must put socio-personal interests in the foreground of its thinking, establish these on the solid foundation of morally just inter-relations of people, and maximize their interests from the angles of culturally wholesome and expan-

[47] *The Spirit of Russia*, II, 509; Krofta, "Masaryk's Political Democracy," p. 17; *Les Problèmes de la Démocratie*, pp. 34, 35, 43, 58; *The New Europe*, p. 68.
[48] Cf. L. P. Jacks, *Constructive Citizenship*, Garden City, N. Y., 1928, for an industrial version of morality.
[49] *The Making of a State*, p. 440.

sive associations of people in all spheres of life. True democracy is a democracy of culture as well as of bread and of votes.

From this standpoint, indeed, it is important to consider Masaryk's view of the relationship of democracy to socialism, and of individualism to both nationalism and internationality. These relations have been the sources of a great deal of confusion. What is the modicum of truth from which each of these sundry viewpoints gains its special strength? This was Masaryk's specific concern. And Masaryk, in point of fact, showed the actual harmony of individualism with nationalism and of nationalism with international democracy. The principle of individuality was the stronghold of democracy: acknowledging and, in so far as possible, providing for the "rights" of men as individual citizens. But nations too, he pointed out, are individuals: natural groupings of mankind, with common backgrounds and closely interacting interests. States may differ widely from nations. The former may be artificial and amorphous. States, at best, are instruments or agencies of nations. Nations are the normal functioning unities of people. Democracy extends also, naturally, between "nations," despite the lag of international morality and lack of democratic understanding in many, if not most, nations.[50] A fundamental problem in the solution of world problems is just this extension of democracy to relationships of nations (and how in the meantime a democracy can interact with non-democratic nations). But between love of one's own nation and internationality there is no cleavage. One cannot be effectively international in outlook and action without due loyalty to one's own country first of all and to other nations via this national loyalty. Proper devotion to or concern for one's own nation involves, in fact, a just regard for the interests of others.[51]

If nations are, however, or at least may be, individuals, this

[50] *The New Europe*, pp. 67 ff.
[51] Čapek, *Masaryk on Thought and Life*, pp. 212-213.

Philosophy and Practice

same obtains for other groupings, such as those who in an aristocratic social order are distinguished as the "workers." Not only are they separate individualities, as persons, and entitled to consideration wherein no man shall use another man mainly as an instrument for his own ends; but collectively they form a natural unity in essential interests and functions. The only problem from this standpoint is that there should be any other healthy adult group than that of those who are workers. "Democracy demands that all shall work." In a democracy *per se*, "there are no men or classes exploiting the labour of others." That would be a violation of the principle of individuality from which democracy obtains its validation and its virtue. "Democracy aims, not merely at work, but at the spirit of industry." It is, as we have stated, "the organization of progress in all branches of human activity," and finds its special power in the unloosening of all energies. Democracy is, accordingly, a principle of labour.[52]

There should be no substantial difference, therefore, from this standpoint, between individualism and socialism. Individualism must itself be social to be democratic and effective, not exploiting but supporting and advancing personalities. Democracy, indeed, "is based on individualism"; not "capricious individualism" such as Stirner's or Nietzsche's, but "rather on the effort to strengthen individuality and the sense of individual responsibility." Democracy bespeaks "the sense of social solidarity."[53] If groups themselves, moreover, are in natural circumstances also individuals, it follows that the emphasis on group interests, whether of the workers or any other natural group, is implicit in the very structure of democracy. Group interests must, in fact, be maximized to provide for individuals. The truth and worth of socialism consists distinctively in this

[52] *The New Europe*, p. 68; *The Spirit of Russia*, II, 509.
[53] *The Making of a State*, p. 464; cf. *Speech on Tenth Anniversary*, p. 22.

emphasis on the values of the inter-relations of totalities of persons, in distinction from some favored few, and above all, on the value of work and the workers. "My socialism," Masaryk said of his own view, "is simply love of one's fellowmen, humanity. Humanity strives to improve conditions through law and order." [54]

This assuredly is not the viewpoint of materialistic communism; but that itself, we shall find, is a violation of sociology and history. It fails to recognize the different kinds of work and human values, and notably the principle of individuality itself.[55] The essential equality which democracy asserts to be the only valid principle for human living in society, entails the right of everyone so far as he is capable to share in every form of opportunity and in all phases of culture. Democracy in substance "proclaims not merely political equality but also economic, social, moral, religious, and spiritual and intellectual equality generally"; and "aims at 'fraternity not merely in respect of daily bread but also in rights, in science and learning, in morals and in religion.'" [56] Democracy therefore requires the definitive organizing of society for facilitation of the lives and individualities of peoples. This is individualism in its best functional form—concerned for building up of individualities. Yet it is also socialism in its true functional meaning: advancing groups (as groups) and work. It is not "communism" in any usual understanding of that term. Yet no simple sharing of all human goods nor any largely mechanistic economics can do justice to the complex spiritually moral brotherhood of man. Only an effective love of men and a politically just balancing of all types of interests can serve men's group life soundly or

[54] *Ideals of Humanity*, Chap. II; Ludwig, *Defender of Democracy*, p. 55.
[55] *Die Grundlagen des Marxismus*, cf. especially Chaps. V, X, XII; also *Ideals of Humanity*, Chap. II.
[56] Krofta, "Masaryk's Political Democracy," p. 2.

Philosophy and Practice 55

adequately and advance human society. This is a function of leadership, science, and work.

There remains then the dilemma of combining demagogy with bureaucracy in a democracy. Here is where Masaryk differed most clearly from Plato. Masaryk had faith that the masses of men could rise to self-government and that philosophical thinking and living is not the prerogative only of philosopher-kings. It is the potentiality and right of the masses. Just as Comenius would have taught metaphysics to children,[57] within the compass of their apperceptive possibilities, Masaryk undertook to teach men generally to think scientifically and philosophically. Not that they could grasp it all at once, but that they could grow in understanding and in critical acumen, and achieve constructivity for the surmounting of issues. They could, furthermore, help to educate their leaders. Leadership was a mutual, interactive, progressive affair; a matter of growth as well as intelligence.

The problem basically, however, is not that of bureaucracy within a democracy but that of the autocracy of demagogues, who try ignorantly to assume authoritative roles. For in so far as experts are employed as advisers, in the spirit of humanity, there is no problem for democracy. Both the preservation and advancement of the rights and duties of mankind for succeeding decades and centuries make the often-unappreciated services of experts unavoidably essential. And in so far as men want to dispense with or lessen their dependence on bureaus or experts, they must themselves achieve such range and depth of knowledge that they themselves no longer are only citizens but experts.[58] This is the prime issue: thorough-going, fundamental education of the masses and their leaders.

Democracy requires of men that they should be prepared at

---

[57] *The Spirit of Russia*, II, 511.
[58] Krofta, "Masaryk's Political Democracy," p. 28; cf. *Speech on Tenth Anniversary*, pp. 15 ff.

least to judge the wisdom of advisers and to be in that more-or-less direct sense self-governing. It stands to reason that democracy cannot be developed or maintained without intensive and inclusive culture. "Democracy means constant training for democracy..."[59] and not in politics or government alone but in general education and culture. Not that demagogy is the sole possession of the democratic systems; dictatorships depend on it for absoluteness. But right there is the danger of autocracy within democracy itself. Absoluteness is the characteristic of ignorant and untrained individuals and groups, or of those whose training has been too narrow or too shallow. Democracies lend themselves in sweeping fashion to this source of exploitation. Between the demagogue and the narrow expert, they are in constant danger within as likewise from without. The demagogue has no basis for collaboration with the expert. The demagogue lets words do duty for ideas and for things: "good round words." He both gains election and also undertakes to solve his nation's problems by slogans and catch-phrases. "Watchwords" are essential, and may express high principles but there is a significant difference between watchwords and catch-phrases. "To speak uncritically [even] of the will, instinct, and sound-common sense of the masses ... the people, the nation, the party, and the like, is generally ... only a proof that the man who speaks thus does not think in scientific terms, that he has no clearly defined political aim, and that he believes in miracles." The demagogue's objective, in fact, in so far as it is not just merely gaining some advantage for himself and partisans, is that of compromise between opposing extremes. He does not have the viewpoint of sound policy based on knowledge of historic culture and of the concrete facts of his State in the actual complex order of his continent or world. Compromise of method and of detail is indeed essential in de-

[59] *Ibid.*, p. 19; cf. *The Making of a State*, pp. 444 ff.

Philosophy and Practice

mocracy, but not compromise of principle nor yet compromise as itself an end.[60]

The issue, therefore, is not one really of bureaucracy within democracy but of demagogy and quasi-bureaucracy. Without the achievement and the preservation, in fact, of a significant cultural level "neither the parties, nor democracy nor parliament can be guarded from demagogy"; [61] and science cannot be brought to function to advance the human interests of the nation. Small wonder that Masaryk arrived, long years ago, at the conviction that to be an honest democrat means to think philosophically; that the problem is one pre-eminently of both science and morals, and that the attitude of the democrat "who reflects" is "not to seek what is called the golden mean between the right and the left" but deliberately to consider "the reality." [62]

This indeed is a large undertaking for the great masses of men, and Masaryk not merely conceded but insisted that it is primarily the function of leaders. Democracy can no more be sustained as democracy without educational, moral, and political leaders, who prepare their people in culture and truth, than political aristocracy could function without men who could be employed as the workers. The analogy, indeed, is close; for democracy demands as the leaders of nations men who while aristocrats of character, knowledge and wisdom, are the nation's main servants. The difference is that democracy is concerned with maximizing humanity and that its leaders are its leading workers.

Democratic politics, in point of fact, is management and leadership, and "democracy therefore has its constant and urgent problem of leadership,—that is, it has to train and edu-

---

[60] Krofta, op. cit., pp. 12, 18-19; *The Making of a State*, pp. 466-467.
[61] Krofta, op. cit., p. 15.
[62] *Les Problèmes de la Démocratie*, pp. 47-48.

cate leaders ..." [63] Democracy "is itself a constant striving for political education and for the education of the people; and education is, in high degree, self-education." Practically this is a question not just of schooling in the academic but a wider sense. "In all democratic countries ... leading positions are now being taken in politics and in the public services by men devoid of higher education. How to preserve the special knowledge that is required in government, administration and in Parliament is a problem that arises in every democracy as soon as the center of parliamentary gravity shifts toward the great popular parties. ... Yet it is true that the academically-educated and capable official is often inferior to the experienced organizer and party leader in knowledge of men and in practical capacity for dealing with parties, Parliament, and the Government; for political sense and statecraft are not to be acquired solely by schooling or even by administrative experience. Moreover, the problem of the educated comprises that of the semi-educated. Semi-education, as a transitional phase of our period of transition from theocracy to democracy, is the peculiar curse of our society and our era. Democracy has therefore to find means of turning semi-education into education" and of making this latter more full-blooded and concrete as well as most soundly basic.[64] This again, however, is a function of the interaction of leaders with each other and with those who are less educated. The masses themselves accordingly must help to educate their leaders.

Quite specifically, furthermore, democracy is a function of the Press. Its members have a direct educative function, without which democracy surrenders to mythology and autocracy. Publicists are or ought to be the nation's leading democrats, providing an extension of parliament to all of the people. But this requires that they be faithful to a responsibility or trust,

[63] *Speech on Tenth Anniversary*, p. 19.
[64] *The Making of a State*, pp. 437, 445-446.

Philosophy and Practice 59

and, rather than betray their public through misconstruing or creating news, that they present the truth with precision and informed acumen. "Hence the responsible and splendid task of journalism in democracy!" [65]

There is no clearer statement of the moral limits of a free yet democratically functional Press than Masaryk's elaboration of his own war-time principles of propaganda: "Not to abuse" or "underrate the enemy; not to distort facts or make boasts . . . to let facts speak for themselves, and use them as evidence . . . to influence by ideas and arguments and remain personally in the background; not to be an opportunist, not to snatch at the things which pass with the day, to have one plan and one standard in everything; and one thing more—not to be importunate. . . . To lie and exaggerate is the worst propaganda of all." [66] "Some among us," he said, "thought that the whole art of politics consists in gulling people. Until we stopped them, they tried to disseminate 'patriotic' untruths, forgetting that falsehoods can be exposed. Our enemies used these untruths against us." [67] These principles of propaganda, Dr. Beneš pointed out, were those of the "scientific and truthful propagation of knowledge." [68] This is an especial responsibility of the Press in a democracy. Negatively, a really democratic Press must be opposed to ignorance, obscurantism, lopsidedness, exploitation, oligarchy, and anarchy.

All this is but to say that democracy is a matter of the practical achieving of a full, realistic philosophy of human culture: that it requires all its statesmen to have a comprehensively informed viewpoint on human principles and values and that they be conscious of its humane import and outlook. Its fore-

---

[65] *Speech on Tenth Anniversary*, p. 19. "The daily press," he said in *The Making of a State*, "enjoys a real albeit not a codified right of initiative and referendum. In this right lies its great responsibility."—P. 448.
[66] Čapek, *President Masaryk Tells His Story*, pp. 252-253.
[67] *The Making of a State*, p. 81.
[68] "The Political Activity and Philosophy of T. G. Masaryk," p. 6.

most problems indeed are not so much technical or theoretic, important as those phases are. Technicians can find ways to cope with them; democracy is allied directly with science. The primary problems of democracy are spiritual and moral: issues of the *quality* of men's mental culture. Men are not democrats at heart when they are derelict in moral or religious perspective. People characteristically think to gain through other's loss. Revolution and reactionism show that men do not tend to think of making changes in society except through substitution of one system of oppression for another. To take the viewpoint of the entire group or nation and of outright mutuality in maximizing interests demands a thorough change in quality of views and in fundamental motives. Democracy requires "a new man, a new Adam. . . . A democratic republic is a matter of principle. . . . To proclaim and to practice the equality of all citizens, to recognize that all are free, to uphold inwardly and outwardly the humane principle of fraternity is as much a moral as a political innovation. . . . As I have shown when writing of Russia, men are wont to make their earthly and heavenly gods in their own image. They are anthropomorphist. . . . Most of them are guided, in theory and practice, by analogy . . . not by creative understanding." [69] Democracy demands that men be moral and that they also be morally creative; that they gain critical yet sympathetic perspective and live in terms not just of social solidarity but of social, cosmic creativity.

"I conceive the State," Masaryk consistently asserted, "*sub specie aeternitatis.*" [70] "The State is not merely a mechanism and politics are not merely a skillful administrative and diplomatic technique; the State is the association of the citizens on rational and moral foundations. . . . The State has a more pro-

[69] *The Making of a State*, p. 443.

[70] Cf. all sources and notably *The New Europe*, Dec. 21, 1916, in which Masaryk wrote his pre-eminently significant article, "Sub Specie Aeternitatis."

found meaning than appears on the surface in the medley of individual political actions. The State has a spiritual meaning, a moral meaning." [71] The real solution of its problems and real advancement of its interests can only be secured when adjustments are prepared upon the ground of continual stability and peace. Its foremost principle is "true equality—alike in the inward and the outward sphere—which extends to every citizen and to every nation." [72] The State indeed performs a cosmic function, when it is organized and advanced on a democratic basis. The State is then the agent of persisting and enlarging moral good; and it conserves and furthers normal individuality in normal groupings and relations. The work of states, accordingly, is advancement of whole nations in accordance with the laws or principles of collective progress.

These principles require efforts from the viewpoint of the universal and eternal. To take the outlook of the purely temporary is not only just to leave all tasks to be done over repeatedly from the start and therefore to provide no solid ground for progress, but it is also to have no concern for net long-run results and to impose thereby on future generations the burdens of a quite hopelessly exploited past. The sense of the enduring character and worth of both persons and nations is a prerequisite for arousing men to constructive, consolidating effort. This means indeed that they must have the viewpoint of metaphysical, besides social, synergism.

Men's democratic culture, none the less, cannot be a matter purely of religion and morality in isolation from techniques and understandings. Both religion and morality, we shall see in succeeding chapters, are functions of men's metaphysics and therefore of their concrete logics. Whole thinking is the logic of democracy. Men must understand and know, and they must know the why of what they know, in order to be morally

[71] *Speech on Tenth Anniversary*, p. 31.
[72] *The New Europe* (periodical), Dec. 21, 1916, p. 305.

and intelligently democratic. The freedom of enlightened consciences is the only basic freedom men can have: the freedom which illuminates and expands the understandings, outreach, and control of life. This is the freedom which democracy in principle affords. Whether this is actualized to any marked degree throughout the diverse spheres of life depends not on democracy but on its advocates and beneficiaries. Scant wonder that Masaryk told the communist radicals in Czechoslovakia in the early days of the Republic, that they already had democracy in principle and that a "purely political revolution . . . in a democratic republic, is madness, a crime against the interests of the working people." [73] The democratic principle applies to all of life, and democracy *de facto*, throughout the compass of human relations, is the end of the social and the philosophic enterprise of men's living.

[73] *Les Problèmes de la Démocratie,* p. 116.

Chapter Three

Sources of Social Effectiveness

THE KEYNOTE OF MASARYK'S EFFECTIVENESS, in democratic social life, lay indubitably in his unusual integration of philosophy with concrete daily life. The degree to which he personally succeeded in this is well illustrated by a statement of Christian von Ehrenfels, who found himself, his family, and his country the mortal enemies of Masaryk in the World War. "I came to the conclusion that I could have murdered him," he said. "*Homo sum*. Yet at our first meeting, I was forced to confess: 'In spite of all, I love this man; I love him as I love the closest members of my family. . . . How is that to be explained? I asked myself that question then, and I ask myself that question now. And I have no other answer to it than the conviction which is as firm as a rock. This man alone, in all questions of life and death, can decide and deal with absolute selflessness." [1]

One cannot, in fact, read any of Masaryk's writings, much less study his life without the sense of the utter immediacy of his philosophy with the direct concerns of the moment. This is true pre-eminently of three major works: *The Czech Question*, *The Spirit of Russia*, and *The Making of a State*. It is true almost as notably of *Suicide as a Social Mass Phenomenon* and *The Social Question or Philosophical Bases of Marxism*. Even

[1] *Die Religion der Zukunft*, p. 23.

The Concrete Logic, which was Masaryk's clearest attempt at philosophical system, undertakes to present a logic of both theory and practice and to show that practical logic cannot be narrower or less penetrating and thorough than theoretic reflection. It must be scientifically inclusive and sound. Any adequate system in turn must take full note of all vital necessities of practice.

Masaryk, it is commonly agreed, was a master of life. He knew how to live, and for him, as for Socrates, virtue was knowledge. There was no needed cleavage, he believed, between wisdom and life. Ludwig Klages and divided personalities might talk for scores of centuries about the battle of the soul with the spirit. They had a dualistic view of life, and they themselves produced the battle by the incompleteness and dissociating jars of onesided, fragmentary thinking. Wisdom is not a divider of life. Wisdom is the best judgment of men, unifying thought on all phases of life and existence and thereby unifying living. He who is master of life is master therewith of thought, for by his mastery in thinking he intelligently organizes his whole living—while seeking trans-personal ends. The primary problem is that of selecting and appropriating sources for one's guidance or the advising of one's judgments. There is, in truth, no more significant chapter in the account of Masaryk's democratic mode of living than that which deals with his deliberate assimilation and assessment of sources. Here would seem to be indeed the major source of his success not only in personal living but in broad social relations.

BRENTANO AND MASARYK

We have presented Masaryk's own statement at twenty-five of his early development. That was the period in which he was least obviously the master of circumstances and yet in which he himself laid the foundations for his own understanding and

Social Effectiveness

evaluation of sources. We have now therefore to take account of those especial sets of influences which entered quite immediately into Masaryk's mature reflection and contributed most effectively to his viewpoint and practice. It is common to distinguish two such special groups of influences: (1) those of his foremost teacher, Franz Brentano and (2) the Czech Awakeners and Czech Brethren. Masaryk himself would have added a third: Charlotte Garrigue Masaryk, his wife. Yet a fourth, and even a fifth, the influence of his colleagues and students and the philosophical problem of the literary philosophers of Germany and Russia, stand out as forces on his philosophical pathway. First attention must, in any case, be given to Masaryk's relations to Brentano.

We shall approach this question of Brentano's influence on Masaryk with the query as to whether or to what degree Masaryk was a philosophical disciple of Brentano. Brentanoists insistently have included Masaryk in the membership of their fellowship of truth, although they have also emphasized that he was not wholly orthodox.[2] Masaryk himself, furthermore, was ever ready to pay homage to Brentano; and the Brentano Gesellschaft in Prague, established on a foundation provided by Masaryk, was a pre-eminent instance of homage—as was, in his Leipzig days, Masaryk's winning of Edmund Husserl to attendance on Brentano's lectures in Vienna.[3] Yet apart from honoring Brentano,

---

[2] Professor Oskar Kraus wrote of Masaryk in contradistinction to Brentano: "His way was not that of psychological analysis and sharp logical inquiry."—"T. G. Masaryk und Franz Brentano," reprint from *Die Drei Ringe*, Vols. 5, 7-8 (1933), p. 3.

[3] *Ibid.*; also Čapek, *President Masaryk Tells His Story*, pp. 104-105, 132; Zdenek Nejedlý, *T. G. Masaryk*, I, 254, II, 111-112. This last is a voluminously complete biography of Masaryk. Describing Masaryk's activity, 1876-1877, in Leipzig, Nejedlý wrote: "But Masaryk was at the same time also making individual friendships and contacts here [in Leipzig], in which connection one name is of particular interest, Edmund Husserl. This now so-celebrated founder of 'phenomenology' was, to be sure, much younger than Masaryk. He was born on the 8th of April

is there actual reason to believe that Masaryk was significantly Brentanoist? The Brentanoists submitted that there is.[4] There are strong evidences to the contrary. We must, accordingly, investigate the brief on which these former rest their case.

They pointed first of all to years of Masaryk's close association with Brentano, as a student, friend, and junior colleague—by means of walks, talks, and correspondence.[5] In 1874, in his fifth semester at the University of Vienna, Masaryk became a

1859, and was then not quite eighteen years old. He had just come from the Gymnasium. Even so they became very close friends, first as compatriots. Husserl was, in fact, a native of Prossnitz and, although a German by inclination, he presented himself to Masaryk as a compatriot. But more than that, of course, it was his keenness which attracted Masaryk to him. Therefore Masaryk went with him to lectures, also to the 'Philosophische Gesellschaft,' and was not infrequently helpful to him in his inexperience. In particular he advised him, as a beginner, not to let himself be led astray by second-rate contemporary literature, but to make a careful study of the principal modern philosophers, Descartes, the English empiricists and Leibniz. But Masaryk himself was also learning from Husserl. Husserl was then studying mathematics and in exchange he in turn initiated Masaryk into foundations of higher mathematics. Through these interests they became personally fond of one another. Hence they did not separate even after Masaryk left Leipzig. While in Leipzig Masaryk had told Husserl much of Brentano, and so in order to know Brentano, Husserl went to Vienna; here he was on as friendly terms with Masaryk as at Leipzig. Masaryk influenced him not only philosophically, but religiously and, as we shall see further, politically. Afterwards their relations languished. Husserl became somewhat of an academic philosopher, and with that Masaryk lost interest in him. But they never broke off completely. They corresponded with one another and do so even today."

In Volume II Nejedlý reiterates: "In Leipzig, as we know, Masaryk gained for Brentano's philosophy another adherent, the now young philosopher Edmund Husserl, who is today highly significant. Masaryk lured him to Vienna by telling him that there he would be able to learn more about Brentano's philosophy from the master himself." (Translation by Mrs. Lida J. Matulka.)

[4] Kraus, *op. cit.*; cf. especially the open letter (written 1918): "An den Philosophen Masaryk," and also Kraus's "Die Grundzüge Welt-und-Lebensanschauung T. G. Masaryks," *Slavische Rundschau*, Vol. II, No. 3.

[5] Kraus, "T. G. Masaryk und Franz Brentano."

Social Effectiveness 67

student of Brentano, and although he took his doctorate in 1876 and spent the following year in Leipzig, he maintained close relations and had frequent conversations with Brentano not only while a Dozent in Vienna (1879–1882) but during that whole period (1874–1882), and in the immediately succeeding years as well—when Professor-in-extraordinary of Philosophy at Prague.

Brentano's own regard for Masaryk is significant in this relation. It was expressed in sundry letters but perhaps most clearly in the statement with which he and Zimmerman approved Masaryk's dissertation on *Das Wesen der Seele bei Plato* (*Plato's Notion of the Soul*)—a work which Masaryk soon burned because of its immaturity and lack of noteworthy content.[6] "The author," they agreed, "has studied the full writings of Plato with a great deal of industry and knows how to produce references from the most various dialogues which throw light upon the question treated. He shows himself, furthermore, widely versed in modern philosophic literature." They conclude: "The author displays not only a capacity for investigation in the sphere of the history of philosophy but in some degree for his own speculative consideration of problems. Long association with the noble and sagacious Greek masters appears to have served equally to develop his own keenness in thinking and to produce in him the tendency to nobility which in numerous ways makes itself felt."[7] In 1883, Brentano confirmed this positive appreciation in a letter to Anton Marty in Prague. "Masaryk was here," he wrote. "I was greatly pleased with him; he spoke with fine balance of judgment."[8]

Professor Oskar Kraus of the Brentano Gesellschaft in Prague summarizes, in consequence, that "if we ask what circumstances called forth the extraordinary interest and good

---

[6] Cf. Čapek, *President Masaryk Tells His Story*, p. 114.
[7] Werner, *T. G. Masaryk, Bild seines Lebens*, p. 29.
[8] Kraus, "T. G. Masaryk und Franz Brentano," p. 2.

will of Brentano for Masaryk, there can be no doubt that the mental gifts and character of young Masaryk made an unusual impression, while Masaryk, in turn, perceived in Brentano an exemplary thinker and fighter." [9] The evidence from associations is thus noteworthy, if indecisive. But Brentanoists adduce two additional considerations: the fact of mutuality in views, and certain parallels of Masaryk's with Brentano's development.

Several parallels are to be noted. Both left the Catholic Church following the Pope's enunciation of Infallibility (1870), and while this might mean merely that both were conscientious and courageous thinkers (as both were), it was Brentano's action in this which first won Masaryk's notice. A more significant parallel was their mutual regard for English empiricism and for Auguste Comte. In 1877, Masaryk wrote that Hume, Comte and Mill had been his teachers together with Plato and Aristotle.[10] In 1884, Masaryk's *Versuch einer Concreten Logik* (along with his reply to Professor Durdík in the Philosophical Society in Prague that Comte must be considered as one of the five greatest philosophers[11]) secured his outright branding as a positivist. Yet in so far as positivism might be attributed to either Masaryk or Brentano, it formed a transitional tendency in the reflections of each. Masaryk, we shall find, went beyond Comte even in *The Concrete Logic*, in his much more positive conception particularly of psychology and religion, while Brentano's point of view, in turn, had closer affinities with that of David Hume than with that of Auguste Comte. Brentano and Masaryk were both indeed susceptible to the methodology of Hume. Brentano ranked Hume higher than Kant; and in his seminars he used a translation of La Place's "Philosophical Essay on Probability." Masaryk accepted Brentano's criticism of

[9] *Ibid.*, p. 3.
[10] Werner, *op. cit.*, p. 140.
[11] Čapek, *President Masaryk Tells His Story*, pp. 151-152.

Social Effectiveness

Kant, who he said was Brentano's favorite target;[12] and from Brentano, rather than from Comte, Masaryk derived the view that abstract ideas are pure fictions—a view which Masaryk at once modified to take account of generalities which are capable of concrete articulation and which are definitely essential for the organizing and resuming of the data of knowledge. It was in Hume, none the less, that Masaryk found the model of empirical method,[13] and for his Inaugural Address, 1883, at the University of Prague, he lectured on "Hume's Scepticism and the Calculus of Probability"[14]—an idea which in Brentano's post-Vienna years assumed for him still more extensive importance.[15] Relation, therefore, unmistakably is evident, but the "what" and "how much" of Brentano's influence is not clearly apparent.

It remains, accordingly, to consider the persisting community of ideas shared by Brentano with Masaryk. Three of these stand out above all others: determinism, theism, and a naturalistic ethics of sentiment. From the standpoint of ethics, Professor Oskar Kraus has pointed out that there are strong traces of Brentano's ethics in Masaryk's *Ideals of Humanity*.[16] Here, if anywhere, indeed, we would expect to find Brentano's influence, inasmuch as ethics was the one field in which Masaryk was able to attend almost all Brentano's lectures. The fact is, however, that the evidences of Brentano's thought are not weighty. That Masaryk states that ethical consciousness is vested primarily in feeling rather than in thought might be

[12] *Ibid.*, p. 105.
[13] Indicated especially in Masaryk's Preface to the Czech edition of *Hume's Principles of Morals*, translated by Mrs. Masaryk, Vienna, 1883.
[14] Cf. Kraus, "Grundzüge der Welt-und-Lebensanschauung T. G. Masaryks," p. 2.
[15] Franz Brentano, "Von der Wahrscheinlichkeit," *Versuch über die Erkenntnis* (1916), pp. 160-184.
[16] "Grundzüge der Welt-und-Lebensanschauung T. G. Masaryks," p. 4.

attributed almost wholly to the influence of Hume, whose *Principles of Morals* Masaryk used extensively in his class lectures and whose ultimate consciousness of human "sympathy" Masaryk found decisive for his own "humanitism." Masaryk did maintain in the direct spirit of Brentano that sympathy is "self-justifying" and needs no further validation; yet Masaryk found validation for it within modern history. That Brentano taught that men should choose the best of all practical attainables and realize the good in the largest measure possible to them, and that Masaryk urged the active love of men in its maximal extension shows no definite connection. Both positions could be ascribed, on one hand, to utilitarianism (to which Masaryk devotes a chapter in his *Ideals of Humanity*), and on the other, Masaryk's especially, to Czech humanism. Both Masaryk and Brentano were humanists in their special fashions, but it is Masaryk specifically who stands out as the philosopher of "humanity." That Brentano mediated influences from French, English, and Greek literature is another matter.

Both men, secondly, held complete determinism to be the only adequate conception of events in human life and universal nature; otherwise we would be faced with an irrationalistic fatalism. "It is evident," Masaryk insisted, "that ethics and sociology are possible only from the deterministic standpoint." Causal sequences in human nature enable us to comprehend and to modify human behavior. "Knowledge gives us power to intervene in the causal order," to determine our necessary goals and to choose the means which are best suited to these.[17] The very law-abiding nature of existence is the causal basis for this. Otherwise control of nature, or of any factors within nature, would be capricious, and data of knowledge could not themselves be effective as directors of action. What both Masaryk and Brentano considered a complete determinism of events does not seem indeed to explain that deliberate self-choice,

[17] Kraus, "T. G. Masaryk und Franz Brentano," pp. 5-6.

self-direction and self-mastery whereby knowledge ceases to be purely mechanistic and becomes a self-initiated quest of truth (and soundness). Nor does their determinism appear to do justice to that element of chance variety and spontaneity which so obviously presents itself in nature. And this is the more problematic when we take account of the theistic basis of existence which both men insisted was necessary. Whence the uncaused and unconditioned? An element of chance at the beginning as well as in the midst of the chain seems therefore inevitable. One of the considerations, none the less, that Masaryk and Brentano were concerned to maintain, is that freedom, in so far as this term is permissible at all, is not chance but determinism on the grounds of knowledge and in accordance with each individual's distinctive integrity. Unquestionably, Masaryk found himself in agreement with Brentano on this issue.

Their common commitment to theism was, indubitably, a different matter. Brentano reasoned with Leibniz and Thomas Aquinas that the fact of existences within our experience which are not immediately necessary, requires a necessary Being as their First Cause. An unconscious Cause cannot be basically necessary, since it is homogeneous with its effects and itself in need of causality. An omniscient and wholly good Cause is essential, though not an unchanging Perfection.[18]

Masaryk's approach to this issue was different. He never enunciated any formal "proof" of God's existence, though accepting teleology.[19] Perhaps this was because Brentano's reasoning seemed conclusive, but more probably because belief in God was not practically the issue, but what specific kinds of theistic faith people have and hold. The problem of suicide among sceptical and subjective peoples in contrast to the Catholic and orthodox objectivists had convinced him of the truth of

[18] *Vom Dasein Gottes*, pp. 410-489.
[19] Čapek, *Masaryk on Thought and Life*, pp. 62 ff.

Dostoievski's formula: "either God or murder." Yet even the most radical subjectivism is not without its god or gods. The highest that men know or acknowledge they invariably make gods, and in ultra-individualisms this is the ego *per se*.[20] The question, therefore, is not that of belief in God but what kind of cosmic viewpoint provides, first of all, for an epistemologically fundamental faith and, secondly, what kind of cosmic superstructure can be most adequately conceived on a realistically rational basis. What and where God is will follow from this. A concrete philosophic view, which takes account of all the facts and values to be critically considered and which provides most soundly and completely for the consolidation and effectiveness of life, has a primacy for religious loyalties and devotions and is essential to the comprehension of true theism. Such a philosophic view, Masaryk held, presupposes teleology on its highest plane. What, after all, is religious theism but the venture of a cosmic Purpose![21] Any other view is inadequate to the data of existence, including or excluding that of human life.[22] That one cannot think of God just in simple terms of human personality does not do away with moral cosmic creativity: a Providence in which all sound existence has its source and which constrains all nature toward constructive destinies.[23] God is, therefore, more than merely human "value." God is highest value, because ultimately supreme existence. Theism is implicit in the evolving and essential solidarity of life and nature, and above all in the integrity of human life and culture.

This viewpoint obviously has affinities with Brentano's Leibnizian Thomism, and Brentano indubitably did contribute to

[20] *Ideals of Humanity*, p. 49; cf. p. 80.
[21] Čapek, *Masaryk on Thought and Life*, pp. 62 ff; Masaryk, *Grundlagen des Marxismus*, p. 234.
[22] Cf. below, Chapter IX.
[23] Ludwig, *Defender of Democracy*, pp. 75 ff, 256; cf. Čapek, *President Masaryk Tells His Story*, p. 225.

Masaryk's comprehension of the issues of theism. But Masaryk's more complex cultural theism reveals the genius of his special viewpoint and shows the way in which his whole philosophy was, in fact, built up—not through isolation of theology from men's concrete world perspective, but through the formulation of an adequate viewpoint on the universe and life. Yet more of this later. The case for influence, indeed, is definitely apparent, but not that of discipleship or any close approximation to it. Rather do we have the instance of a broadly independent and far-reachingly inquiring mind who used Plato, Comte, Kant, Comenius, and others as well as Brentano, as his guides—within the limits of the constructive possibilities in their viewpoints—and went beyond them all in both synthesis and the pursuance of his problems.

Masaryk had, in fact, been studying philosophy independently for several years before attending any of the lectures of Brentano. Čapek states that Masaryk went to Professor Zimmerman on matriculation, in 1872, to ask how he could "set about the study of philosophy in a business-like way." Zimmerman replied that he "should read the whole history of philosophy and then choose the philosopher who interested" him most for detailed study. Masaryk recounted, "I had read the history of philosophy and the works of some of the philosophers while I was still at the high school, and had already discovered my predilection for Plato. . . ." [24] Masaryk, in point of fact, as we have seen in his *Curriculum Vitae* for the doctorate in 1876, had discovered at sixteen that his interest in the natural sciences led him to philosophy and he had told his boon companion Fojtik, as they talked about their futures, that he hoped to be a philosopher.[25]

Brentano, after all, was only one of Masaryk's several teach-

[24] Čapek, *President Masaryk Tells His Story*, pp. 79-80.
[25] Werner, *op. cit.*, p. 135.

ers in philosophy at Vienna and Leipzig,[26] and Masaryk never attended all of any series of Brentano's lectures due to demands on his time as a tutor. He did hear most of the lectures on ethics, but secured notes on Brentano's metaphysics and logic from others. Masaryk's study was pursued in consequence almost wholly on his own initiative. He was aided greatly by his conversations with Brentano, but his own omnivorous reading habits and extensive recourse to the most scattered of sources lent themselves to independent philosophical thinking and effort.

None of Masaryk's writings are, in fact, related closely to any of the writings of Brentano. His habilitation thesis, on *Suicide as a Social Mass Phenomenon*, raised the question whether he should receive his appointment in history, philosophy, or law, but since his study issued in the question of the functional connection of philosophies with suicides and was in import a philosophy of history, Zimmerman and Brentano approved appointment in philosophy.[27] The *Prologomenon to Concrete Logic* took its inspiration fundamentally from Comte, along with Comenius and Bacon, and centered in the issue of the unity of science. As Professor Kraus suggests, this was not logic in Brentano's, or in most common usage. Yet this was the point around which Masaryk gathered his creative thinking; this logic was his "system" of reference for guidance in solving all types of issues. Masaryk's *Social Question*, or *Philosophical and Sociological Bases of Marxism*, perhaps holds more of that penetrating criticism which should link him closest to Bren-

---

[26] Cf. above, *Curriculum Vitae*, 1877. Masaryk, as indicated in Chapter I, tells that from 1873 he had devoted himself exclusively to philosophy and that his teachers in Vienna besides Brentano were: Zimmerman, Brücke, Meynert, Langer, Stefan, Menger, Conze, von Eitelmeyer. In Leipzig, 1876–1877, Masaryk audited the lectures of Drobisch, Zöllner, Wundt, Roscher, Curtius, Schuster, Ziller; and of the theologicans: Luthardt, Kanis, Fricke.—Werner, p. 140.

[27] Čapek, *President Masaryk Tells His Story*, pp. 124-125.

Social Effectiveness 75

tano, but this is a much later work (1898) with Masaryk at his own epistemological best. By 1913, in his volumes on Russia, he had gone so far in his thought that in contrast to Brentano, he emphasized and re-emphasized the importance of the work of Kant. Only incidentally, therefore, do we find clear similarities of Masaryk's with Brentano's views, and these are but close enough to show little more than just mediate influence. The two doctrines for which Brentano is most noted, his theories of truth and of value, or of insighted judgments and self-justifying feelings, are scarcely traceable at all in Masaryk; and quite notably is this true of the former.

"Masaryk and I," Brentano once wrote, "approach issues and think in far too different ways." [28] Their whole conception of philosophy was different. Brentano thought of it as a special form of psychological analysis, discovering, one could say, the logical within the psychological—and Brentano was a logical and a psychological surgeon! [29] Masaryk was a broader thinker, concerned with total syntheses of knowledge and with sociological values. He took account of practicality, individual and social, and of its foundations in metaphysics and science and sought that "whole philosophy" which would be adequate to all needs and possibilities of life. Philosophy for him was world outlook (and defensible thinking) *in life:* in ethics, sociology, politics, and all the spheres of human culture. It must be true to be effective, but it must be functionally effective also to be wholly true. Masaryk was an arch-democrat among definitive philosophers; Brentano an aristocrat in political position.[30] Both were founders of philosophies, and to think of calling Masaryk a Brentanoist would be as inaccurate as to speak of Brentano as a Platonist. It was the genius of Brentano, none the

[28] Kraus, "T. G. Masaryk und Franz Brentano," p. 3.
[29] Čapek, *President Masaryk Tells His Story,* p. 132. Here Masaryk says of Brentano: "He was a great man with a mind as keen as a razor."
[30] Kraus, "T. G. Masaryk und Franz Brentano," p. 5.

less, to develop independence in his students. Witness Husserl, Meinong, and Stumpf. Masaryk was one of those privileged with the guidance and the stimulation of this great critical and courageous teacher and to become in partial consequence a most notable philosopher-statesman in history.

GOETHE, TOLSTOY, AND DOSTOIEVSKI

Next to Brentano and the influences which he crystallized one must consider those of the literary philosophers: Goethe, Tolstoy and Dostoievski. These were much more important to Masaryk's viewpoint and life than compartmental purists would approve. They filled, in fact, a role quite equal to the scientists—though not in opposition to them—both in the degree of attention which they received and even more distinctively in the increment which they afforded for Masaryk's philosophical conceptions. This is quite intelligible if we take account of Masaryk's view that philosophy most notably is vision (or world-view) and his recognition that the artist, in the truer and the larger sense, comprehends the world concretely and directly. Artists lead the way in insights and interpretations, and afford conceptions of which the philosophic thinker must constantly take note. Literature and art, in any case, are needed complements of science. Literary philosophers in particular, are teachers of mankind,[31] even though their works may have the sharpest limits.

Masaryk's relationship to Goethe was of primary import for his cultural development. To Goethe he attained when but a boy in the fourth and fifth *Gymnasial* classes; and Masaryk earmarked his youthful savings to obtain a full six-volume set of Goethe's works. Goethe was, he afterwards insisted, the first and greatest of his literary teachers—whose multi-sided cultural

---

[31] Cf. *Spirit of Russia*, II, 513; cf. Čapek, *President Masaryk Tells His Story*, pp. 98 ff, especially pp. 102-103.

universality set a master-type. From his lyrics and his novels, Masaryk passed on to his dramas and the *Faust:* that analysis of man of the nineteenth century. "Goethe has had a strongly formative influence on my development," Masaryk stated in his eighties, although "I have not uncritically taken over my teacher and prototype. . . . Goethe opened my eyes with his strong egosim, his sheer profligacy; but he reconciled me with his truthfulness, which did not falter even at a not just-involuntary confession." [32]

How different from the case of Tolstoy, whom Masaryk visited in 1887, 1888, and 1910! Yet how equally instructive! Masaryk disagreed with Tolstoy and his moral anarchism from the first. They spent days, in 1887, debating non-resistance to evil and defense of human good in war. Tolstoy's lack of social consciousness extended quite beyond the bounds of pacifism in its common reference. He was opposed to church and state and all social culture. Ethical communion at the moment took precedence over sanitation and every social precaution. Tolstoy would rather drink from the same cup as a syphilitic than to show the slightest sign of discrimination which might bestir humiliation in the latter. Cleanliness, he held in any case, is aristocratic, involving labor on the part of many people. The simple life in its least accomplished, least organized and almost primeval sense is the moral basis of society.[33]

Masaryk's point of view was totally at odds with this: "The simple life! My God! The problem of town and country cannot be solved by a sentimental morality and a declaration that the farmer and rural life are the pattern for all. Agriculture today is becoming industrialized." "The peasant lives wretchedly because he is poor, but not for the sake of asceticism. . . .

[32] Masaryk, "Mein Verhältnis zu Goethe," sonderabdruck *Prager Rundschau;* cf. Werner, *Th. G. Masaryk: Bild seines Lebens,* pp. 21-22.
[33] I. Silberstein, "L. N. Tolstoy und T. G. Masaryk," *Slavische Rundschau,* Jahrgang VII. Nr. 3 (1935), pp. 141-166.

To sew one's own boots, to go on foot instead of travelling by train, all that is only time thrown away; think of all the useful things you could have been doing in it!" [34]

Masaryk, on his second visit, took Tolstoy his own system of ethics. Tolstoy, however, was not impressed with it. Ethics for Tolstoy was a matter of concrete inspirations rather than of conscious system. He did attempt to generalize from these, but Tolstoy lacked methodology and a theoretical basis.

Tolstoy, none the less, was pleased with Masaryk's other writings. He liked his *Suicide*, and especially *The Bases of Marxism.* "What a masterly book!" Tolstoy wrote on reading *Die Philosophische und Sociologische Grundlagen des Marxismus.* "I am greatly pleased that Brockhaus ranked it foremost in his Bibliography of Socialism." [35] Tolstoy, in fact, had eight of Masaryk's books in his own library at his death in 1910.

Nor is it to be presumed that Masaryk's attitude toward Tolstoy was by any means entirely negative. His readiness to consider Tolstoy's ultra-sentimentalism shows the philosophical tolerance of Masaryk's scientific mind. In fact Masaryk made an effort, in 1888, to live like Tolstoy, to see if practice might confirm the latter's view. It was unsuccessful. Masaryk, furthermore, joined Tolstoy's anti-alcoholic society, pledging himself not to drink wine or beer of any kind, not to buy alcohol or treat other men, and to inculcate the harmfulness of alcoholic drinks. In this, he was successful. But Tolstoy's artificially primitive moral anarchism, with its non-consciousness of group loyalties and relations, Masaryk continuously and uncompromisingly rejected. He went to Tolstoy because he wished to know him personally, and Tolstoy in person could not validate his views. Tolstoy himself in fact did not make a success of life.[36]

---

[34] Čapek, *President Masaryk Tells His Story,* pp. 164-165.
[35] Silberstein, *op. cit.*
[36] Čapek, *President Masaryk Tells His Story,* pp. 162-165.

Social Effectiveness

In Dostoievski, by contrast, Masaryk found one of the most significant of all literary philosophers. His *Brothers Karamazov* Masaryk appraised as the most outstanding novel in the literature of all ages. Dostoievski was a kind of higher synthesis, indeed, of Tolstoy and Goethe. He set the modern scene of human struggle in the city, with its reactionary revolutionisms and its atheism, the hiding place of crime and vice. He let faith face the fire of unalleviated doubt, and would in no way spare the cleavage between scepticism and belief. And Dostoievski overcame the supermanishness of Goethe and the solipsism of his Fausts not by mystic altruism, as Tolstoy advocated, but by a sociology of daily work. Dostoievski's multisided and well-grounded sociological interest in the questions of the time, along with his actively incisive efforts to arrive at their solution, appealed definitely to Masaryk.[37]

Masaryk, Dr. Horák said,[38] was the first European who understood Dostoievski's work both as a whole and in its variously independent parts. Russian critics in the nineties were themselves so close to Dostoievski that they could not recognize his greatness. Western Europeans, on the other hand, were only superficially acquainted with Dostoievski's total work. Their views, in consequence, could not but be fragmentary. Masaryk knew all of Dostoievski's writings, as well as conditions in Russia, and Masaryk found Dostoievski to be a great psychological clarifier both of the unusual mentality of Russia and of the universal modern quest for soundness in faith and meaning in life.

As a philosophical artist, indeed, Dostoievksi stood so near to Masaryk's own realism that the latter could, in his *Spirit of Russia*, examine Dostoievski's criticism in relation not just to

---

[37] "Masaryk and Dostojevski," *Central European Observer*, Jan. 6, 1933, p. 8; *Slavische Rundschau*, Nov.–Dec. 1931, pp. 627-632; "T. G. Masaryk und Die Russische Gedankenwelt," *Prager Rundschau*, 1938.

[38] *Central European Observer*, Jan. 6, 1933, p. 8.

Russia but to Europe as a whole. Masaryk early urged, in fact, the significance of Dostoievski's work for modern life in general, contrasting his sense of the reality of the spiritually moral with the naturalistic realism which characterized the French. Masaryk himself started out, he said, from Dostoievski.

Still Dostoievski was decadent. He tried to find the keynote to life in the Russian monk; religion for him was an otherworldly matter. He was orthodox at heart and Czarist, and thought that Russia could attain to truth by dint of lying. He wished to think that dishonesty and trickery would somehow win out. "Neither in the case of Russia nor in our own," Masaryk wrote, "do I believe it" (that falsity can win). Masaryk's differences from Dostoievski grew sharper as his own thought developed. Yet Dostoievski continued to be one of the two most esteemed of Masaryk's literary guides.[39]

The significance of Dostoievski for Masaryk is not to be appreciated, in point of fact, without reference to Masaryk's political interests and motives. His interest in Russian literature and life gathered more and more about the problem of revolution. "These studies," he pointed out in his *Spirit of Russia*,[40] "might well be entitled 'The Russian Revoluton,' for since the days of Peter, Russia has been in a chronic condition of revolution. Since the time of the great [French] revolution the problem of revolution is one of the leading interests of all philosophers of history and statesmen in Russia" and has been "a standing item on the agenda, practically no less than theoretically." Dostoievski, accordingly, was by no means just a source of literary interest. Rather he was one of Masaryk's primary sources for solution of such social maladies as suicide and

---

[39] Cf. also *The Making of a State*, pp. 347-348, 449; Čapek, *President Masayrk Tells His Story*, p. 161; Ludwig, *Defender of Democracy*, pp. 94-95, 96.
[40] II, 528.

Social Effectiveness 81

neurosis and more notably still of revolutionism, its grounds and its defensibility in Russia.

Dr. Jakowenko argues that Masaryk was wrong in taking Dostoievski as his psychologic guide to Russia: that Russian revolutionism is much more akin to Tolstoy's moral anarchism.[41] It can be countered, though, that Russian unpredictability and revolutionism had basically religious causes, and that Russian Bolshevism particularly was the product of the impact of the most radical Western ideas on the stationary outlook demanded by the Russian Church, a fruit of inorganic union. "The Bolshevist," Masaryk diagnosed, "is the Russian monk, excited and confused by Feuerbach's materialism and atheism." [42] The Russian Faust is, in fact, the "idiot" or moral fool, as Dostoievski demonstrated.[43] This Slavic Superman needed both ethical and epistemological enlightenment for reformation of his outlook and culture. Else revolution and reactionism! Dostoievski led Masaryk to, if he did not himself effect, this analysis.

Other literary thinkers afforded other insights and conceptions, humanizing the data discovered and reaffirmed via science. Little wonder that Masaryk maintained that he lived in literature.[44] It was his primary key to human nature and culture.[45]

CZECH AWAKENERS

The most insistent problem which confronted Masaryk throughout life was that of the goals and values for Czech life

[41] "Masaryk und die russische Philosophie," *Festschrift*, II, 111-112.
[42] "The Slavs after the War," *Slavonic Review*, June, 1922, p. 12.
[43] "Masaryk and Dostojevski," *Central European Observer*, Jan. 6, 1938, p. 8; cf. Jiří Horák, "T. G. Masaryk und Die Russische Gedankenwelt," *Prager Rundschau*, p. 87.
[44] Čapek, *President Masaryk Tells His Story*, p. 242.
[45] *Ibid.*, p. 102; cf. also *The Making of a State*, sections on England, America, Germany, and France.

within (or without) Austria-Hungary. He had, we shall recall, given himself after his first experience in parliament to the study of Czech history and the Czech "national rebirth." Here Havlíček and Palacký were his chief guides. Dobrovský (1753–1829) and Jungmann (1773–1847) had been active philologically in restoring Czech linguistics. Kollár (1793–1847) and Šafařík (1795–1861) rekindled literature from a romanticist perspective. Palacký (1798–1876) and Havlíček (1821–1856) undertook realistically to face the problem of political advancement for the Czechs. Palacký, particularly, made an historical approach. Though not questioning the authenticity of the Zelená Hora and Králove Dvur manuscripts, he pointed out none the less that the foremost era of Czech history was Hussite and that the strength of Czech national life lay in morality and culture. Palacký framed the first Czech political program on a socio-moral basis, urging the Czechs to work not for political independence but for reconstruction of Austria-Hungary as a federation. Science and culture, he held, are the only ultimately effective weapons. Palacký advocated comprehensive education grounded in the methods and the facts of all sciences.

Havlíček was more of a democrat and still more of a realist. He was a journalist rather than historian, yet hated superficial thinking. He stood for "natural," in distinction from "historic," right. Palacký had been driven by an alliance with nobility between historical and natural right. Yet for both Palacký and Havlíček rights issued from the people. With Palacký, Havlíček advocated Austro-Slavic federation and opposed romanticism and reactionism with the bitterest of satire. He was revolutionary in political science and culture, demanding that politics be made non-political.[46]

Masaryk built his national philosophy around Havlíček especially. This was witnessed, first of all, by a notable biography

[46] *The Czech Question*, Chaps. I-III.

Social Effectiveness 83

of that short-lived martyr to Czech humanistic realism, and more expressly and completely by a whole series of activities concerned with reforming Austria-Hungary and advancing Czecho-Slovak culture. With Drtina and Kaizl, in 1893, Masaryk founded the paper *Naše Doba*, "Our Era." He conceived this review as a living organ of the methodology of cultural realism, whereby to effect a reconstruction of Czech national life. He obtained the collaboration of a significant number of specialists, while he himself wrote indefatigably on proportional representation, teachers' salaries, the need for a second university, the intelligentsia and workers, liberalism and anarchism, and even on children's literature, on Bourget and Ruskin, Kollár's view of Slav reciprocity, present tendencies and desires, the Idea of Cyril and Methodius, John Huss: articles several of which grew into monographs and books.[47] His participation in the Hilsner murder case, in which he showed the utter falsity of the evidence for a Jewish ritual murder, was an inevitable portion of his work for scientific culture, though he himself did not seek any relation to that travesty of justice.[48] In 1905 he published lectures on "The Nationalist Philosophy of Modern Times." In these he formulated a sociological concept of nationality: tracing national consciousness in language, state, race, economic and social conditions, and all phases of cultural life, and locating both the content and program of nationality in the historic genius of the nations themselves. He drew upon philosophies of history in France, England, and

[47] V. Škrach, *T. G. Masaryk*, pp. 8, 9.
[48] "Hilsner was a young Jew who was accused in 1899 of murdering two girls . . . and using their blood for rites connected with the Jewish religion. He was tried and convicted, and the trial let loose a storm of anti-semitic feeling."—Čapek, *President Masaryk Tells His Story*, p. 187. Masaryk at first, he states, "took no interest in the case" but a former student of his came from Vienna and prevailed on him to take up the issue. "Masaryk was convinced, from a study of the evidence, that Hilsner was innocent, and flung himself into the campaign to prove it."— *Ibid.*

Germany, together with the national philosophies of Russia, Poland, and Bohemia.[49]

Yet Masaryk lived to see the hopelessness of a politically cultural reformation within Austria-Hungary. The question of the social justifiability and necessity of revolution became to him insistent. He studied therefore all the phases of this complex issue and published his results on the eve of the war.[50] Revolution aiming at reform, he held, was not only justified but morally essential, if reformation could not be achieved without it. True revolution involved constructive transformation. Palacký and Havlíček had not advocated breaking away from Austria-Hungary but this was ultimately involved in their political conceptions. It was Palacký, in fact, who in 1866 proclaimed: "We were before Austria and we shall be after Austria"[51]—a statement already fulfilled if but momentarily.

CLOSE PERSONAL FORCES

Here another set of influences came out to meet him, the foremost of which was that of his wife: that one collaborator to whom more than any other Masaryk ascribed his moral strength and spiritual perspective. "It was my own great good fortune and happiness," he stated in *The Making of a State*,[52] "that in my journey through life, I met Charlotte Garrigue, in whom French blood and American vigor were united. Without her I should never have seen clearly either the sense of life or my own political task." She mediated, indeed, French, English, and American viewpoints and culture in their best forms. "I see that her unusual character influences me more strongly than I had first thought," Masaryk wrote to a friend of his

---

[49] Škrach, *T. G. Masaryk*, p. 16.
[50] *The Spirit of Russia*, II, 529-534.
[51] Palacký's political testament, "Mé Posledni Slovo"; cf. Vladimir Nosek, *The Spirit of Bohemia*, p. 164.
[52] P. 323.

Vienna days. "The distinctive clarity of her thought, simplicity of morals, fineness in social grace, practical abilities of every kind, together with a very marked enthusiasm for science and art and a strong sensitivity to the beautiful and good, seem to me to be the essentials for a woman whom every one must love." [53] In conversation with Čapek [54] Masaryk said, "She had a magnificent intellect, better than mine. It is characteristic of her that she loved mathematics. All through her life her desire was for precise knowledge: but she did not lack feeling on that account. She was deeply religious; death was to her as the passage from one chamber to another, so unshakable was her belief in immortality. In regard to morals she had not a vestige of moral anarchism which is so widespread in Europe, that is, on the Continent; for that reason, too, she was decided and firm on political and social questions. She was absolutely uncompromising, and utterly truthful: these two qualities had a great influence on my development; through her the best elements of Protestantism became part of my life: that unity of religion and life, practical religion, religion for every day. In those debates we had together in Leipzig, I had got to know her depth: her poets were, like mine, Shakespeare and Goethe, but she saw deeper into them than I did, and could correct Goethe by Shakespeare. We did everything together, we even read Plato together: our whole married life was co-operation. She was very musical: she loved Smetana, and wrote an analysis of his second quartette in my paper *Naše Doba;* she said that that quartette reveals his spiritual unrest. She wrote other studies of his work; perhaps they will be published some day.

"From American she became Czech, morally and politically. She believed in the genius of our nation, she helped me in my political battles and in all my political activity. I never worked without her co-operation till I was abroad during the war.

---

[53] Werner, *T. G. Masaryk,* p. 40.
[54] *President Masaryk Tells His Story,* pp. 121-123.

Even then I knew that I was working in harmony with her. There were many moments when, far away from her, I was acutely aware of our unity of thought. I do not think it was telepathy, but the parallel thinking and feeling of persons who are in complete harmony and who look at the world with the same eyes. She believed that a woman does not live only for her husband, nor a man only for his wife: both must seek the laws of God and fulfil them."

Yet numerous other personal influences also entered into the concrete articulation of Masaryk's conceptions. Throughout his life Masaryk had gathered groups about him who became imbued with the truth and force of his ideas. In Vienna, 1876, when as a student he and a number of other young men were walking one day, they all acknowledged that they needed a motive for living. They formed a club, took as their motto, "Knowledge is power," and agreed to meet every ten years to recount the results.[55] They never all met again as a club, but some were linked together as a consequence. "The lonely Slovak in Prague"[56] thereby became the rallying point of a widesweeping influence which aimed at nothing less than the ideal of humanity in informed social practice. Masaryk himself, in turn, became pressed by his students and friends into direct social leadership, and on their account especially he was led to complete and apply his democratic philosophy of culture.

The story of Eduard Beneš' relation to Masaryk is a further tale in itself. Though we cannot treat it here, since it would be more a story of the development of Beneš' philosophy rather than Masaryk's, we can point out the import of the associations of two men thirty-four years apart in their ages and yet united in activity by a common viewpoint and loyalty. The force on Beneš of Masaryk's thinking and life did not at first make itself

---

[55] Werner, *op. cit.*, pp. 27-28.
[56] Cf. quotation from Hermann Bahr, cited by Steed, *Slavonic Review*, March, 1930, p. 470.

Social Effectiveness

felt. Beneš was but twenty years old when he first heard Masaryk's lectures. Yet that at twenty-five he should have come to much the same view, while studying abroad (in France, England, and Germany), and that at thirty he should have become Masaryk's most notable colleague is especially symptomatic of the intellectual strength of Masaryk's position and of both the moral and intellectual force which Masaryk exercised on associates.[57]

These had in Masaryk a critically independent thinker who knew the values of sources, who gained from all channels, from those of the most immediate members of his household to those of the inner circles of anarchism and decadent literature. Thus he enriched and advanced his philosophy. Yet this philosophy never was an end in itself for Masaryk, essential and organic as philosophy was to sound and humanly productive life. The end was life itself. Thus he enriched and advanced human living.

[57] Valuable sources on Eduard Beneš include his *War Memoirs* (Allen and Unwin), London, 1928; Louis Eisenmann, *Un Grand Européen* (Paul Hartmann), Paris, 1934; Kamil Krofta, *Éduard Beneš* (Orbis), Prague, 1934; Boris Jakowenko, *Eduard Beneš als Denker*, *Internationale Bibliothek für Philosophie*, *Periodische Sammelschrift*, Bd. I, No. 2, 1935; and W. Preston Warren, "The Democratic Diplomacy of President Beneš," *Furman Bulletin*, April, 1939.

Chapter Four

Philosophies as Modes of Life

WE HAVE CITED the chief sources of Masaryk's social effectiveness, and must now undertake to present his philosophy in substantial detail. This was both broader and profounder than is common among social theorists today, and yet in closest touch with practicalities. The union of the practical and theoretical was Masaryk's especial genius; and that he effected this without the sacrifice of either, places him well in advance of our best pragmatic philosophers. Nor does it lessen his status as a scholar or pre-eminently philosophic thinker. Masaryk's philosophy indeed was not only a union of the theoretical and practical but of the concrete and abstract. It was a rounded view, though not so much in actual system as in approach to all issues.

It is dangerous to apply an epithet to any individual or any of his views, in spite of all the qualifyings which one may insist upon. There is no doubt, however, that Masaryk was a functionalist, or at least a functional realist, in his philosophic outlook, and a functionalist of a more basically functional type than contemporary varieties. He might be called a pragmatist by a superficial classifier, since he insistently demanded that philosophy be practical, and made practical effects a test of valid theories. He broadened out the reaches of philosophy and decried the academicisms which ignored philosophies of politics and nationality *per se*.[1] Practicality in its broader sense was

[1] *The New Europe*, p. 16.

Philosophies as Modes of Life

indeed a primary philosophic datum and any theory which neglected this was *ipso* invalid.

Masaryk's, however, was no mere philosophy of practicality. Practicality itself was a function of right viewpoints and sound theories. Practicality required an outlook and sufficient structural basis. A knowledge of the world beyond and undergirding all immediate expedients was a value to be entered into for its own sake in order to be fully functional. Functionalism, in Masaryk's view, entailed a metaphysics of "actual entities" —to use a phrase of Whitehead—for practical effects depended in due course of time on an informed perspective of realities in their creative interrelations.

Nor was anything more practical than man's perspective itself: his outlook on the world and life. Metaphysics was inevitable in human living if not consciously in human thought, and all attempts to ignore or denounce metaphysics were efforts tending but to rob man of his orientation and vision. Even sheer scepticism, on the one hand, and credulous mythology, upon the other, were metaphysical standpoints implicating extreme individualism and naïve objectivism respectively.[2] Both of these standpoints had far-reaching consequences in and with regard to life which showed their invalidities. Pure pragmatism and utilitarianism, by way of seeming contrast, were make-shift positions, without due regard for truth and fundamental values. They left men without intellectual assurance or cosmic status. Theirs was a metaphysics of opportunism and chance, conceiving the universe as a vaguely ambiguous mine to be exploited so long as it lasts, with no questions asked as to what then or what for.[3] Masaryk himself indeed denied any

[2] *The Making of a State*, pp. 340 ff; *The Spirit of Russia*, Vol. II, Part III; *The Modern Man and Religion*, etc.
[3] Cf. *The Spirit of Russia*, Vol. II, Chap. 22, etc.; cf. also Čapek, *Masaryk on Thought and Life*, pp. 11, 13, 14, 19; *The Making of a State*, p. 230.

special interest in metaphysics and yet he insisted that metaphysical outlooks were crucial for living.

It was with respect to the factor of cosmic perspective that Masaryk first began his major philosophic writing, through analyzing out the function of philosophies in life; and in this factor of perspective he found the unity of theoretic thought with practicalities of life. It was in an effort at the diagnosis of our recent social malady of mass suicides [4] that the factor of metaphysical outlook first gained primacy for Masaryk, and received therewith an early, clear-cut formulation. Masaryk had been appalled in boyhood that anyone should wittingly cut off his life, and more appalled with added years, to find that one hundred thousand people annually consciously destroyed themselves. His first major writing was a thorough study of this circumstance, analyzing in quite modern fashion the different factors which conduce to suicide, in order to determine by accurate and reliable methods, on grounds of detailed evidence from more than thirty countries, what can be the primary cause or causes.

He studied the effects of nature, terrestrial and cosmic—distinguishing rates of suicide in different climates at different times of the year, week, day, in diverse weathers and living conditions, in both city and country—and he concluded that effects of nature might be predisposing influences but not determining causes of a mass suicidal wave. Decisive causes must be sought within the lives and relationships of men themselves.

Influences among men are of five different types. First, there are physical relationships, including body differences, due to age and sex as well as injuries and health. Masaryk found no clear relation of suicides with these. They have a dispositional influence at times, but are not in themselves determining.

Second, this is also true of the influences of social circum-

[4] In *Suicide as a Social Mass Phenomenon of Modern Civilization* published in 1881.

Philosophies as Modes of Life

stances: density of population, family life (marriage, divorce, concubinage, singleness, widowhood), imprisonment, vocation. Their influences are not great and close enough to be more than motivating causes, although concubinage, widowhood, and inconstancy in marriage seem to conduce to a distinctly higher frequency of suicides.

Third, political circumstances—involving race, nationality, forms and crises of government, military service, war—relate quite variously to suicides. Military service lends itself distinctively to higher suicidal rates, except in times of war when these show a decrease—to be followed once again when war is over by a sudden rise. Yet here again, the correlations are not close or clear enough to explain the range and intensity of the phenomena. Political relationships are themselves, in fact, resultants of those deeper-lying social forces which govern both the tendency to suicide and political developments.

Fourth, economic circumstances seem to be heavy contributors to suicides. Statistics show that 20-30% of suicides are due to discontent with pecuniary circumstances. Misery has a peculiarly weighty influence. It puts an individual in a pathological condition in which suicide appears as the end link of a long chain of indescribable distresses. Every economic crisis gives a special impetus to suicides, as do uncertain speculations. Trade and industry are worse in suicides than agriculture. Yet men's whole modes of life from place to place, with their social relations and standards of living, affect their liabilities to self-destruction. Suicide is no matter merely of sheer poverty or wealth. Economically people are far better off than their progenitors. But the tendency to suicide is almost insuperably greater in current living. The issue of distributing wealth has become, indeed, of paramount importance, as we should expect from the large accumulations of a few men while many people still are in differing degrees of really urgent need. But even this is relative in its influences on people, and notably conditioned by their viewpoints and thinking. The modern era indubitably is materialistic and satisfaction seeking. In such a time dissatisfactions must develop which will attain in many instances to sheer weariness with life. It is not wealth, therefore, or its absence, which so pervasively incites to suicide, but the erroneous valuing of goods.

Fifth, we are brought, therefore, to relationships of spiritual culture: intellectual, moral, and religious—and to life-conceptions in their totalities. Other relations, we have found, are almost wholly predisposing, and not in any clear-cut sense, determining. It now remains to ask, what can be determining? To this, there can be just one answer: the individual person. "Every voluntary act corresponds," in fact, "to the character of the human agent and is the more characteristic the weightier it is for that person. Now there can scarcely be a weightier decision than that of life or death, and it is therefore clear that suicide corresponds in a distinctive way to the whole character of the individual (who commits it); and right in this regard, it is a question of the whole life-and-world view of the person, a question of the judgment which the individual can pass about the worth of human life for the universe and especially for mankind. This decision is *man's verdict about the world.* [Italics added.] How horrifying this sounds when one takes account of the vast number of suicides of the present! What in comparison is the significance of all the whining and scoffing of pessimists *à la* Schopenhauer! . . . The immediate cause of suicide is always a misfortune which the individual concerned takes to be so great that he cannot bear to go on living . . . but the objective judge gives evidence in the great majority of instances that the cause was too trivial in relation to the loss . . . and he soon perceives that almost always an intellectual or moral defect has beclouded judgment."[5] *Perspective* has been lost or is otherwise inadequate.

[5] *Ibid.*, pp. 63-64.

Philosophies as Modes of Life

Suicides, in truth, are most characteristic of subjective peoples, in contrast to the Catholic and orthodox objectivists. These latter have a unitary world-view, so long as they can wash away the acids of reflection. But protestantism is confronted with the problem of overcoming scepticism by something other than a new appeal to absolute authority. In its German form—under Kant's, Fichte's, and Hegel's influence—it has swung to radical subjectivism. The outcome is that men have lost their peace of mind, along with their framework of reference, and have grown restless, inconstant, and nervous. The modern man is, in indubitable truth, a nervous creature who commits suicide from sheer weariness with life. Suicide is the crucial symptom of a subjective and a psychopathic age, the function of an ego-centered philosophic outlook, which thereby refutes itself. It is the arch disingenuity of half-trained, half-informed, and only half-philosophizing life, which has thought enough to get away from credulous mythology, but has not thought enough to reach beyond the attitude and philosophy of mere sophisticated doubt.[6]

Masaryk gave a striking picture of this type of quasi-thinking in his *Modern Man and Religion*. "Let us," he wrote, "take Gram in Garborg's *Wearied Souls*. And the generation sit by the road and helplessly drop their hands. They look worn and vacant like the insane. There is darkness ahead, darkness behind. Meaninglessly, aimlessly, above endless marshland dance the will o'-the-wisps of the sciences . . . !" And science is conceived as a system of doubts. "Is there a God? We do not know. Is there a soul? We do not know. . . . Am I living, do I really exist?—We do not know. What, then, do we know? Is it possible for us to know anything at all? We do not know. And this systematic 'we do not know' is called science! And people clap their hands above their heads and cry exultantly: 'The progress of the human mind is incomprehensible! We no

[6] Cf. especially *The Making of a State*, pp. 345 ff.

longer need faith in God, for science has observed that water boiling in a pot lifts the lid and that rubbed resin attracts straw. . . .'"[7] And in this superficial renunciation of all the meaning to reality and life, they lay the bases for their disillusionment and death.

Suicide, indeed, may be looked at in a broader light: to include self-destruction which is not immediate or witting. Psychoses and suicides, in fact, are part and parcel of one and the same ego-centered predicament; and "decadence" ranks with suicide, psychosis, revolution, war, as a set of symptoms of something definitely destructive in personal and group life—a defection in men's viewpoints and lowering of functions, to be viewed as acute by the sociology of history.

Decadence was a key predicament to Masaryk: a problem in the moral health and solidarity of both individuals and nations. He treated this not in his work on suicide but in a number of writings. He studied decadence first of all with regard to its estate in France. He had been drawn to this question, in 1876, by Funck-Brentano, who "after Comte was the first in France to make sociology the exclusive object of his researches," and who maintained that a union of the French and Slavs was needed for the saving of humanity. The French had been till then in the vanguard of civilization; now they were in definite decadence. The Slavs alone could not revitalize humanity; they lacked culturally basic and realistic techniques. They had, however, freshness of faith and vision and must unite with the French to renew the cultural health of France and safeguard civilization for society. Masaryk objected to this sort of reasoning that Funck-Brentano had not really shown that France was basically decadent. In recent years, he urged, the idea of decadence had been emphasized quite widely. German writers particularly, and notably the German Protestants, had inculcated this idea. Laveleye's *Le Protestantisme et le Catholicisme*

[7] *Modern Man and Religion*, p. 28.

Philosophies as Modes of Life 95

undertook to show that the French, vanquished in the war of 1870, were enfeebled, senile, without intellectual and without moral vigor, condemned to disappear. This, Masaryk maintained, was not supported by the facts, but by a wholly verbal theory of conquest. Were that theory in fact true, the French under Napoleon would have been the most virtuous of peoples.[8]

With the World War, none the less, Masaryk's concern for French decadence assumed different proportions. "I felt it important," he pointed out, "to ascertain how France and, particularly, her intellectual class would stand the hardships of war. True, I did not accept the arguments on which the pan-Germans based prophecies of the final decadence of France and of the Latin peoples. But even temporary decadence has its dangers; and in the case of France, they were the more threatening because the depopulation which alarms the French themselves is certainly connected with moral decadence. And this danger, it seemed to me, would not be wholly averted even by an Allied victory. . . ."[9]

Masaryk recounted that though he had early had a "severe attack of French Romanticism," he had soon seen its moral chaos and natural tendency to degeneration. "I was struck," he said, "by the peculiarly morbid and even perverse sexualism in the French Romantics, a trend of feeling of which I believe de Musset has hitherto been the most typical exponent. In this element of Romanticism I sought—rightly, I think,—the influence of Catholicism on quasi-Catholic people; for Catholicism, with its asceticism and ideal of celibacy, turns the mind too much towards sex and magnifies its importance even in tender youth. The sexualism of French literature—and, in this respect, France is truly representative—I attribute especially to this Catholic education. The pro-Catholic poet, Charles Guérin,

[8] V. Škrach, "Masaryk et le positivisme française," *Festschrift, Th. G. Masaryk*, II, 9-10.
[9] *The Making of a State*, pp. 107-108.

expressed it as the 'eternal duel between the fire of the Pagan body and the celestial yearning of the Catholic soul.' It is not asceticism alone but exaggerated transcendentalism as a whole that leads skeptics and unbelievers of Catholic origin to the extremes of extreme naturalism. I compared the French and the Italians with the English, the Americans and the Germans. Among Protestant (and Orthodox) peoples and writers there is neither this sexual romanticism nor the peculiar kind of blasphemy that arises from the constant and obvious contrast between the transcendental religious world and the ascetic ideals, on the one hand, and the real world of experience on the other. This contrast disturbs and excites. Protestantism is less transcendental; it is realistic. In Baudelaire the romantic association of the ideal of a Catholic Madonna with a naturalistic Venus finds graphic and typical expression—the same somersault is turned as when Comte surrenders Positivist science to fetishism. Zola threw this somersault in his naturalistic novels, which are strange mixtures of unpositivist Positivism and of gross Romanticism.

"Carrère's literary studies on Romanticism, which I had not seen before, were a pleasant surprise. He says many things that I had already said in my essays. One of the chief tasks in French spiritual development has hitherto been to analyze and to criticize Romanticism. De Tocqueville, as afterwards Taine and Brunetière, condemned it. To-day its adversaries are numerous, for instance, Seillière, in his 'Away from Rousseau,' and his pupils, Lasserre, Faguet, Gillouin and also Maurras—names which show that opposition to Romanticism may spring from divergent views and aims. It is, above all, a moral problem. The Revolution against the old Régime—in the last resort, against Catholicism—degenerated in France into an exaggerated naturalism and into a sexualism that was unhealthy and therefore decadent. In this tendency I see a grave question not only for France but for the other Catholic nations and, indeed,

Philosophies as Modes of Life

for the whole modern era; and its gravity is not lessened by the fact that the tendency has prevailed in so marked a degree over the more powerful French women writers like Rachilde, Colette, and Madeleine Marx." [10]

Despite decadence in French life, there were strongly moral movements which constantly regenerated. Yet decadence was a basic fact of French, and German, and American life, bespeaking loss of strength from devitalizing cultures, based on *unwholesome philosophies of actuality*. Whereas in Europe, "decadence is attributed to over-population and its consequences," nevertheless, America displayed the morbid symptoms of decadence regardless of the "comparative sparseness of her population. Who can tell how the blending of the races . . . is working out morally and biologically? Nervousness and neurasthenia are widespread, and the number of suicides is increasing, just as in Europe; and there is constant talk of the nervousness—I would rather say the 'nerviness'—of American women." America indeed has her own realistic critics, who oppose Romanticism, Idealism, and modern English Transcendentalism. "They wage war against the Churches, against machinery with its moral and material effects, and therefore against industrialism, capitalism and mammonism. They assail narrowmindedness, Pragmatism in philosophy, and the tendency to exaggerate the value of science." But in "opposing one-sidedness they are radically one-sided. Their aims are hazy and negative, superficial with a typical American superficiality." They "grow rhapsodical over 'free love' and fall into excessive sexuality." [11] They are lopsided and unpenetrating in perspective.

While in America, in consequence, there was no clear system of ideas to make for healthy solidarity of culture—apart

[10] *Ibid.*, pp. 106-109.
[11] *Ibid.*, pp. 229, 232; cf. Čapek, *President Masaryk Tells His Story*, p. 278.

from "simplicity and openness" and a certain pioneering idealism which readily passes into plundering—contemporary German culture was marked by far too great a philosophic set. Current German culture was mechanistically external and more utterly materialistic than America's dollar lust. It stood in opposition to the true German humanitarian artists and thinkers—Leibniz, Kant, Lessing, Schiller, and Beethoven—and was the actual modernizing of Scholastics. German Universities were intellectual barracks. "There is nothing so absurd but that the German Professors cannot cleverly defend it." Indeed, "German scholastics is at its best in theology, namely, in the so-called modern theology; in the Prussian theocratic system the State has the largest share, and therefore its theology is nothing but politics in ecclesiastical and religious guise. Ludwig Feuerbach and his criticism of theology is in substance a criticism of Prussianism." [12]

"It is in Lagarde," Masaryk wrote, "that I find the most impressive formulation of Pan-Germanism; not unlikely, for the reason that he was a theologian.... I am aware that those who hold the point of view in Germany today would insist that their doctrine is not to be confused with pre-War Pan-Germanism," but "present day Pan-Germanism, which has taken on the form of National Socialism, has, as I see it, not gone beyond Lagarde; the thing it has done has been to carry out his teaching in detail." In that respect, "the National Socialists have gone far," [13] and have tried by every desperate means to push their war-time failure to overt success. Yet Pan-Germanism permits of no such final victory. It is a *cul de sac*, a self-defeating-and-destroying philosophy of existence and culture.[14]

[12] *The New Europe*, p. 40.
[13] Ludwig, *Defender of Democracy*, pp. 203, 205.
[14] *The Making of a State*, pp. 337-351. "After Kant," stated Masaryk, "and in large measure through his influence, German thought took the wrong road." "I look upon Hegel as a synthesis of Goethe and Kant and an anticipation of Bismarck. He accepted the Prussian idea of the State

Philosophies as Modes of Life

"There is an essential connection," Masaryk related, "between 'supermanishness,' 'militarism,' war and suicide. . . .

as the highest expression of nationality and a guide for the whole community. His pantheism and fantastic philosophy are a transition from the idea of the Universe held by Goethe and Kant to the mechanical materialism and violence of Prussianism. By his doctrine of 'Absolute Idealism' Hegel supported the claim of the Prussian State to absolute authority, forsook the universal outlook and humaneness of Goethe and Kant, and created the basis for a policy of force in theory and practice. It was not for nothing that Hegel was originally a theologian; and even in theology he propounded the principles of Prussian theocracy. Bismarck and the Emperor William were always calling on God, the Prussian God; and Bismarck and Bismarckianism swallowed up Goethe. The Prussian State became the infallible director of the nation and of its spiritual life and culture.

"Marx, for his part, after running through Feuerbach's philosophy that 'a man is what he eats,' turned Hegel's pantheism and Absolute Idealism into materialism. He took over the mechanism of the Prussian organization, with its State authority and almighty centralization, even though he conceived the State itself as subject to economic conditions. His relationship to the method and the tactics of Prussianism explains the circumstance that, in the world war, the German Marxists associated themselves for so long with the pan-Germans and gave uncritical support to Prussian policy despite their Socialism and their revolutionary tenets. Indeed, the undemocratic notion that large economic units are indispensable corresponds to Prussian 'supermanishness'; and Marx's own view of the Slav peoples was not different from that of Treitschke or Lagarde. And Nietzsche sought refuge from economic isolation—from 'solipsism'—in the Darwinian right of the stronger. The sway (and the Church) of a new aristocracy were to be founded upon the 'blonde beast,' Christian theocracy being replaced by a theocracy of the superman.

"Yet I do not conceive the antithesis between Goethe and Bismarck, Kant and Krupp in the sense of a Parsee dualism, for a psychologist might find elements of Prussian 'Realpolitik' even in Kant and Goethe. The real antithesis would be between Beethoven and Bismarck. In Beethoven I see a German genius unspoiled by Prussia. His art springs from pure, true inspiration. It speaks from heart to heart, as Beethoven sometimes thought it did. The Ninth Symphony is a hymn of humanity and democracy. . . . And with Beethoven I couple his great teacher, Bach, and Bach's religious music; and, in philosophy, Leibnitz, whose yearning to melt the Churches into one is the natural outcome of his doctrine of the Monads and of his fundamental conception of uni-

Modern militarism, especially Prussian militarism, is a scientific and philosophic system of objectivization, of compulsory escape from morbid subjectivity and suicidal mania. I repeat 'modern militarism'; for the fighting spirit of savages and barbarians, or even the fighting spirit of mediaeval knights and mercenaries is, psychologically and morally, very different

versal harmony. Pan-German chauvinists see in Leibnitz's humanitarian aspirations an effect of his Slavonic blood. I, however, look upon his philosophy as a continuation of Platonism, albeit with strong traces of the subjectivism which Kant and his followers were presently to overdo. . . .

"'Expressionism' is preeminently German, an aspect of German subjectivism, and therefore damned from birth. The expressionists are nothing but interpreters of Kantian or neo-Kantian doctrine and of subjectivism after the manner of Nietzsche. Expressionism, as Herman Bahr describes it, creates a universe of its own. The expressionist poet and critic Paulsen—it is something more than an accident that he should be the son of the philosopher Paulsen who was a follower of Kant—explains that the poet bears in himself the 'finished forms' (a Kantian term) out of which the whole world grows. This is subjectivism in all its violent absurdity. Paulsen says rightly that expressionism is essentially German. And I do the Germans no wrong if I say that, during the war, their literature was more chauvinistic than any, in quantity and quality, or that German writers and journalists drove their people towards war, in Berlin, Vienna and Budapest. There were exceptions, like Stilgebauer, Unruh, Förster, Schücking, Nippold and Grelling, but they were exceptions. . . .

"Inadvertently," Masaryk points out, "my analysis is confirmed by the German historian, Lamprecht, who sought, with so much vigor and enthusiasm, to vindicate the Germans in the war. In his history of Modern Germany, written before the war ("Zur jüngsten deutschen Vergangenheit," published in 1904), he rightly describes the epoch as one of 'irritability,' and adduces both the Emperor William and Bismarck as its characteristic types. In truth, the German superman, the Titan, is a nervous creature who seeks relief from chronic excitement in death or war, that is to say, in an excitement still more acute.

"However true this may be of all nations, it is especially true of the Germans. Their philosophers, artists and other active minds pushed subjectivism and individualism to the point of absurd egomania, with all its moral consequences. Nietzsche's superman, the Darwinian 'beast,' was to prove a remedy for the inhuman folly of 'solipsism.' "—*The Making of a State*, 337-340; cf. 344, 351.

Philosophies as Modes of Life

from the scientifically coördinated military system of the modern absolutist State. Savages and barbarians fight from aboriginal savagery, or driven by want or hunger; but, in the World War, disciples of Rousseau and Kant, Goethe, and Herder, of Byron and de Musset stood in the trenches. And when, in the spirit of Hegel, Werner Sombart praises German militarism and boasts of the Fausts and Zarathustras in the trenches, he fails to understand how severely he is, in reality, condemning German and European civilization. The fighting of these modern, civilized men is a violent effort to get away from the perplexities that arise in the ego of the superman; and, for this reason, the *intelligentsia* were no whit behind the peasants and workmen in fighting spirit, but rather outdid them. This phenomenon struck me first when I saw the Serbian *intelligentsia* in the Balkan wars. In modern war, adversaries do not face each other eye to eye, hand to hand. They destroy each other from a distance, *abstractly, invisibly, killing through and by ideas* [italics added]—German idealism translated into the tongue of Krupp. Even defensive war, which alone is morally admissible, thus becomes repugnant; and this is why Democracy has so hard a task in training democratic soldiers, in building up a democratic army composed of soldiers consciously on the defensive, not seeking to conquer and to subjugate by main force, yet brave and ready to sacrifice their own lives. Militarism and modern war are of a piece with Rousseau's 'State of Nature,' with Comte's lapse from Positivism into Fetishism, and with the Romanticist yearning for an unreasoning, animal, vegetative life. Neither the great theorist of modern Democracy nor the founder of Positivism nor the Romanticists saw that the 'State of Nature,' Fetishism and animality signify barbaric blood-lust and a war of all against all. The natural man knows naught of suicide from modern weariness of life, exhaustion and neurasthenia. If he ever kills himself it is in rage at some affront or at the failure of some vigorous effort, whereas the modern man suffers from morbid suicidal mania, from lack of energy, fatigue or dread born of mental and moral isolation, of barren megalomania, and supermanishness. Militarism is an attempt of the superman to escape from diseases which nevertheless it aggravates. The German 'Nation of Thinkers and Philosophers' had the greatest number of suicides, developed the completest militarism" and pressed the world into war.[15]

Such, in part, was Masaryk's analysis of the socio-personal force and inadequacies of philosophic viewpoints within current culture. Marxism and Russian anarchism were likewise symptoms of this culture, radically reacting from its sharpest limitations. Their especial limits we shall compass later. The Bolshevist at best, we have already noted, was but "the Russian monk excited and confused by Feuerbach's materialism and atheism," while the true-blue Marxist, if not necessarily and destructively a revolutionist, was none the less negative and reactionary in his point of view: a dogmatic and primitive materialism which fills its adepts with intellectual, moral, aesthetic, and religious darkness and corrupts all whom it regards as the emancipated and elect.[16] Marxism was submoral and intellectually untenable as philosophy, while mechanistically subhuman as a mode of life. To say, in fact, that any metaphysic has no relationship to concrete human life is to ignore the meaning and the motive-force of every world-view or concept of ultimate principle for personal programs and actions. It makes every difference how a man conceives his world; and his metaphysics, in its most abstract sense, is his view of what is final in that world. Beneš' statement is germane here: that democracy perforce "rejects materialistic conceptions, which in their consequences necessarily lead to force generally, just

[15] *The Making of a State*, pp. 345, 348-349.
[16] *Grundlagen des Marxisms*, p. 516; cf. "The Slavs after the War," *Slavonic Review*, June 1922, p. 12; cf. also the preceding chapter.

Philosophies as Modes of Life 103

as it rejects the nationalistic nature of authority as the basis of national and international politics." [17]

The foregoing, then, was not the total picture of our modern culture. There was another side which expressed the actual spirit of "humanity," which revolted against bonds of iron-clad anti-human systems, and which demanded the achievement of an expansive system of ideas which would illuminate and be adequate for life. There is in fact no clearer simple development of this philosophy of the function of philosophy itself than in Masaryk's striking monograph, *Ideals of Humanity*.[18]

There he shows how philosophic systems, or Ideas, are themselves ideals for living and how they really actualize themselves as human modes of life; how socialism, individualism, utilitarianism, pessimism, evolutionism, positivism, Nietzsche's superego are all humane in fundamental motive and also metaphysical in their essential characters; how each is incomplete and superficial as a mere ethic or practical philosophy but requires elaboration as a whole viewpoint on existence and value; how *time*, through social consequences—a consideration which contemporary experimentalists have been highly wont to circumscribe—changes the emphases or fulfills the characters of philosophic systems, and brings them round toward more "humanity"; and how it is essential for any nation's thinking to take account of all mankind's achievements in reflective culture. All of Masaryk's writings are expressions of this viewpoint, but most notably his *New Europe* (1918) and *The Making of a State* (1927)—in which the *Ideals of Humanity* (1901) finds concrete elaboration.

Our era, quite particularly, is a time of striving toward an ideology which will be adequate to life. We have our antimetaphysical and our anti-socialistic human viewpoints. Strife of systems is indeed the order of the day, and has been so

[17] Krofta, *Eduard Beneš*, p. 13.
[18] 1901; English trans., Allen and Unwin, London, 1938.

increasingly from the eighteenth century. Philosophies of life and of trans-human actuality battle with each other for the governance of life, and each presents a problem by reaction and one-sidedness which is itself an impasse for our culture. Neurosis, suicide, decadence, revolution, war are symptomatic social functons of these sundry systems. The worst irrationalities of life are products and by-products of conceptual systems, and most notably of those which conceive themselves as non-philosophic. Man's problem therefore is distinctly philosophic: what can make for health and solidarity of life through wholesome unity of ideological outlook and culture?

Perspective, Masaryk found, is basically conceptual. Men are governed by ideas even in emotions and habits, and philosophical conceptions have an outreach and expression in their lives whether those conceptions purport to be philosophies of life or of non-human nature. Every culture, in fact, embodies a philosophy or group of variously distinct philosophies, which are lived out by the generations which accept their implications, and which disclose their human values by results in human lives. Cosmic conceptions and perspectives yield in fact men's principles of life, and while these may be primarily implicit—and there will always be recalcitrant factors and forces—both the order and disorders of living are variously functions of ideas. The question is: What particular ideas? And how do these provide for solidarity and the satisfactoriness of life? Masaryk's concern for these especial outcomes placed him on the other side of our recent cultural register; for he stands, as he continuously stood, for clear integrity in culture.

Plato indeed has had no more realistic interpreter in theory or in practice than Masaryk, the philosopher-statesman. Both in the belief in the determining influence of Ideas—for better or for worse—and in effective comprehension of the methods of their actualizing, Masaryk made Plato intelligible to the most

Philosophies as Modes of Life 105

unphilosophic or unpenetrating minds. Masaryk himself became, in fact, the actualizer and embodiment of Plato's philosophy.

Masaryk was more than a Platonist indeed, in the usual apprehension of that term. He was an heir of the ages in thinking and acting, combining an Aristotelian thoroughness in concrete, scientific method with a Socratic aptitude for intellectually social endeavor. But in his insistence on philosophic conceptions as the heart of all living and culture, he was as "Platonic" as Plato himself had any occasion to urge.

Perspectives of all men, Masaryk held, need ideological analysis. Mythology and mysticism lend themselves unerringly to aberrations. Concrete comprehension of the reaches of philosophical conceptions into life is an essential for living. These must be made articulate for socio-personal good. This was witnessed especially in the issue of the "manuscripts" concerning the historic genius of the Czechs—and numerous other events. It was the business of such an institution as the reestablished Czech University of Prague to stand uncompromisingly for facts of history and for scientific soundness in culture.[19]

This, in fact—Masaryk had already pointed out—is the primary business of philosophy. "What does it mean to me," he asked in 1884, "if you tell me that Comte or Descartes and others, were philosophers? I study Descartes. I learn to distinguish mathematical, historical, biological, psychological, ethical, logical, and other points of view—pure sciences—but where

---

[19] A Czech branch of the University of Prague had been conceded by the Hapsburg Government, 1882. With gaining of their independence, 1918, the Czechs insisted that 1882 was the occasion of the renewal of the original Czech University established by Charles IV in 1348. That King Charles viewed the University of Prague first and foremost as a Czech University was evident by the predominance in voting power which he gave to the Czechs and which led to the withdrawal of the German students from Prague to form the University of Leipzig.

now in addition is philosophy? I ask a philosopher [20] if he will recommend a compendium of his specialty. He shrugs his shoulders: 'Friend, that is just the difficulty; we still have no handbooks like the natural sciences possess; but study this and that work! I study, therefore, and, in fact, in order not to overlook anything, I study the recognized philosophers chronologically. I study several histories of philosophy but in the end I know no more than I knew in the beginning. I analyze the definitions of philosophy—a sad business that! I investigate the content of what is said to be philosophy, and again I fail to achieve my goal. For everywhere I see special sciences, as for instance in our *Hochschulen* where the philosophical faculty is a composite assembling of diverse sciences. But what philosophy is I do not clearly see or hear, although I feel that it exists and must exist since I perceive indeed a certain difference between various specialists. . . . I study my philosophers again and again, and let myself, so to speak, from despair into research. Then there occurs to me, what indeed should surely have occurred at once: that I should separate and classify the 'philosophic' disciplines in distinction from the special sciences in order just to see in these themselves what is 'philosophic' and what 'scientific.'

"I now see that in distinction from mathematics and the natural sciences, the sciences of spirit (*Geisteswissenschaften*) usually are designated as the philosophic disciplines. Yet that too is not wholly right, for no one takes law, for instance, for a philosophic study. Again, I am at loss until, *Gott sei Dank*, I have the happy thought to classify not just the mental sciences but the whole ensemble of the sciences. This idea leads to concrete logic, and through concrete logic, I finally learn what philosophy is and is not, or better stated, what it should be."
For "when we separate out all independent special sciences in

---

[20] Professor Zimmerman? Cf. Čapek, *President Masaryk Tells His Story*, p. 79.

this way, there is only metaphysics left," though about its "nature and position in the system of the sciences we still have gained no knowledge."[21] After pages of discussion about meanings of this term, Masaryk concluded that while metaphysics is the science of being in its universal and essential nature it is best comprehended as the integrated content of all sciences. It is, therefore, in its most intelligible sense, unitary scientific world-conception. While far from unavoidable in this sense, metaphysics is humanly inevitable in some sense and basically prerequisite in this specific sense to solidarity and effectiveness in life.

It savors of counsel of perfection that anyone should urge on men an outright scientific solidarity in culture. It is, however, a counsel of protection. Man, Masaryk declared in the introduction to his *Concrete Logic,* "is not a rational but a rationalizing being" who gropes planlessly along a fate-determined path. Life questions of the greatest moment are decided at haphazard venture. Feelings and impulses are more manifold than intellectual operations and much more intense. The result is that intelligence is much more subject to effective strivings than feelings and impulses are to intellection. It cannot be doubted that blind forces direct men more frequently and dynamically than does the goal-conscious activity of reflection. Reflex action, surplus energies, habits, fixed ideas, arbitrary choices motivated and impelled by feelings, these are most immediate determinants of living. Men's wishes, furthermore, are father to their thoughts. Were man, in fact, an intellectual being, the products of his mind would realize themselves of their own force. They are made, instead, to travel the cross roads of passion and of error. Thought and life seem highly incommensurable.

How easily indeed our mind itself can go astray! How readily we are satisfied with prescriptions of others! And how we

[21] *Versuch Einer Concreten Logik,* pp. 250-251.

delight in the pictures of inflamed phantasy! Of exact thinking, we find little in men. The greatest of philosophers, even, frequently turn back to the inaccuracies of ordinary inconsistent, and intellectually disordered life. We must, in consequence, give our minds a reliable guide, a sound logic, and good method. Science gives the power of actual knowledge, and concrete logic, which knits together all men's accurate conceptions, involves the combined logic of all sciences.[22]

Despite their irrationalisms, and partially indeed because of them, men are more subject to ideational influences and, in fact, to philosophical conceptions than they generally acknowledge. The revolt from metaphysics, in point of fact, is not basically a revolt from metaphysics but from the tendency toward the superimposition of a cosmic theory on concrete facts from, or in view of which, it was not derived. Men will have cosmic outlooks and conceptions, though they be negative or simply unavowed. Even the disorder and travesties of life are, as we have instanced, resultants variously of men's world conceptions. Men's foremost need, in consequence, is to form a true idea of reality and their lives. This, Masaryk emphasized, is the special *motif* of philosophy and notably of that philosophy which is built on concrete logic.

It is this insistence on the intelligible meanings of life and existence throughout which constituted Masaryk pre-eminently a Platonist. The prime difference certainly between Masaryk and the great preponderance of others of our age is that whereas we surreptitiously admit the high *suggestive* value of ideas—for advertising, salesmanship, and propaganda—and use a marked proportion of our effort to forestall critical reflection, Masaryk *consciously made the fact of man's susceptibility to ideas the occasion and groundwork of a definitively constructive philosophy;* and he insisted that every man requires clear, true, co-ordinated ideas for satisfactory living. Which type of

[22] *Ibid.*, pp. 2-10.

Philosophies as Modes of Life

approach operates with anything that approximates enduring success is not difficult to discover. We have seen the workings of the makeshift approach in recent diplomacy. One makes for human incapacity, social imbecility, and essential anarchy as we have had it in various phases of our life of late; the other conduces to solidarity and man's intelligent participation in the constructive processes of nature. Strength, scope, and effectiveness of life lie with Masaryk's Platonic functionalism.

Were one to undertake to use younger contemporaries to interpret Masaryk's functional realism, he would be tempted to consider Masaryk as a synthesis of Whitehead and Dewey: of Dewey in his practical social insistence; of Whitehead in his metaphysical and comprehensively cultural viewpoint. Whitehead's mathematical logic would have a place also in Masaryk's functional outlook, whereas for Dewey, this was considered at odds with the functionally genetic method of dealing with issues.[23] Masaryk was not himself to any notable degree a mathematical logician, but he was a believer in science, in organized, unified science and in *mathematical analyses* and *precision*. Mathematics was, in fact, for him the basic science of a realistically functional philosophy.

Masaryk was also, like Whitehead more than like Dewey, a philosopher of history, who judged movements of history in the light of sound gains to life and who saw in historical succession not the rightness or validity of a social system but its momentary opportunity to rule. Time and human values would assess its solidarity and right, though any system of sheer force stood condemned from its start. The concept of problem-solution seems to have been less vague to Masaryk than Dewey, as were his concepts of knowledge, of truth and of right. The notion of the almost total socio-philosophic failure of the past was

[23] John Dewey, "Whitehead's Philosophy," *Proceedings and Addresses of the American Philosophical Association*, X (1936); cf. also Whitehead's reply in the same volume.

not his view of history either intellectually or practically. The basic solidarities, first, of historical processes from the quite ancient Greeks to the twentieth-century moderns, and, secondly, of science from mathematical logic to applied sociology, are points that combine the inclusive standpoint of Whitehead with the practical experimentalism and social emphasis of Dewey.

Masaryk's experimentalism was of a definitely socio-historical type. History moved forward not just by trial and error, action and reaction, but also by conscious efforts to enhance the contents and the worth of life. Modern history was especially portentous.[24] It had tended to flexibility in social controls; though at the cost of revolutions. The World War was a clear-cut revolution in which men joined together on behalf of humane principles and values. That this was followed by reactionism of both upper class and proletarian types was but witness of the often unreflective dialectic whereby men characteristically approach the truth of life and nature. But that both types of social reaction were ideological, even when ideologically materialistic, was witness of the inevitable philosophic genius of men, striving toward an adequate cosmic viewpoint and life and testing out ideational constructions as these become implicit in their thinking. Philosophies, accordingly, were hypotheses for experiments in human life, in reference to trans-human actualities; and the philosophic test of adequacy to life was an indispensable test of their adequacy to actuality.

The logic, certainly, of each philosophic system would be elaborated by successive generations of philosophers themselves, and might, as in the case of English empiricism, definitely disprove the system—*reductio ad absurdum*. There was a more inexorable logic, none the less, to life itself. It asked for inward consistency and consolidarity, and for the possibilities of significant activity in relationship to other life: with oppor-

[24] *The Spirit of Russia*, I, 204 ff.

Philosophies as Modes of Life 111

tunity for sound expansion. That life should find itself frustrated, in a philosophic *cul de sac*, meant not that logic was gainsaid but that it was continuously reaffirmed and significantly implemented. By its inevitable logic, life proved and disproved philosophies. These either gave it better comprehensions and more significantly valid outlets and interests, whereby life itself could be increasingly established, or they led it to its own White Mountain.[25] Philosophies, in either circumstance, were its guiding principles and motives, giving ordered unity to both thought and life, controlling men's horizons and governing their status in the universe, and validating themselves through their adequacy to actuality for that human living part of it which tried to interpret the entire order of nature and could not help living accordingly. Ideas were in this sense instruments of action, but they were immeasurably more. They were keys to reality and important actualities themselves, to which men attain haltingly yet likewise insistently. But first of all they were agencies and constituents of human vision.

The problem of both philosophy and life was not one, therefore, of any isolable genius or inspiration but of organized and integrated culture, wherein men might know the truth in its substantial detail and relations and live as informed citizens of a whole universe of facts and values. This was the enduring quest: the quest of a soundly ideational perspective on existence, and thereby of a culturally valid *modus vivendi*.

[25] Battle, 1620, in which the Czechs were defeated, following which their nobility were exiled or executed and their peasantry subjected to 300 years of Hapsburg absolutism.

Chapter Five

The Logical Structure of Culture

MASARYK, IT WAS HELD by gentlemen's agreement, was not a philosophic "system builder"—like Wilhelm Wundt and German philosophic writers generally.[1] Masaryk spared himself that "doubtful honor," it was indicated, by writing variously on widely scattered topics and then becoming a diplomatist with no chance for systematic philosophic writing. His system, Professor J. B. Kozák states, was written in his personality, which spelled philosophy so full and true in all the spheres of human action that Masaryk ranked among the very greatest in philosophic social living.[2] Masaryk was a practical rather than a theoretical philosopher.

The claim, however, that Masaryk had no written system must be qualified, and perhaps remoteness from the scene of his uniquely philosophic personality and voluminous production will enable us to see his "system" in a clearer light. For "system" he advanced in early philosophic works and "system" he insisted on for all of human culture. His *Concrete Logic*, in particular—the second of his major writings—was the formulation of his system, and while he modified his views in significant details, that system remained substantially his system

---

[1] J. B. Kozák, "Der Philosoph," *Masaryk: Staatsmann und Denker* (Orbis, Prague, 1930), p. 91.
[2] "Masaryk as Philosopher," *Slavonic Review*, March, 1930, p. 478.

throughout his life though expanded realistically to meet philosophically cultural demands. This was the work, in fact, which after more than fifty years, Masaryk was, up to his death, September 1937, putting through a final revision. It comprised his frame of reference for his thinking and his life. For though philosophy never was a sheer end-in-itself for Masaryk, all of life's issues demanded an adequate system of reference whereby to judge wisely and clearly, and guide men's activities toward sound results. For such a sound yet cultural philosophy Masaryk strove consciously from his early university years.[3]

We have viewed Masaryk as a functionally social realist who was signally effective as a statesman and as a philosopher of life: and therein is his genius pre-eminently depicted. We must now proceed to treat him genetically at least as a Comtist and, in the sequel, as a Kantian; for Masaryk's philosophy of life and social practicality derived from Comte and Kant, as well as Plato and the others we have cited. The import of these facts should be apparent as we advance, but that we may not be confused, to start, by thinking that there was no community between Plato and Comte, we must remind ourselves of the synthetic scope of Plato's ideology. Plato soft-pedaled indeed on the biologic phases of existence. Yet there was a sweeping compass to his methodology which was every whit as broad as Aristotle's epoch-making *Organon*. Nor was there greater rigor anywhere than in Plato's *Parmenides* and his later philosophy of numbers. Plato was a comprehensive and a penetrating thinker who had a profound sense of human values—individual and social—and was an artist in appreciation and expression. It was Plato who was first, in fact, to grasp the meaning of ideas not just for intelligible thinking but for any apprehension of existence. With Whitehead, Masaryk could readily have said that all of European thought is a series

[3] Čapek, *President Masaryk Tells His Story*, p. 124.

of footnotes to Plato.⁴ Plato stood for full integrity in thought and did not make that cleavage between the purely intellectual and affective understanding which has so limited and almost despoiled logic.

This was the point, in fact, at which Masaryk joined Comte with Plato and for a time at least passed from Plato to Comte; for it was Auguste Comte who "made the first complete attempt to effect a natural classification and organization of the sciences" and thereby to establish the unity of knowledge.⁵ The author often wondered, in his college days, why there should be any great concern about the order and relation of the sciences; this seemed a wholly academic issue. For Masaryk, from his college days, this seemed the foremost theoretic problem and for the reason that only through the unity of science could there be a unitary world-outlook ⁶ and thereby a substantial unity to human life and culture. The solidarity and security of life depended on the natural integration of a scientific culture. No dilettantic liberalism or eclecticism could give soundness to man's thinking and by way of thought to life; and no mere fortuity of circumstances could long save men from their own stupidity and disjointed notions. Culture, even scientific culture, did not simply care for, and consolidate, itself. This was witnessed by conflicts between politics and science, on one hand, and science and religion on the other; by departmental jealousy in almost every sphere of intellectual operations and by a chaos of conceptions that made for social conflict and experimental social anarchy, with a common disregard of everything that savored of a fundamental culture.

People stood during Masaryk's life, as they now stand, at a

⁴ *Process and Reality*, p. 53. This would also seem to be the motif of Whitehead's *Adventures of Ideas*.
⁵ *Versuch einer Concreten Logik*, p. 39.
⁶ *Ibid.*, pp. 215-217; cf. pp. 13, 39, 202-218, 280.

Logical Structure of Culture 115

conflict in conceptions, and knew not why the issues were confusing. The different meanings of the terms by which they tried to live and on which they staked their social faiths, their failure to distinguish them or consistently maintain some one interpretation: all this was symptomatic of illogic in their culture. The modern age, for instance, had been individualistic, and individualism was the self-consciousness of "humanity." Yet "Kant conceived individualism also as subjectivism," and set the stage for egoistic anarchism such as Stirner's and Nietzsche's.[7] Marx, *par contra*, leaped to anti-individualistic socialism and thereby wronged the cause of men as much as he had hoped to help. Functional individualism and functional socialism were both quite different matters, social systems which would strengthen men and not by methods which made for the despoiling of others.[8]

Men were mythological in every phase of life: religion, politics, social theories and practice, aesthetics, and philosophy.[9] And mythology was a positive antagonist of science. It had even entered into and confused science. When men like Bertrand Russell, mathematically precise thinkers of our day, were guilty of such vague and confused positive conceptions as Masaryk cited in Russell's *Principles of Social Reconstruction*,[10] how could others think and conduct themselves who

[7] *The Spirit of Russia*, I, 212; cf. *Making of a State*, pp. 340 ff, also *Ideals of Humanity*, Chaps. III and VIII.

[8] *Ideals of Humanity*, p. 51; cf. Ludwig, *Defender of Democracy*, p. 55; cf. also *Making of a State*, p. 465.

[9] J. B. Kozák, "Masaryk as Philosopher," *Slavonic Review*, London, March, 1930, pp. 479-480.

[10] Reviewed by Masaryk in *The New Europe*, March 29, 1917. Russell proposed an actively constructive pacifism as the solution to international ills. His psychology, however, Masaryk pointed out, proved a difficult chapter. Impulses must be offset by counter-impulses. Reasoning functions in a very minor aspect. Thoughts spring out of intellectual impulses and provide some blockage to the other impulses. Constructive

were guided by sheer sentiment? They were victims of almost every wishful gleam of uncritical imagination. Witness again the battle of the manuscripts and, more obviously, the Hilsner Jewish ritual murder case. This is, Masaryk urged, an age of science and of substantiated accuracy in thinking. It is, and it ought to be, a realistic era, in which men face the facts in lieu of garnishing or avoiding them. It is a time of practicalities instead of useless culture. Yet clarity in human thinking and practicality in life were not to be achieved without first of all the isolation of our facts and terms for full analyses; and, secondly, the enlightened relating of these facts and terms to each other. It was men's lack of full, accurate science which left them at the mercy of their feelings and imaginations. For even when they resorted to science they stopped short, if not at full rigor, at full correlation and scientific synthesis.

Masaryk fought two different battles on behalf of sound thinking as the ground-work of life. The first was for scientific exactness or rigor, against the mythology of Czechs, Austrians, and Russians; the second, for integration not only into specialized theories but also into a full system of all of the sciences.

---

organizing of all impulses either in the individual or society is not provided for; spirit functions largely on the blinder side of life.

Russell's treatment of religion is similarly discrepant. He favors a religion which will be creative, but does not show how this can be the case. He contents himself with criticisms of prevailing ethics and the churches, and neglects the fact that morals and ecclesiasticism do not exhaust the issues of religion.

We can, Masaryk maintained, accept many of Russell's proposed objectives: promotion of freedom and of individual creativeness, substitution of law for force, and multiplication of voluntary organizations or agencies. But it is not the proposal of noble aims which we expect from a new philosophy of politics, but the critical elucidation of its fundamental notions and the elaboration of a sound method. Russell's politics are mixed together in confusing fashion. There are good passages on education, but the criticism of existing views of patriotism is too circumscribed. His whole point of view is dangerous because of its vagueness.

Logical Structure of Culture 117

Science, it was commonly taught, is a matter of the separation of each problem from all others for experimental study, but that this is just one stage of science was not by any means generally realized. That all sciences need to be knit into one comprehensive system of thinking appeared to be grasping too much. The human race after all had survived up to date and progressed—at least some of it had. But human living, none the less, was speeding up, while becoming more and more complex, and was subject to controls for most devastating ends. It now required the guidance and the leaven of a scientific philosophy of all human culture. The social schemes of political adventurers, together with the reckless makeshifts of undiscerning leaders, demanded counteracting, or else validation, from the point of view of an inclusive logic. There was no recourse in modern social life from sheer knowledge and its counterpart in fully integrated scientific vision. That this must be a social product or attainment did not lessen its necessity or excuse its lack in current politics and education.

There has been no more rigorous insistence on the accuracies and evidence of science than that of Masaryk, the analyst of manuscripts and life. He urged persistently that Humian exactness [11] was needed for clear and reliable experience, and that without this men could not but be mythologists. They must take their cues from concrete experience and validate their ideas by the degrees to which these fit all of the facts which they are supposed to explain. Concrete, detailed facts were the primary data for each valid judgment. No mere impressionism could be depended on for guidance of thinking and life. Men must have recourse to empirical science, analyze out all of the relevant data that concerns any problem, and test out every suggested hypothesis.

This was the prime keynote of Comte. He appealed to concrete description against all transcendent techniques and ush-

[11] *Versuch einer Concreten Logik*, p. 300.

ered in a new positive era of science by exposing mythology in history and in contemporary life. His was a hard-headed viewpoint, with no sugar-coatings or glossing-over of facts. He submitted to science, accurate, observing, metrical science, and made no allowance for human psychology of any kind or degree. An ultimate fetishism of humanity comprised, in fact, a reversal of this point of view, but this was not intrinsic to the Positivism for which Comte took his firm, clear, non-anthropomorphic stand.

Masaryk appealed, therefore, to Comte against the hazy, wishful thinking of contemporaries, and prepared a résumé of the whole six volumes of Comte's *Positive Philosophy* for daily reference in his classes. He made a full translation, likewise, of Comte's *Sociology* and pointed social living back to a whole philosophy of science.

Yet Comte was only incidental for Masaryk to the solution of life's basic cultural problems. One could maintain that Masaryk's own genius consisted fundamentally in taking count of factors which are characteristically neglected or read out and that, as pointed out in Chapter IV, the factor of men's world-perspectives was one which he found crucial for life. Yet it was no isolated insight that produced the consciousness of these commonly neglected factors. It was Masaryk's own wholeness of perspective and complete scientific approach to the diagnosis of issues. His was characteristically an inclusive, cultural logic, built up through broad yet equally intensive study. He deliberately undertook to achieve such a logic, since it was clearly essential to sound human living that logic should embrace whole thinking on all of existence and culture. In this, we have seen, Masaryk was quite independent of the direct influence of Brentano.

Professor Oskar Kraus has suggested that Masaryk was not a philosopher primarily but an *ethico-politicus homo;* and Professor Kraus has adduced, we have earlier noted, that even

Logical Structure of Culture 119

Masaryk's logic was not logic in the common usage of that term.[12] Here again, indeed, we find a close relationship of Masaryk to Dewey, in that logic was not narrowly delimited to formal issues, but was instrumental to solution of all types of problems of which the sagely intellectual was but one group or type. Masaryk, however, had full regard for older logics, including them within his broader view [13] and pointing out that in the sense of whole reason in concrete cultural thinking his employment of the term was not only justified but now preeminently in order. Logic was the methodology of knowledge and all defensible thinking; and as Masaryk wrote: knowledge logically considered is relationally intelligible and, therefore, unitarily one. Although the organizing of the sciences into systematic unity has been as an historical event always incomplete, the time must now, in fact, be ripe to think in logic of a natural system of all scientific thinking and to attempt the task which finds its closest analogue in recent natural history, to put in place of artificial inventories the actually organic system.[14]

Masaryk undertook therefore to determine the relations of each science with all others from the points of view of content and method and by showing the *rapport* of all sciences with each other to establish the integrity of all scientific culture and assure a unified world-view. To see, in fact, how each science can and does contribute to the others is essential for advancement of each of the sciences as likewise for metaphysics and logic.[15]

The relationship of philosophy to science was strikingly clear in the thinking of Masaryk. We have cited, in Chapter IV, his own summary of his early efforts to determine this. In

[12] *T. G. Masaryk und Franz Brentano*, Sonderdruck aus der Monatschrift *Die Drei Ringe*, Hefte 5 und 7/8, 1933, p. 3.
[13] *Versuch einer Concreten Logik*, pp. 202-218; cf. concluding observations to this chapter.
[14] *Ibid.*, p. 39.
[15] *Ibid.*, pp. 48-50, 216, etc.

The Spirit of Russia [16] Masaryk traced the history of this relation. "From the history of European thought," he said, "we learn how among the Greeks there occurred a gradual severance between mythical and critical thinking. . . . Thenceforward the opposition between mythology and philosophy had become established"; philosophy was critical reflection; mythology, credulous suggestibility. "After Aristotle," indeed, "philosophic thought grew weaker, mythology stronger. The mythical thought of the East was superadded to that of Greece." A syncretism occurred which explains the mythical element in Christian theology. This took on the form of "Greek metaphysics with a mythological gloss." Theology, in fact, through its appeal to dogmatism instead of reflection became the agent of myth in contrast to science, while philosophy characteristically assimilated critical methods. The separation out from philosophy of the different special sciences advanced instead of weakened the cause of philosophy, which was the instrument or organon of specialized science. In the final analysis, indeed, "modern philosophy" is synthetic scientific "knowledge of the All in all its parts." It is therefore the complement and completion of science and, in this sense, *scientia generalis*.

It is indubitably true that Masaryk viewed philosophy commonly enough indeed as something less than a full synthesis of all sciences, but that it was a scientifically critical synthesis of scientifically determined data was a view for which he stood throughout. For even when he wrote in *The Making of a State*

[16] I, 208-213; II, 500. *Russland und Europa*, a two-volume magnum opus on the history, literature, and philosophy of Russia, was published in 1913 in Jena. It appeared in English as *The Spirit of Russia* (1919). A third volume was to have soon followed, treating Dostoievski most particularly, but the outbreak of the War with the subsequent developments blocked completion of the writing. This volume, none the less, with the new edition of the *Concrete Logic*—was the work on which Masaryk was engaged just prior to his death. Professor J. Horák, a student of Masaryk, has been preparing this third volume, which Masaryk definitely formulated.

Logical Structure of Culture 121

that "in my eyes philosophy was, above all, ethics, sociology and politics," he pointed out both that he "sought to develop a critical faculty as a preservative against shallowness," insisting on "strict and pitiless analysis even in history and sociology," and that "the analytical method" was for him "a means, not an end. The end was synthesis and organization, as all my writings show." [17]

And this distinctively was the genius of philosophy. Philosophy projected from innumerable angles its problems of the truest and the wisest of ideas. It reached out beyond established knowledge and accurately determined probabilities to the best that anyone might think in light of all the facts and factors to be relevantly treated. Philosophy was best indeed conceived as philosophy of history. Interpretation of events and processes of history was essential to the comprehension of genetic or developmental meanings. In Aristotelian terms, in fact, things were not what they appeared to be at any moment or period but as they did or could become in their whole lifecourses. With the rise of the historic sense, indeed, history came to be "conceived as a history of the future" and underwent expansion from history of the human race into "history of the world and of the universe." [18] In this sense, therefore, of the critically constructive interpretation of things as well as events in history, all philosophy was philosophy of history, and yet in need of grounding in the data and the methods of all of the sciences. That one might make preliminary syntheses on bases of incomplete and scattered knowledge was not only human but, within limits, philosophic; but that he should thereby expect something other than preliminary glimpses of the nature and the possibilities of existence was not philosophic, or yet scientific, but unthinking.

The primary problem of philosophy, therefore, was the problem which Masaryk set himself in 1883 and which he still pur-

[17] Pp. 318-319.   [18] *The Spirit of Russia*, I, 204.

sued at eighty-seven as his final philosophic study: the organizing and the integrating of all sciences into one comprehensive system. The history of the relation of science in general to the special sciences afforded, in truth, the best course of entry onto this task, for not only was the past of science one of growing separations but also of increasing effort at inclusively co-ordinated system. "The first attempts at classification were commonly just surveys of the variously independent spheres of knowledge. All the genealogical tables and schematisms of the older logics afford us only scant advice about the natural system of the sciences. It was Auguste Comte," [already cited], "who made the first complete attempt to effect a natural organizing of the sciences, and it was his philosophy, too," Masaryk asserted, "which most motivated me to the following endeavor." Yet, from Plato and his more empirical follower, Aristotle, to the work of Bacon and Comenius and that later of Bain, Harms, Bourdeau, Erdmann, Wundt, Dilthey, Ratzel, and Palacký, there had been efforts at the systematic integration of all sciences. And knowledge of the entire history of this problem was essential for its resolution.[19]

The philosophic value of each science differs and needs, accordingly, to be concretely determined; each science differs from all others in its methods and its data. Each science had accordingly to be studied in the light of its specific history to establish its objectives, methods, sphere of interest, and position in the total system of acknowledged culture. Only, in fact, through knowledge of the distinctive nature and functions of each science could its relations with all other sciences be defined and a systematic scientific viewpoint fully established.[20]

The modern period was distinctively the age of conscious effort to achieve system among the sciences, just as it has been the age of widely extended experimental accuracy in science.

[19] *Versuch einer Concreten Logik*, pp. 24-39.
[20] *Ibid.*, pp. 215 ff.

Logical Structure of Culture 123

From Bacon on, in fact, concrete logic has been advanced along with logic of pure method. Bacon himself did little more than set the problem in outline relief, but his is the credit for that, however general his thinking.[21] The work of Comenius, following Bacon, was highly significant to Masaryk. For while the advancement of scientific knowledge had not reached the stage in which Comenius' work could be carried to completion or be widely acknowledged, Comenius was the first to comprehend the instrumental values of each science for the other sciences and to apply this principle to the unifying of all sciences.[22]

Pansophia was his objective and motto. *Pansophia* meant an inclusive outlook on the universe and life based on all the sciences. *Pansophia* entailed not only comprehensiveness in knowledge but integration of all scientific data for a full cosmic viewpoint. *Pansophia* could not consist in mere discrete informational tidbits or in the bare juxtaposition of the multitudinous findings of science. The content of all sciences must be brought together as *cohaerentia* and ordered so to serve as stages to each other. "The entirety of knowledge must accordingly be so graduated that in our study we begin with the lowest stages and so advance to the final ones that we always start out with new stages where the others end." [23] This encyclopedic system would then correspond as accurately as possible to the actual order of existence.

It is uncertain, none the less, Masaryk pointed out, whether such a hierarchy of knowledge really parallels the structure of existence. This ought not, at all events, to be arbitrarily assumed, but to be subject to determination by the methods of a fully scientific logic. We must question any logic which proceeds on preconceptions. Nor is the issue of a natural hierarchy among all sciences by any means as simple as Comenius assumed. Serial stages in the normal order of most sciences may

[21] *Ibid.*, p. 27, cf. p. 215. [22] *Ibid.*, p. 51. [23] *Ibid.*, p. 53.

correspond substantially to the gradations in things. Yet this parallelism must not be construed in so naïve a manner as Comenius believed, or as, after him, even Comte maintained. For in view of the fact that knowledge must be able to establish or vindicate itself to show its credentials as knowledge, the process and theory of *knowing* becomes thereby itself the sphere of a science. Knowledge, in point of fact, is a two-way process of reference. It relates not only to its direct objects but also to the special conscious process in which these objects are referred to, demarked, and identified. This process, moreover, needs not merely to be psychologically described but justifiably conceived so that one may have adequate reason to believe that he knows what he knows about knowing and other objects. We must find a place, in consequence, in the system of sciences, not just for knowledge as the content and technical procedures of all sciences, but as also in itself a special object of study. Yet what does knowing correspond to in the structure of existence? And what the theory of knowledge? For both of these, there are no objects in the world of overt things. We must, therefore, beside and in addition to the usual special sciences, distinguish logic and epistemology as special sciences of knowing.

Comte's view was more readily conceivable than that of Comenius, inasmuch as Comte's view was simpler, more scientifically advanced and natural. Comte found six abstract sciences to be the kernel of the system of all sciences and he arranged these in a hierarchy on the basis of their universality and comparative independence. Mathematics, astronomy, physics, chemistry, biology, and sociology comprised their linear order. Whoever wishes, Comte held, to attain a knowledge which would enable him to think and judge scientifically about comprehensive matters of existence must proceed in this order. He must begin with mathematics, since it is independent of all other sciences—with the exception of logic. Then, pro-

Logical Structure of Culture 125

gressively, he must achieve a mastery of astronomy and the sciences which follow until he comes to sociology. This presupposes all the other sciences. Comte admitted no alternative for sound judgment or thinking. Science must proceed from its abstract and universal phases and foundations to its less basic and more interwoven phases. These latter can be rightly carried on and comprehended only on the groundwork of the former.[24]

This general view, Masaryk agreed, is the starting point for any sound system of scientific thinking. Yet even Comte's formulation was not to be accepted without serious criticism of its details. Comte was wrong, first of all, in that he considered astronomy to be an abstract science; whereas actually it is both abstract and concrete, and dependent not only on mathematics but on other sciences, most notably on physics. Comte was wrong, in the second place, in that he assigned psychology to the compass of biology instead of recognizing the uniqueness of its subject-matter and function. Comte's view, thirdly, was too simple. He did not undertake to show how logic, linguistics, and aesthetics are related to the different serial stages in the framework of the sciences.

Comte's gross error followed from the phenomenalism with which he viewed all sciences as substantially alike and arranged them as if all were merely parts of one inclusive science. Knowledge ought indeed to be an intelligible whole, but this does not entail that all sciences are qualitatively alike. Mathematics, for example, as the deductive science of pure quantity, has a quite different character from the natural sciences, despite the fact that J. S. Mill attempted to maintain that mathematics is basically inductive. Psychology, furthermore, as we noted, is not simply to be grouped, as part of physiology, with the natural sciences. Every claim to knowl-

[24] *Ibid.*, p. 57.

edge requires that we take Descartes' "*cogito ergo sum*"[25] as the starting point of valid thinking and recognize accordingly the uniqueness and finality of consciousness. Otherwise, we must leave all sciences in that equivocal position in which their own agent, the intelligence of men, can give them no assurance of their soundness or grant them any hearing whereby to justify their findings. If intelligence, in fact, is not *sui generis* and final, science never can have validation. Both psychology and epistemology in consequence must be recognized as distinctive sciences. Comte's whole system, however, admits no actual reason for its own acceptance. Comte made no attempt at all to justify his view but merely urged it as the latest thing in evolution. How he knew that this was so, he did not and on his view he could not show.[26]

Comte's view, in fact, reduced man to a complex of mechanical relations, and suspended its system in the thin air of pure credulity, which it had set itself initially to give no quarter. Comte's view was, therefore, but the starting point for a unifying of the sciences. *Geisteswissenschaften* (as those sciences of mind or spirit) were indeed as natural as any of the sciences, yet had a quite different character and status. They were, in fact, more basic and needed to be granted that essential place which would do justice to their philosophic value and scientific functions and thereby bring all the knowledge and the wisdom of the ages to the understanding and the aid of *homo sapiens*.

It is not essential to consider here Masaryk's treatment of the other major modern students of this problem. It is enough, with Robert Flint, to mention Masaryk's knowledge of the growing literature. "The English authors he refers to most frequently are Bacon, Bain, Faraday, Rowan Hamilton, Sir

---

[25] "Because I think, I am."

[26] *Versuch einer Concreten Logik*, pp. 57-58; cf. V. Škrach, "Masaryk et le positivisme français," *Festschrift*, II, 33.

Wm. Hamilton, Hume, Locke, J. S. Mill, Newton, H. Spencer, and Whewell; the French, Descartes, A. Comte, Pascal, and Roberty; and the German, Dubois Raymond, Dilthey, Fechner, Harms, Kant, Leibniz, and Wundt. That Italian authors are so much overlooked is to be regretted." [27]

Masaryk's own system was both dualistic and tripartite: an interacting tripartitism in a framework of philosophical complementation. It was tripartite, firstly, in that it distinguished three qualitatively different groups of sciences: mathematical, psychological, and natural. Natural sciences were distinguished by established usage. The caption, "natural" science, did not really mean that other sciences were unnatural, but that natural sciences delved distinctively into external "nature." Mathematics was essential to the "natural" sciences, while both mathematics and the "natural" sciences were sources for psychology. There was a linear relationship accordingly in the contributoriness of sciences, giving rise to a hierarchical order of relations. Seven sciences comprised this serial system, in order, mathematics, mechanics, physics, chemistry, biology, psychology, and sociology.

But this was only the beginning of the story of the relations of the sciences. Three sciences or spheres of study were left outside this system: (1) linguistics, including *Sprachlehre* and *Grammatik*; (2) aesthetics; and (3) logic. Their relationships were not those of linear contributoriness or dependence. Logic, in particular, obtained material from all sciences and gave both system and foundation to them. Logic with epistemology, from which it could not actually be separated, ranked with the sciences of mind and spirit as an intellectual normatively cultural science, concerned with the determinants of knowing instead of simply with the objects that are known. Sciences of mind and spirit had, in fact, a function both at the peak of the

[27] Robert Flint, *Philosophy as Scientia Scientiarum and a History of Classifications of the Sciences*, p. 275.

system of sciences and also at its basis. Mathematical and natural sciences are debtors to intelligence, deriving both their articulation and their validation from rational reflection. All sciences, indeed, depend on human knowing, regardless of their objects or techniques. The simple fact of hierarchy is a first principle for co-ordination of the sciences, but that knowing is itself, in some degree at least, a self-justifying process is a denial of pure linearity in sciences and, in fact, of the finality of science in distinction from philosophy. The fact of rationally organic unity with other sciences conditions every science and gives ultimacy to the more philosophic studies.

Masaryk's system was tripartite, secondly, in the modes as in the basic kinds of science. He demarked the concrete from the abstract sciences, and made place, furthermore, for all sciences which are practically applied. All must be included in the union of the sciences and yet be logically distinguished. Concrete sciences corresponded naturally to the abstract sciences, as witnessed in mathematics by geometry; in mechanics, by acoustics, hydrostatics, hydrodynamics, etc.; in biology, by botany and zoölogy; in psychology and in sociology, by sciences of individual and group life, such as special histories of men. History was notably a concrete science, while sociology, as the theory of the principles of group life, was characteristically abstract. There were abstract dynamics, assuredly, in history: ideas, forces, and groups as such governed events. Yet individuals occasioned and precipitated these processes and changes, and results were always, if variously, specific. The task of sociology was to isolate the laws of change or progress in society and so to deal in general factors of history. Concrete sciences were dependent on the abstract sciences for their groundwork and first principles; abstract sciences, in turn, abstracted data and principles from the concrete wholeness of existence. Abstract sciences, furthermore, were more notably deductive; concrete sciences characteristically were empirical and inductive.

This difference of the abstract from the concrete sciences was significant. Abstract sciences were concerned with universal characters: sameness, unities, general principles, necessities. Concrete sciences dealt in differentials: novelty, variation, and fullness. They treated individualities and contingent circumstances, and had in that regard a special function. To undertake, like Mill, to minimize this difference of character and function was to gloss distinctions and confuse the tasks of science. To deal in basic common characters and ultimate essentialities is one function; to treat of special concrete facts and phases is another. The fact that these two enterprises must be interwoven in the interests of each does not modify their difference or dispense with their necessities. Concretion and abstraction are essential and distinctive modes of science.

Applied sciences, finally, (such as agriculture, engineering, medicine) were readily distinguished from "pure" or theoretic sciences. They were, and could afford to be, no less scientific. Nor would Masaryk admit that practice generally could be sharply dissevered from theory. "I have never," he said, "recognized an antagonism between theory and practice, that is to say, between correct theory and right practice; and just as I opposed one-sided intellectualism I stood out against practice divorced from thought." [28] Practicality he considered a technical issue for science as well as a philosophical datum.

While theoretic sciences were both abstract and concrete, applied sciences derived immediately from the theoretic concrete sciences and in light of these served human needs and interests. Applied sciences, none the less, were dependent on abstract general sciences and required a basic orienting in the entire scientific system. How each science can and ought to

[28] *The Making of a State*, p. 318.

serve all others for the maximum effectiveness of science was, in fact, as much an issue of the practicalities of science as it was of scientific theory. No science could achieve its best (and its best alone was fully valid) until it learned to use all aids from other sciences which it could advantageously employ and to make accessible to every science its especial functions. The natural and effective unity of all the sciences was in truth a crucial issue for human practice as for theory: the foremost condition indeed for effective solidarity in technical and broader culture. And this precisely entailed the integration of all applied sciences with all other sciences.

Masaryk listed seven groups of practical sciences, paralleling the seven groups of both the abstract and the concrete sciences. There were, first, the practical sciences of calculation and measurement. Secondly, there was technology in its broadest sense, or the making serviceable of the forces of nature. Third, there were the sciences of physical and hygienic education: phytotechny, zoötechny, hygiene, and medicine. Fourth, came the training of understanding and character, involving politics and ethics together with pedagogics and didactics. The fifth was applied grammar. Sixth was practical art or applied aesthetics. Seventh was applied logic. "Obviously," wrote Flint, "some of them would have been better placed among arts.... Sciences and arts may be intimately connected, but to call either arts sciences or sciences arts is an error, and must lead to confusion...." [29] For Masaryk, however, science tended to have less mechanical rigidity than in much modern thinking; and arts, for him, were sciences as well. His was the science of the scientific and philosophic artist; and one is led to wonder whether science can be fully scientific without the qualities of art. In any case, it is apparent that science is applied in art, though often quite unwittingly, and that the science of the artist is, at least, a special case of science. It is evident, further-

[29] *Philosophy as Scientia Scientiarum*, p. 275.

more, from what has preceded, that Masaryk was concerned not just for the harmonizing of the sundry academic fields of scientific research but for the extension of science to all phases of life and the unifying and consolidating of all fields of culture.

It is not germane to treat the detail of Masaryk's particular analysis of the variously different sciences and their severally philosophic values. It is enough to state—with Robert Flint again—that these were quite well done for a young man of thirty-three who claimed expertness only in "some sociological and psychological departments." His "description and distribution of the mathematical sciences," for example, "seem to be about as accurate as could possibly be given in fifteen pages by one professedly not a mathematical expert; and show how carefully he has utilised not only the well known works of Comte, Bain, and Wundt so far as they bear on the subject, but also such works as Baumann's *Lehren von Raum, Zeit und Mathematik in der neuesten Philosophie,* Clifford's *Common Sense of the Exact Sciences,* Cantor's *Vorlesungen über Geschichte der Mathematik,* De Morgan *On the Study and Difficulties of Mathematics,* Duhamel's *Des Méthodes dans les sciences de raisonnement,* Kroman's *Beiträge zu einer Theorie der Mathematik und Physik,* and Schmitz-Dumont's *Die mathematischen Elemente der Erkenntniss-theorie.*" [30]

Nor is it necessary here to inquire into the exact arrangement of all sciences in Masaryk's system. Masaryk's view developed, we suggested earlier in this chapter. This was true especially of his conceptions of religion and ethics in relation to science. In his *Syllabus on Sociology* (1900), ethics gained status as a philosophical study in place of a science, i.e., applied philosophy in contrast to logic and metaphysics, which were theoretic. At the same time, religion achieved standing as science, whereas in the *Concrete Logic* it had been appended inse-

[30] P. 277.

curely to philosophy. Theology, in consequence, became a scientific study rather than an unscientific, and even antiscientific, system of conceptual projections.

In recent years, Masaryk had quite constantly been reworking his position further. Depleted energy prevented his completion of this work while serving as his nation's President. With his retirement in December, 1935, he had more time and strength to give his more-than-fifty years of thinking on this subject its full written formulation. His death, September 1937, deprived him of this possibility. His students then took up the task of finishing this revised edition yet under international circumstances which were not conducive to an early publication. Still this is neither necessary nor important for the essentials of his system. These have been expressed not only in the *Concrete Logic* but in numerous other writings. His essential system pervades indeed his entire work. The interacting solidarity of all sciences, and their dependence on, as well as basically essential contribution to, philosophy, is the foremost datum of his viewpoint. Neither science nor philosophy can adequately serve men's intellectual or men's practical necessities without this synthesis of sciences: in elaboration of a full scientific philosophy of existence and culture. This is essential to soundness in thinking, guidance in practice, to outlook and understanding proceding from a realistically adequate vision.

Masaryk's system is therefore a system of logic for all reaches of thinking and life. Wisdom is here no fortuitous emergent in unprepared or chaotic minds. Wisdom is built up, in both theory and practice. The one constant or enduring ground for assured conviction and dependably constructive activity is in adequately integrated, comprehended, and well-applied science. This is the keynote and core of any soundly effective philosophy, without which men must live off-balance and in perspectival disorder.

Two final observations will enable us to see perhaps more

Logical Structure of Culture 133

clearly the integrity not only of all sciences with each other but with philosophy and with concrete human culture. The first concerns the question of the relation of pure logic to a logic of whole culture, the second, that of logic to the theory of knowledge. The relationship of abstract to the concrete sciences applies likewise to logic. Abstract and concrete logics denote pursuits which are not to be rightly confused, though each is interwoven with the other in the formulation and pursuit of its objectives. Abstract logic deals in universal rules of inference and judgment; concrete logic is men's scientific culture in its synthetic *toto* or wholeness. Abstract logic finds its cues in concrete situations, while maintaining a formal detachment. Concrete logic is built upon the undergirding which abstract logic affords. Yet concrete logic gains and consolidates cultural data which were not implicit in the abstract science. Neither of these logics can indeed ignore or do without the other. Both are complemented and completed in the systematic logic of the syntheses of all sciences; and there, in truth, all partial ways of thinking achieve their wholeness and completeness. Abstract and concrete logics are but phases of *whole reason*, which is a unifying of the universal and immediate, of the theoretic and applied.

We come, therefore, to our second observation. We noted previously that logic and epistemology cannot really be dissevered from each other. That abstract and concrete logics have quite different functions does not alter the immediacy of their relationships to theory of knowledge. The question of the rules of valid judgment is bound up with the question whether there is any valid judgment or under what conditions judgments are or may be valid. "I believe therefore," wrote Masaryk, "that those are in the right who, like Ueberweg, admit no independent theory of knowledge along with [and in separation from] logic," though this is not to say that epistemology "because of its importance should not be treated [in and] for itself." [81] Logic passes into theory of knowledge and theory of knowledge is prerequisite to logic. Both are fundamental to the concrete logic of the unity of sciences. These latter make no claim to justify their respective standpoints and methods, apart from quite provisional pragmatics. Both their inner logics and their different points of view in knowledge rest back on theoretic logic and epistemology. These, ultimately, are the unifying and the validating grounds of science and philosophy.

Science and philosophy, moreover, are not independent spheres of thought or action, though each maintains its special private enterprises. Philosophy and science comprise, in truth, a structural whole, and each depends upon the other for its special enterprises. Science finds its basis and its certifying in a philosophy of knowledge. Philosophy, in turn, looks to science for its concrete and real universe. For either one to undertake to carry on its several functions without this consciousness of unity would be, at best, but partial science, or else pseudo-philosophy. An honestly reflective realism in philosophy or science can take no other view than that of fully integrated culture on a scientific basis.

What particular significance has this for our common human life? It is of paramount importance. Certain sciences quite directly are sciences of effectiveness in life: ethics, sociology, politics, and economics notably. Human life depends on these for the stabilizing and the maximizing of its interests. Mankind can dally until human history abandons its course at guess work and at pseudo-science. They can try all conceivable expedients of uninformed imagination. But until they link their work and dreams to the direct sciences of life and establish these upon the solid structure of achieved knowledge and of validated methods, they shall live and die at haphazard venture. There is and can be no real mastery of life or conquest of

[81] *Versuch einer Concreten Logik*, p. 203.

its tragic ills without employment of full science. Social order and disorder reflect the depth and order of men's knowledge.[32] More significantly still, the orienting and the anchoring of life are dependent on achievement of a unity in informed perspective. Intermittent and disjointed cultural efforts must give way to an ordered scientific culture in which men's life-conceptions and programs are governed by a comprehensive and yet concrete outlook on existence.

This is not at all to intimate that Masaryk believed that society or individual life could by mere mechanics be advanced, but that *it could be positively and creatively controlled.* When men proceed upon the grounds of fact, and therewith of all the facts to be critically considered, and when men treat every problematic situation as one which must be worked out in complete detail—instead of played with on occasions—life can be controlled and its interests both protected and advanced. The motives and personal equations of men will not then be overlooked but honestly and factually considered; that motive, above all, that human life must have a satisfactory cosmic outlook and an adequately effective human meaning. This was a prime motif of Masaryk.

[32] *Ibid.,* p. 217; etc.

Chapter Six

Criticism: Its Philosophical Nature and Value

WE HAVE NOW TREATED Masaryk as a "system-builder" or systematic builder of sound culture. And all the knowledge and the effort which his system demanded surely took the joy from life for those who wished some simple verbal trick whereby to cope with human problems. Yet the problem of men's thought and culture was not as simple even as the concrete logic which we have presented. For whence came the sophisticated faith that science actually yields knowledge or that a total synthesis of scientific culture conduces to wisdom? What are the final criteria for science, literature, ethics, and art whereby men can know that they have knowledge or sound judgment? And how do those commend themselves defensibly to human life and thinking? Masaryk was confronted by these questions when once he had preliminarily advanced his concrete logic—questions which were forced on him not so much, however, by positive demands of theory as by the illogic of the Marxists, Comtists, Voltairians, and even more especially, by mythological Czechs and Russians. Each of these became, therefore, the object of all-sided criticism.

It is as a *critic*, in fact, that Masaryk was known chiefly during his pre-war life: a critic whose criticism reached to literature, art, politics, religion and sociology, together with philosophy and education. It was as a critic that he was thought of especially in philosophy, since he was not reputed to have a "system"; and it was as a *philosopher* that he was held to be a critic—for even in his political and literary activity his criticism was not only rigorously ethical and sociological but also epistemological.

Masaryk, it was not uncommonly maintained, was too intellectualistic.[1] He had no notion of art for art's sake and no appreciation of literature apart from its sociological and epistemological significance. Masaryk, in truth, had scant praise for art which could not justify itself to other spheres of life and thought. "Art for art's sake," he believed, should not mean the right to violate all standards of morality and thought, but rather the distinctive genius to add something which commends itself at least from the contemplative point of view to life—and which does not detract significantly at any point from life. But "art for art's sake," in the common comprehension, was wont to be both dilettantic and decadent, besides incoherent in its standards and its values. If these were valid values, they could justify themselves to human thinking, and just so far as they were unintelligible they were meaningless alike to the artist and philosopher. Art, for Masaryk, had a wide outreach into life. It crystallized and refined ideas, socialized and enlarged feelings; or it made for human mystifying and disintegration. Art, he found, could lead men nearer truth by affording insights and instructing their imagination. There was indeed no better way to grasp the spirit of a nation than by its literature and art.[2] Both as means to knowledge, therefore, and as a moral force or agent, art was more than purely art. It was a significant phase of human culture, bound up with all other phases. And its tests were more than simply aesthetic. Whence,

[1] Pavel Fraenkel, "Der Kritiker der Literatur," *Masaryk: Staatsmann und Denker* (Orbis, Prague, 1930), pp. 125-136.

[2] Čapek, *Masaryk Tells His Story*, p. 102; cf. Herben, Hartl, Bláha, *T. G. Masaryk: Sa vie, sa politique, sa philosophie*, p. 141.

therefore, were its standards? Could these stand the test of an all-sided criticism? Was there any reason to believe that art actually gives knowledge of reality or offers any other basically essential human values? In so far, indeed, as art aspired to be an autonomic system, it should show reason for the faith which modern men place in it and not just stake its case on aesthetic gnosticism or mythological dogmatism. It ought to be self-validating. Art, moreover, if self-justifying, must not be at odds with other fundamental human values. It must commend itself to and be capable of the sanction of a fully philosophical, rather than just an artistic, criticism. The latter would be unintelligibly impressionistic without the groundwork of the former; and so with all other phases of our culture. They, too, must finally find their validation in a comprehensive and yet basic criticism.

Such criticism was the function quite especially of philosophy. Philosophy in its most basic sense was criticism: criticism of both thought and life (i.e., of life through thought). But philosophic criticism needed to be distinguished from all common forms. It was criticism of all criticisms. Nor was it purely analytic and experimental in the sense of modern science; nor yet simply socialistic and political, attacking evils of society. Philosophic criticism was more ultimate than any of these special criticisms and more penetrating. It demanded the final squaring of accepted ideas with each other, and a formulation of a point of view or faith in the light of which one could think most satisfactorily or intelligibly. This was the sense in which Masaryk appealed to philosophic criticism as the ground of all defensible beliefs and conceptions.

It was Masaryk's study of the social culture of Russia, it is claimed,[3] which won him for "criticism" in the strictly philo-

[3] Boris Jakowenko, "Masaryk und die Russische Philosophie," *Festschrift*, Vol. II, pp. 105-120; cf. E. Rádl, "Masaryk und Kant," pp. 153-162.

sophic sense, in distinction from the empirical science of J. S. Mill and Auguste Comte. Previously, it is held, he had been a critic in the shallower and more dogmatic sense of positivistic science and had undergone conversion from the solely scientific to the really philosophic criticism. It is pointed out that in the *Athenaeum* and *Concrete Logic,* 1885, Masaryk set the concrete exactness of Comte in contrast to the mythological abstractionism of Kant because Kant dissevered philosophy from science and set the former drifting in an ocean of abstractions; whereas in his *Russland und Europa* (1913) Masaryk reversed himself and opposed Kant to Comte, maintaining that "Comte, with his positivism, endeavored to rest content with scientific thought as developed in the special sciences, and to justify such thought historically as the latest stage of evolution. But such a naïve historical outlook," Masaryk concluded, "is inadequate; it is necessary, with Kant, to establish *epistemologically* the opposition between mythopoiesis and scientific thought" and to find a defensibly intellectual basis for one's thought and faith. "It is a case of *criticism* versus positivism." [4]

Fourteen years earlier, however, in his *Grundlagen des Marxismus* [5] (1899), Masaryk had already made a positive appeal to Kant, in assessing socialistic criticism such as Marx's and Engels'. These had staked their faiths on simple positivism, both Feuerbach's and Comte's, yet not so scientifically as Comte. Masaryk showed the intellectual dogmatism of any such position. Positivism itself, he emphasized, contains no reassurance. Philosophy and life, in fact, have before all else their noetic or epistemological problem, and even science needs a philosophical foundation which can only be secured

[4] I, 208.
[5] A comprehensive study of the whole "Social Question." Tolstoy said that Brockhaus had rightly ranked this work as first in his *Bibliography of Socialism.*

through dialectic reasoning. All ideas and beliefs must square finally with each other for any intelligent confidence in their reliability and rightness. This, Masaryk pointed out, is the especial meaning of the whole development of philosophic thought from Berkeley via Hume to Kant. This historical development, through scepticism to criticism, puts the problem of criteria against the background of our non-authoritative modern individualistic thinking and asks not only how we know what we know, if we know anything or nothing, but how we know that we know *either* anything or nothing. Positivism has no answer of any type to this question of a philosophically defensible or consistant faith. "A consistent positivism is theoretically and practically impossible." Positivism asserts itself as a sophisticated type of dogmatism. It dogmatizes an extreme analytical impressionism into a philosophical theory. Comte, indeed, borrowed both Hume's radical empiricism and his scepticism and was content to be agnostic with regard to everything but the disconcerting poverty and elementism of immediate experience. Comte made a fetish both of science and the special sciences, and thereby he denied them any actual *raison d'être*.[6]

It was the business of criticism to delve into the problems of intelligible convictions and of actual authority. This was its paramount function. And this was where socialistic criticism revealed its ultra-superficiality. Just such errors actually as were made by Hume and Comte were made also, but more glaringly, by both Marx and Engels in their effort at the formulation of a social plan for human life and practice. Their case is quite illuminating since it bespeaks the type of thinking which has captured men's imaginations. Yet Marx and Engels started not with science as the ground of their conviction but *materialism as a bald assumption*. Marx merely presupposed the con-

[6] Škrach, "Masaryk et le positivisme français," *Festschrift*, Vol. II; cf. especially pp. 33 ff.

trary of Hegel's dialectic, which took its origin from the Critiques of Kant. Whereas, in fact, for Hegel the thought process was "the demiurge of the real which only forms its outer aspect," for Marx it was the direct converse: ideas and ideals were "nothing other than materials transplanted and transformed in human heads." [7]

Marx and Engels were positivistic, indeed, in their materialism, appealing to the facts and laws of science. But they proceeded from materialism to positivism, instead of scientifically; and they confused materialism with positivism, as a methodology. Engels actually defined materialism as positivism: to comprehend the real world—nature and history—as it gives itself to everyone who faces it, without idealistic whims; unhesitatingly to sacrifice each idealistic whim which does not allow non-phantastically comprehended facts in their own connection to be brought in harmony with itself; and beyond this materialism signifies nothing. Marx similarly declared the materialistic to be the only scientific *method,* not only thereby confounding positivism as a methodology with materialistic metaphysics but making the unwarranted assumption that positivism necessarily is materialistic; whereas his own emphasis on clear-cut facts required the recognition of both the material and the non-material.[8]

Neither Marx nor Engels had, furthermore, anything like a clear conception of science. Though both spoke frequently of science, and most characteristically of "scientific socialism" and a really "scientific history," nowhere, Masaryk contended, do we find in the works of either one an elaboration of what is meant by science or what is scientific. They helped themselves plentifully to positivistic terms—such as "laws" and "study of the facts"—yet nowhere was there any accurate defining of those words and phrases. Small wonder that Marx disliked J. S. Mill! Mill was positivistic, too, and could have aided

[7] *Grundlagen des Marxismus,* p. 59.   [8] *Ibid.,* pp. 63, 64n.

Marx to formulate a scientific view of the laws in social science. Mill was clear on scientific method. He worked out detailed formulae for determining social laws. Mill, furthermore, carried out his abstract logical conceptions in his economics—a most instructive work for purposes of Marx and Engels. They were clear regarding neither laws nor facts; and they appear not to have even cared to be exact, despite their talk of science. They made no efforts to define their terms or use them with consistency.[9]

Nor did Marx and Engels comprehend at all the relations of philosophy to science. They undertook to do away with all philosophy except the simple theory of historical materialism with its epiphenomenal "scientific" perspective. Rejecting ideology of every type—religious, moral, metaphysical—Marx recognized only simple *Weltanschauung* which was but a naturalistic copy of the process of production. Consciousness became itself illusion, the illusion of illusions, since the consciousness of being conscious was the most illusory illusion. Yet what illusion was or is Marx did not clarify. How historical materialism could then defend its case since it itself was but an upshot of consciousness (and one of its many illusions), was not indicated. Assuredly its particularly puerile credulity was no sort of defense.

Masaryk summarized that neither Marx nor Engels "have deepened the problem" of the relationship of philosophy to the special sciences "neither anywhere in logical nor in social aspects. Nowhere do we find a more accurate determining of what the new philosophy is or can be, and in what relation it stands to religion and theology. Marx and Engels could object that religion, theology, and philosophy are already abolished, that it is no longer necessary to treat of their relations. But even were this true, an explanation of these relationships as they concern the past would be essential." Nor is philosophy

[9] *Ibid.*, pp. 71-72, 204.

Philosophical Nature of Criticism 143

so negative as Marx and Engels depicted. It is as positive as the sciences, to which it stands in closest relations. Marx's and Engels' theory of the sciences permits no clear conception of philosophy.[10]

(Engels' comprehension of the relations of the sciences was singularly naïve. He made a three-fold grouping of all sciences, in terms of: (1) sciences of inanimate nature—mathematics, astronomy, mechanics, physics, and chemistry; (2) sciences of life or of organic nature; (3) sciences of history, including living conditions and social relations of people, laws and types of state, with their cultural standpoints in philosophy, aesthetics, and religion. "Obviously," wrote Masaryk, "Engels has no suspicion of the significance of the classifying of the sciences, what an important task here devolves on him"—since he rejects all earlier thinking and organizings of society. His historicism leads him to consider as historical just the sciences of mind or spirit (*Geisteswissenschaften*). It does not seem to have occurred to him that organisms and non-living things likewise have a history, and that *par-contra* studies in religion and aesthetics are affairs not only of history but also of persisting cores of fact and essentialities of culture, that every study has its reference to evolving nature with its processes in history.[11])

Marx and Engels derived their positivism actually in first instance from Feuerbach, especially their notion of the evils of anthropomorphism in human thinking. Yet neither Marx nor Feuerbach understood the problem of anthropomorphism as fully as did Kant or even Comte; and Marx, like Comte, could not teach himself that anthropomorphism occurs not just in religion but in every sphere of human thinking: sociology, psychology, physics, and even in mathematics. Neither Feuerbach nor Comte, in fact, glimpsed the substance of the problem of adequacy in thought (and also in life). For if sound thinking develops by historic stages, as both of them main-

[10] *Ibid.*, pp. 74-75. [11] *Ibid.*, p. 75.

tained, there still exists the question of the evidence of its sufficiency and rightness. Wherein are our criteria of adequacy and truth? And what specifically is the relationship of anthropomorphism to clear thinking? Must there be no human norms at all in interpretation of reality? The determination of historical advances is itself a matter ultimately of the psychology of knowledge and trans-positivistic criticism. Only epistemologically can it be solved, for positivism itself requires, as we have seen, a philosophical foundation. Positivism simply does not validate itself as a *later* stage of historical development, or yet by any of the novelties of its viewpoint or results. It must be justified on critically constructive grounds, through dialectic or rational synthesis. For Feuerbach, however, and in a lesser sense for Comte, philosophy had a wholly negative significance: to criticize theology and despoil it of its myths. Feuerbach did propound a new philosophy, in which man was to be thought of non-mythologically, and even non-anthropomorphically, as himself deity. But Feuerbach only posited this: he never worked it out in clear or significant detail. Feuerbach never really reached beyond negation of all earlier thinking, especially the theologies. He never grasped the actual character of criticism as exact analysis, psychological and noetic, of mythology in distinction from scientific and scientifically philosophical thinking, and thereby he maintained an erroneous conception of religion and theology in contrast to the sciences and philosophy. In religion, he saw just naïve philosophy. A religion of humanity, he held none the less, provides the only positive philosophy.

Marx's position was similar to Feuerbach's. Hume had thrown out both theology and metaphysics through his sceptical empiricism. Kant had undertaken to refute Hume and to save in religion by criticism whatever ought to be preserved. And Kant inquired to what extent mythology is not only permissible but necessary since it is unavoidable in some degree

Philosophical Nature of Criticism 145

in thinking. The fact that Kant finally admitted a subtle anthropomorphizing in his transcendental criticism meant a higher estimate on the possibilities in mythology than it is customary to acknowledge. Comte returned essentially to Hume's position, though later he admitted myth again, in a fetishism of humanity. Feuerbach consciously proclaimed the religion of humanity as the only truly positive philosophy. Marx proceeded via Feuerbach on the winds of Humistic deism and the humanistic atheism of Comte. Marx's views on anthropomorphism were not unified. He treated it most commonly, in the Comtian manner, as a function of religion, though sometimes he acknowledged it in politics as well. Most frequently for Marx, however, anthropomorphism meant deistic theology, as a culturally primitive and crudely philosophic method of conception; and religion from this viewpoint was the most persistently prevailing of all superstitions. With religion, Marx rejected morals and all ideology, recognizing only simple (non-ideational) world-perspective. This took the form of "historical materialism." That historical materialism was itself at least a quasi-intellectualized conception, especially in its historical and scientific pretentions, Marx did not clearly recognize.[12]

Historical materialism was, moreover, Masaryk reasoned, a violation of first principles of human life and history, and a denial that it can have meaning for anyone.[13] It explained con-

[12] *Ibid.*, pp. 66-71, 155.
[13] Engels' cultural history is skillfully constructed to construe itself entirely as an economic function. The development of capitalism and its evil rule is explained as an unhappy dialectic movement within social evolution; and where, in fact, the course of evolution definitely does not lead, an Hegelian *negation of negation* appears upon the scene to save historical materialism. Innocent Adam precipitates the capitalistic fall into anti-socialistic sin. The unsophisticated materialistic primeval man becomes an ideological capitalist. Engels gleans such satisfactions from the savage crudities of primitives that he affirms with total earnestness that the death penalty introduced by growing culture is worse than the

sciousness as illusion, whereas all socio-historic forces center notably in three psychological categories: understanding, feeling, and will. "Our [Bohemian] reformation," Masaryk emphasized, "that shows history most distinctly . . ." was "a religious and a moral movement." The reformation assuredly had economic consequences, particularly in non-ascetic morality, and in the fact that political leaders and the nobility misused it for material advantage. "But I ask the disciples of economic materialism to clarify how Huss's zeal for faith, how Luther's power of faith may be explained primarily as economics. History shows us how Huss learned from Wycliff, how on Huss his Bohemian and his German predecessors under Charles IV had effective influences, but all of these relationships, and most notably Huss's faith and zeal for reformation definitely do not lend themselves to economic explanation." There is no meaning to the effort at an economic explanation of the power of

---

blood revenge of primitives. He pictures Greek life disadvantageously, decrying the amount of slavery, and emphasizing Rousseau's general theory of decadence. The matriarchal *gens,* and indeed the whole constitution of the family tribe, presents an issue for Engels, since it was organized not through economic processes first and foremost but through family bonds. Yet Engels took undue delight in the simple communism of this early group, in which "without soldiers, gendarmes, and police, without nobility, king, governor, prefect or judge, without prison, without lawsuits, everything goes its appointed course." Clan societies, none the less, were organized against each other and contained in themselves the lively germs of unproductivity and of self-destruction. Engels misconceived the ideality of their history in view of his own preconceived theoretical position. He failed to comprehend that early communism was not positive but negative: that it entailed the sharing in the absence of privileges rather than the exercise of significantly mutual rights. Where, in fact, could one hope to find a stronger case of anthropomorphism than in this idealizing of the limitation of primeval life? The simple fact is that neither economic nor yet sexual communism existed in the measure that Engels emphasizes both. His decadent emphasis on the absoluteness of the sex urge is, in fact, bound up likewise with his preconceived materialism, which in turn denied to consciousness any actual sense of values.—*Grundlagen des Marxismus,* pp. 330 ff.

Philosophical Nature of Criticism 147

Dante, the painting of a Michael Angelo, the scientific work of Newton. Religion, morals, art, and scientific work—in brief, the total field of ideology and culture—are ultimates for men's consciousness, and human consciousness itself is the starting point of any justifiable philosophy.[14]

To explain consciousness as illusionary means disillusionment, in fact, not only with regard to all higher values and ideals but also with respect to all thought and perception, including the view itself of consciousness as an illusionary by-product of relations of production. For if consciousness is illusory and illusionist, historical materialism as a philosophy of the reality of life and of the universe is one of its illusory conceptions and has no more reason for acceptance than any other theory. It has, actually, no basis for acceptance, since it refutes itself and ends in utter scepticism. Any philosophic viewpoint, to commend itself, must establish consciousness as a critically final fact, the significance of which is of such a grade as to permit self-vindicating certainty. This is the crucial problem of all modern thought, deriving notably from Hume and Kant. Yet neither Marx nor Engels was concerned for this. Neither one of them allowed any of "his hair to gray" because of Hume or Kant. Both jumped to materialism without seeing, much less showing, their way. They were critical enough of others, however negatively, but uncritical of their own assumptions. And criticism without self-criticism, Masaryk pointed out, is both philosophically and sociologically dangerous.[15]

Marx himself, in fact, was an embodiment of the Hegelian *negation of negation*. His positive philosophy arose plainly by eclecticism. Frightened of subjectivism and sentimentality, Marx and Engels denounced individualism and conscious "humanity." Afraid of philosophic criticism, since it led them to the

[14] *Ibid.*, pp. 144, 156.
[15] *Ibid.*, pp. 61, 133, 154-155, 514-516.

canyon of reflection with its subjectivities, they tried to find a mechanistic kind of objectivism in mass solidarity. They did not realize that philosophy and human life have, before all else, their noetic problem and that pure dogmatism and inaccuracy are both socially and epistemologically untenable. They did not see that crass materialism is not merely an offense to rational intelligence, but that it demoralizes and desocializes those who regard themselves as its initiates. Marxist materialism, Masaryk stated, has in it "something quite close-fisted and ungenerous." Marx himself, in fact, was totally a party man. He had no sense of social solidarity. With his revolutionary hatreds he aggravated antisocial feelings. His inhumanity, surely, was no worse than the perfumed indifference of the higher classes, but it was no less negative and reactionary. It gained its positive content through grasping everything in mode: naturalism, positivism, Darwinism, liberalism, Zola, and decadence—all in motley interpenetration. It had no basic unity of system except its dogmatic, primitive materialism which "fills its adepts with that intellectual darkness which corrupts those who regard themselves as the only chosen." [16]

The "crisis in Marxism," therefore—of which Masaryk was one of the very first to call men's notice, and in which ideology became acknowledged by the later Marxists—was a crisis of the "system" and not some incidental phase or phases. The whole point of view was wrong, untrue to thought and life. Acknowledgment of ideology indeed was renunciation of materialism as the lone principle of actuality.[17]

The cause, however, which it undertook to serve was no less worthy, because so falsely served. "I would not wish to produce the impression," Masaryk stated in his *Ideals of Humanity*, "that my opposition to some theoretic forms of Marxism extends likewise to the workers and the masses. Not to recognize the moral force and devotion of the workers would be a grave

[16] *Ibid.*, p. 516.   [17] *Ibid.*, pp. 585 ff.

Philosophical Nature of Criticism 149

injustice. To condemn completely the movement of the workers because we cannot approve some of their theoretic views or political defections would be equally one-sided. We have not heretofore concerned ourselves about the masses, and now we are surprised that they are organizing themselves and, to some degree, against us." [18] The privileged and oppressive collectivities which we accept and represent are naturally the foes of those whom they oppress. These are now insisting on a new, a fairer order of humanity.

The issue of society and thought was at once an issue, therefore, of individualism versus objectivity. This was the antinomy which needed to be bridged through philosophic criticism, by criteria which are ultimately authoritative yet non-arbitrary. To provide for individuality and yet find non-subjective standards of the right and true is the function finally of epistemology.

In *The Spirit of Russia* Masaryk attacked the issue of criticism directly and showed its utter urgency for normal human living. Masaryk was, in 1913 and previously, the best authority on literature and life in Russia, and so acknowledged by informed Russians. True, academic Russian philosophic thinkers resented his neglect of their specific theories—which they themselves naturally took seriously enough—but Masaryk, first and foremost, was concerned for essential characteristics of Russian thought and life, whereas all academic philosophers and writers were under direct sanctions of the absolutist government. Masaryk maintained therefore that "those who take the trouble to examine sketches of the history of Russian philosophy will find that, while many noted Russian names are not to be found in the present work, on the whole my choice of representative thinkers will appear justified." [19]

And "one conclusion emerges with especial force," Masaryk pointed out in his analysis of Russian history and literature.

[18] *Ideals of Humanity*, pp. 32-33.   [19] *Spirit of Russia*, II, 466.

Russian thought "lacks epistemological foundation." Whilst Russia has numerous literary and in fact ethical critics, and has ample positivists and reputedly empirical scientists,[20] "the country knows little of" and has "no interest in" epistemological criticism. "Kant's criticism as epistemological reflection concerning the range and limits of cognition was rejected by Russian thinkers, who regarded it as a form of subjectivism." Russian thinkers "preferred Schelling and Hegel to Kant. . . . Schelling, as against Kant, introduced mythology into philosophy; and Hegel, despite his opposition to theology, furthered both theology and mythology by his dialectic with its suspension of the principle of contradiction. . . . The Russians failed to accept Kant because they were and still are more inclined toward mythology than the Europeans. Under European influence, Russians could be induced to negate myth, to negate theology, but they could not be induced to criticise myth and theology." The teaching of the church had "accustomed the Russian to accept a ready-made and objectively given revelation. . . . This explains why Russian negation remains believing negation. The educated Russian abandons the faith of his childhood, but promptly [and uncritically] accepts another faith—he believes in Feuerbach, in Vogt, in Darwin, in materialism and atheism." The Russian monk was the archsymbol of his country, and revolution was his first reaction to the influx of new thought or knowledge. Russians were simple objectivists in a very large part of their thinking, and naïve objectivism was esotericism with its mythology. What Russia needed therefore was philosophic criticism such as Kant's. Criticism meant, however, the overcoming of scepticism as well as mythology, whether this latter occurred in dogmas of science or in the more nebulous forms of anthropomorphism.[21]

It was the overcoming of mythology which must first indeed

[20] "Positivism in its various forms held the field."—*Ibid.*, II, 468.
[21] *Ibid.*, pp. 467-472.

be undertaken. Yet this itself required a philosophical surmounting of scepticism. Mythology is not overcome when its alternative is but sceptical agnosticism. The latter state is not more valid than the first, it is a transition condition. Transcending of mythology requires achievement of a critically constructive philosophy of knowledge. This is now, and has long been, in the process of achievement. Yet mythology to date has had little more than some partial eclipse. Analysis of the functions of mythology in both history and the present gives plentiful evidence of this.

Masaryk's treatments of mythology were distinctive contributions to the study of that field and merited consideration of the students of mythology for their constructive besides critical significance. These treatments, which appeared most fully in the *Concrete Logic* and in *The Spirit of Russia*, disclosed the steps of progress in Masaryk's own thinking from scientific to philosophical criticism. And even in his early study, which he said was written hurriedly one summer, his treatment was distinctive. For while his view was positivistic in that work, it was positivistic in a sense which went beyond the atheism and the apsychologism of Auguste Comte. It might, in fact, be called full positivism in distinction from the negativism in the view of Comte, though Masaryk did not positivistically confine himself to immediate experience.

"If science then inquires about the causes of phenomena," he wrote in 1884, "it reaches from secondary to primary causes and finally to the first cause. This indeed we only can conceive of anthropomorphically, for with all the logic of his thinking man cannot rise beyond himself; he is himself, in fact, the measure of all things. Science seemingly thereby returns to the original mythology; but only seemingly. The logically trained mind restrains its primitive tendency to myth and replaces spontaneously impulsive habits with reflected conclusions. And just as we perceive a great difference between the common man who in his opinions of causal relations follows custom in both theory and practice, whereas the philosopher himself fashions his theory of cause and effect, so likewise there is between the mythical theism of the crowd and the theistic views of a Leibniz a great difference." [22] One bespeaks the credulous opinions of the highly prejudiced and quite uninformed, the other represents the wisdom and the vision of the cosmically scientific citizen and thinker.

Mythology arose, indeed, as Comte agreed, to serve a basic function in the life of early man. "The first man had assuredly the same life-problems to solve as we have. He had in fact, as we have, many questions to answer; the relation of cause and effect interested him particularly, as it does us. We see the still untrained man confronted by an overpowering nature. We see him surrounded by numerous enemies from the animal and human worlds; and we see him wholly helpless against sickness and constantly encompassed by death, fighting for his daily bread. How shall the first man, in this situation, find his way?

"Surely man needed, in that circumstance, a general theory of things. This theory indeed must have suggested itself; it must have been utterly simple, yet with all its simplicity sufficing all cases.... For when once man somehow had been able to explain the world, society had next to be organized; for this also a theory was necessary. Primitive man, in a word, needed a philosophy, as we do, for both living and dying.

"This primitive philosophy ... was furnished by the spontaneous tendency of man to personify all external objects," as "psychologists and sociologists have long taught." The "disposition to personify is really quite natural—and for early man likewise most necessary. We must not forget that primitive man had gathered almost no experience at all. He only knew one fact: that he himself existed; for he perceived events of his inner life directly. Not that he would study this inner life of

[22] *Concreten Logik*, pp. 280-281.

his; no, he did not consciously observe himself. On the contrary, he was wholly lost in 'sensible' perception of the external world. Yet just on that account it is evident why at this stage of reflection man explained events after the analogy of his own inner processes. It is intelligible, too, why he especially used his will as model for this explanation. Since he perceived himself pre-eminently as a willing and an acting being, he transposed this property immediately to external things in order to explain thereby their causal connections."

Mythological thought was a function quite exclusively of imagination. It bespoke lack of acquaintance with things and events, mal-observation and inattention. It had to give way with each mental advance to something more realistic and more reflective. "Only gradually," however, "with growing experience, does man learn to observe." Yet "therewith is the first step taken toward a scientific world-conception. As man becomes increasingly acquainted with things and events, he conceives himself of their impersonality and his superiority [to them]. Those few experiences which he has naturally to enter into most frequently lead him, to begin with, to the sense of this impersonality. . . . Other experiences, likewise, must be frequently re-had in order to be recognized just as simple facts. The circle of these experiences widens very gradually indeed; attention becomes steadier; quiet observation leads to comparisons, comparisons to estimates. While myth conceives each entity as a unitary whole, comparing observation undertakes analysis and a study of the parts. With comparison, there simultaneously grows the capacity for abstraction. Abstract and general ideas are formulated, and with these ideas, as Aristotle stated, knowledge ultimately is given. Once wild roving phantasy gives place to attentive observation, man then begins to study objects in and of themselves, whereas previously he had only seen himself in them. And whereas he had formerly attended only to the overpowering and unusual, now he learns to note and watch the smaller and more customary. In place of dreaded beings, things emerge which man can use for experimental verifying of conclusions. Original astonishment, mother of myth, gives way to attention, the mother of science.

"Man attained, accordingly, as he became accustomed to things, to calm, clear, scientific comprehension and explanation, which, in contrast to personifying myth, consists in this: that each phenomenon is studied in and explained from itself" and yet also "each phenomenon is thought of in relation to the rest of phenomena and traced thereby to a universal law."

Before man accustoms himself wholly, none the less, to exact views, he sees objects quasi-mythically, half-scientifically. Scientific abstractions are themselves personified. Plato's theory of Ideas denotes this stage of thinking, as do Kant's Categories, Schopenhauer's Will, and von Hartmann's Unconscious. Men postulate and hypostatize physical, intellectual, and moral fictions to serve them in the explanation of events. Mythology and science interpenetrate continually. What to us, in fact, even at our cultural level, is art and above all poetry but a kind of personifying "of feelings and thoughts," a non-scientific projection and hypostatizing of subjective factors and conceptions?

We see, therefore, Masaryk maintained, how science grows not only in a struggle with the inaccuracies and ineffectualities of negative non-science, but also that it had and has a positive opponent. The tendency to myth is an imaginative course of maximum ease, and the conflict of mythology and science is the main motive force of intellectual progress.[23]

We stated earlier that Comte, with Feuerbach and Marx, conceived mythology as the function quite specifically of religion. Masaryk repudiated this view completely. Pointing to myths in all spheres of thinking, especially in politics and social life, he denied that mythology in its narrower sense is even

[23] Ibid., pp. 278-283, 285.

inherent in theism. "Usually," he stated in the *Concrete Logic*, "people talk of the antagonism of religion and science and see in these two natural enemies. Between religion and science, I see no necessary cleavage." There is an antagonism between the "theological" and scientific, or the scientifically philosophical, methods, in so far as the former is demarked from the latter. But religion pre-eminently is feeling and attitude which attaches to the world of one's philosophical conception and may be as scientifically right as theology can be religiously wrong. Everything depends upon the guidance of its ideation, whether this is mythologically uncritical and credulously blind or scientifically clear and exact. Atheistic humanism, as in Feuerbach and Comte, involves a clear-cut case of myth; whereas theistic thought like that of Leibniz is an achievement of reflection beyond which we have not yet gone far.[24]

"Following Plato's example," Masaryk summarized in his *Spirit of Russia*, "I wish to take my stand with those who replace the term anthropomorphism by the term myth, and to speak therefore of mythopoiesis, which is contrasted with critical, scientifically precise thought and behaviour of human beings vis-à-vis the world. Behaviour of human beings, let me repeat, for we are concerned, not with religion alone, but also with morality, with the whole conduct of man in relation to the world and to society. At a certain stage of development man is not only characterised by having a mythical religion, but in addition his philosophy is mythical; mythical too are his poetry and his art, his ethics and his economics, his language. To express the matter briefly, the essence of myth is found in man's purely objective attitude, in man's complete self-surrender to the object, in his explanation of the world and of himself by analogies, and by hasty analogies. Contrasted with this are scientific and critical thought and conduct. By the critical

[24] *Ibid.*, pp. 275-276; *Spirit of Russia*, I, 208 ff; "Sub Specie Aeternitatis," *New Europe*, Dec. 21, 1916, p. 300.

mind, things are deduced from other things as a result of careful observation and comparison; the critical thinker generalizes and makes abstractions; he thinks, in fact, thinks scientifically and critically." [25]

Mythology is, none the less, a special liability of theology, if and just in so far as theology opposes science, for to that degree theology is inaccurate and uncritical. The Middle Ages made, in fact, the separation of theology from philosophy, wherein the worldly wisdom of the Greeks was set in sharpest opposition, and subordinated, to the wisdom of the church and sacred wit. None other than Augustine first carried out this separation. Theology became thereby the special agency of myth, since it denied the right to reasoned thinking about the intelligibility of its teaching.

Theology, however, was not then, nor is not now, confined by any means to ecclesiastics or to theologians. Divorcing of belief from understanding was historically accompanied by a dual organizing of society, under other-worldly and mundane powers respectively. These worldly powers themselves soon claimed, in turn, the same finality of voice which was supposed to characterize ecclesiastical princes. The kings of the earth, therefore, themselves aspired to be, and in fact were, theologians.

Dictatorial absoluteness was the overpowering method of theology. This stood out for Masaryk as the full antithesis of science and epistemology. Theology, accordingly—if juxtaposed to philosophy or science—was but mythological dogmatism; yet this might obtain in politics and government, in morals, education, or religion. Like philosophy, in truth, of which it undertook to be the conscious negative, theology can reach and govern every phase of life. Dogmatism may well be called theology, regardless of its sphere, since it presumes to some divine prerogative and presupposes one at least of the many possibilities

[25] *The Spirit of Russia*, I, 207.

Philosophical Nature of Criticism 157

in theocratic world-conceptions. This explains why all absolutist systems were theocracies to Masaryk, including even those which undertook to be anti-religious in nature.[26] Democracy alone of social points of view or systems was philosophic instead of theocratic. It was basically theistic while scientific and anthropocratic.

The modern era held denouement of a really philosophic world conception, though this was just in process of emergence. Intellectual conditions were unsettled. All shades of theology obtained, from the most dogmatic to the most modern rationalism. Traditional philosophies persisted, going back variously to Plato and Aristotle. Still, the constituting and advancing of the special sciences paved the way to the establishing of a scientific world-view, and the development of critical philosophy. This depended on and proceeded with the development of all sciences. The crystallizing of a fully scientific view, in turn, required self-validating trans-scientific dialectical criticism.[27]

Comte, Masaryk insisted, made a vital contribution to this outcome. He laid solid grounds for the explanation of the phenomena of nature and the progress of philosophy. He offered a real antidote for myth: an indispensable standpoint and method for accurate factual thinking, wherewith men might guard themselves from sheer suggestibility and work positively and soundly in accordance with reality. There can be no clear hope for men without the accuracy of science, and no limit to fatalities which can and may attend them. They themselves, however, have agencies and methods for their own protection and advancement: exact yet integrated science in service of life. This was Comte's great contribution, and Masaryk frankly said in appraisal of Comte's work: "If Comte had not written his *Sociology*, I would have written it myself in

[26] *Ibid.*, II, 507-517; *Concreten Logik*, p. 297.
[27] *Ibid.*, p. 299.

almost the same spirit." Despite his criticisms, Masaryk considered Comte among the foremost thinkers of his century. Comte stood for factual clarity in human thought and solidarity in life.[28]

Kant, contrarily, Masaryk first maintained, fell into rationalistic unclarities. In failing at a circumspect psychological analysis, myth gained the upper hand with Kant and still more so with his followers, Schopenhauer, von Hartmann, and others. Doctrines such as "the thing-in-itself," "phenomena," and "noumena," were imaginative fictions. Kant's "Pure Reason," virtually made metaphysics a part of logic and gave rise to that word-philosophy (euphemistically designated "dialectics") which not infrequently was offered in the place of scientific method. Kant placed philosophic history in reverse by severing philosophy from science; for thereby went, first of all, the scientific method and with it the scientific content. By taking philosophy, furthermore, to consist primarily of logic, Kant emphasized too much the static moment in world explanation. To offset this defect, Hegel formulated his philosophy of history; yet it too lacked psychological sobriety. Kant set the stage, in fact, for subjectivity in both thought and life and thereby turned the Titans loose to destroy themselves in suicide and war. Kant lost the world of concrete fact, and gave to German thought the turn which issued in its self-destroying inhumanity.[29]

This was Masaryk's early view of Kant, and this remained his view, to some considerable degree, throughout his life.[30] But Masaryk had some second thoughts on Kant, which had a more marked value for his own system. He urged Kant as the antidote alike for Hume and scepticism, on one hand, and for mythology and Russia, on the other. Comte's achievement,

[28] Skrach, "Masaryk et le positivisme français," *Festschrift*, II, 12, 14.
[29] *Concreten Logik*, pp. 301-302; *Making of a State*, pp. 341-351.
[30] Čapek, *Masaryk on Thought and Life*, pp. 36-37.

Philosophical Nature of Criticism 159

Masaryk urged throughout, was not great enough. He had only gone part way and inadequately that part. Comte stopped with dogmatism on one side and agnosticism on the other. Not that Comte was wrong in insisting on exactitude and the systematic organizing of all sciences; it was certainly essential to demand clear observation and analysis as the pre-conditions for reliable syntheses of scientific data. It was a naïveté, however, to *reject all quests for causes*, the efforts to explain the world of thought and life. These have always been the primary quests of men. It may be that mankind will learn the futility of search; yet that itself will be a *critical*, non-positivistic discovery. *Knowledge* of the very limitations of men's minds and of their pervading ignorance is itself a critical achievement of epistemology. Comte was superficial, in spite of emphasis on science. He stopped short with scepticism and a mythology of science. Scepticism has, indeed, a high methodological importance, but taken as a final attitude or theory, it is scientifically and philosophically inadequate. Philosophy and life alike require that men advance to fuller and more penetrating criticism, in the Socratic sense and, more especially, that of the Kantian Critiques.[31]

Kant's critical philosophy was thus of epochal importance. The "world-historical" significance of Kant's philosophy consisted actually not just in rejection of mythical objectivism but also in its attitude toward sceptical subjectivism. "Once for all," indeed, "Hume and Kant destroyed the myths on which childlike faith can alone be established, and all attempts to reconcile scientific philosophy with [mythical] theology have since their day been of necessity fallacious and fugitive." "Epistemologically considered, criticism as a philosophical doctrine signifies critical and cognitive reflection of a sceptical character, as opposed to the blind faith that has hitherto pre-

[31] *Concreten Logik*, p. 302; Škrach, *op. cit.*, II, 32-36.

vailed." Kant's criticism, in fact, like Hume's scepticism, was "directed against theology, for theology makes belief in authority the basis of our entire outlook on the universe." Yet this was just the negative aspect of its function. The constructive interest of the Kantian Critique lies in "the way in which it conceives the attitude of the critical thinker towards the world and towards himself," not only as opposed to myth but also as *opposed to scepticism*. "Kant demonstrates that a critical awareness of the powers of the human intelligence is the only possible and the only correct attitude for the philosopher to assume. This is the historical, the world-historical, significance of criticism." "Regarded from the outlook of universal history, Kant, as opponent alike of theology and the scepticism of Hume, signifies that with the coming of Kant mankind is ripening to an age of reflection," and that both mythology and scepticism are being transcended. Mankind as a race is awakening to wisdom founded on validated knowledge.[32]

In final analysis, in fact, critical philosophy is a philosophy of religion: a philosophy of informed faith and enlightened devotion. These are basic to life, and they are key aims of reflection. For "if the new philosophy is so frequently conceived as hostile to religion, all that this really signifies is that between philosophy and historically extant religion, the so-called positive religion, an opposition exists, that there is hostility towards the doctrine and the practice of the church." Inasmuch, none the less, as ecclesiasticism and theology pervade all reaches of living, philosophy, "as philosophy of religion, is criticism, not merely of theology, but in addition of theocracy, of church doctrine, church morality, church politics —of official doctrine, morality and politics in general."[33] Kant, indeed, provides the basis of the anti-theological enlighten-

[32] *The Spirit of Russia*, I, 205, 207-208, II, 468, 469, 478.
[33] *Ibid.*, I, 205, 206.

ment. "The modern man has begun to consider the course of his own development cognitively and critically" and to try to find a basis for intelligible conviction.

It is not only, therefore, as a critical assessing and refining of theology, secular and sacred—so that it will be respectably intelligible—that Kantian and post-Kantian thought is philosophy of religion. It is also, and more basically still, in its constructive efforts to find a solid and enduring ground for faith. Kant himself declared that "he had formulated his criticism in the desire to find his way back to faith," but this was only "one of the numerous examples of Kant's inconsistency." "Epistemologically," Masaryk held, "Goethe is right when he insists, as he does more than once, that no one can return to faith, but only to conviction. His meaning is that faith (credulity) constitutes the essence of myth. That which theologicans ever extol and demand as child-like faith is nothing but the blind belief, the confident credulity, of the uncritical human being. One who has understood Hume's scepticism and Kant's criticism can no longer 'believe'; he must *know*, must *seek*, and find conviction." Today, in fact, the religious problem can be formulated: Can there be a critically defensible and philosophically intelligible religion? "Can the scientific or critical thinker, can the philosopher, have a religion; and if so, what religion?" [34]

This was the problem to which Masaryk addressed his *Modern Man and Religion*, 1897–1898, in which he juxtaposed Pascal as the still believing Catholic to Hume, the unbelieving Protestant, and endeavored through Kant to mediate religion on the grounds of pure reason. "There is but one great question of our time," Masaryk asserted in 1902: "the religious question." This is the kernel and the cornerstone of all else in life. "All my life experience and study has confirmed me in this con-

[34] *Ibid.*, I, 205-206, 210, II, 469, 478; *Modern Man and Religion*, pp. 9-10.

viction again and again." [35] The modern man must have something in which he can intelligently believe, on which to base the whole organizing of his life. "Religion constitutes the central and the centralising mental force in the life of the individual and of society. The ethical ideals of mankind are formed by religion." [36] Man's fundamental problem is to find a basically informed ground for his cosmic outlook and life. All concern of modern philosophy lies, in point of fact, in such a constructive revision of Hume, in thinking through of empiricism critically, i.e., in the sense of philosophic criticism.

The view that religion is a matter chiefly for the unthinking masses of men, who need superstitions as primary motives, Masaryk dealt with in the opening part of *The Modern Man and Religion*. He treated there of Garborg's *Wearied Souls*, who know not why they live, have neither God nor their own soul, and find no meaning in or sense to life. Their very dilettantic scepticism is the ground of their psychologically weak and seriously diluted living. They might save themselves momentarily by falling back on some still unestablished faith. Yet this would solve no problem for themselves or others, and they would have the entire round of thought to start out on once again when their minds were strong and frank enough to undertake the philosophical adventure. Neither sceptical agnosticism nor yet arbitrary dogmatism afford solidarity, with strength, in life. Where can one find a basis for enduring and effectively informed faith? Spiritism, symbolism, and all formulations of occultism are evasions of the issue: a return forthwith to myth. Modern man has no alternative to critical philosophy. He must think life's standards and objectives through to a constructive climax, unchurch and de-theologize his life. Science and epistemology lie athwart the way to religion of the

[35] "Los von Rom," address in Boston, 1902, concluding section; *Modern Man and Religion*, p. 9.
[36] *The Spirit of Russia*, II, 557.

spirit with its honest, understanding faith.[37] Science and epistemology must themselves be bulwarks of that faith.

Here, indeed, Kant did not prove Masaryk's final helper. Masaryk said that he discovered Kant through Russia, and it has been clearly acknowledged that Masaryk's early criticism of Kant was subordinated to a more fundamental issue in *The Spirit of Russia*. He had been led increasingly to recognize the basic import of the Kantian dialectic, while disapproving still Kant's subjective and non-empirical abstractionism. The early emphasis on concrete and objective facts had never ceased to be a prime concern of Masaryk, but he had long been convinced that refuting Hume, who set the problem for all modern thought, was much more than a matter of empirical science. Kant's positive construction was subjectivistic. It did issue in results which were destructive. Yet the "whole Kant," including Practical besides Pure Reason, was not understood except when taken as a fundamental unity. Kant went definitely beyond both Comte and Hume in his diagnosis of this crucial modern problem. Yet it was not given him to enter or subdue the land of intelligently established faith. Religion within limits of Pure Reason allowed him to approach no nearer than its own Mount Nebo.

Masaryk's chapter on Kant, in *The Modern Man and Religion*, bears the title:"Religion is Morality." The great virtue of Kant, Masaryk declared, is in the utter honesty with which he faced the whole problem of knowledge and belief and in *his recognition of the fact that thought ultimately must be made to square with itself;* that no hypothesis, however scientific, which fails to permit of this is ultimately justified. There is no doubt, said Masaryk, that Kant by means of his Critique has well characterized the activity of the human mind, its con-

[37] *Modern Man and Religion*, Chap. II ff; cf. also Kozák, "Masaryk's Stellung zur Metaphysik," *Festschrift*, II, 205-206.

tinuous search for truth, reflection over and penetration into things. More significantly, too, Kant disclosed the essential unity, wholeness, and logical connection of our knowledge. Yet Kant separated reason sharply from all sensibility, and his religion on the grounds of necessities in moral faith was epistemologically undemonstrated. Our whole conscious life is fundamentally one. The denial of certainty from the point of view of dialectic thought does not leave still other channels open. Either thought can balance its equations or it cannot; and separation of pure reason from sensory, affective, and from moral life precludes the very possibility of an actually enlightened faith. This means that morals and religion are left to rest on sheer suppositions. Kant, therefore, definitely failed to refute Hume; and Kant, furthermore, had recourse himself to subtle myths.[38]

Masaryk, on the other hand, had found a way preliminarily to surmount Hume's scepticism, back in 1882, and had in fact made a public balancing of his philosophical accounts in his inaugural lecture in that year at the University of Prague. His address was entitled "Hume's Scepticism and the Calculus of Probability." The mathematicians, he stated, have made it clear "that the conclusions of what is known as imperfect induction are not founded exclusively, as Hume affirmed, on habit. Hume had reasoned on the basis of analyses of experience that we have no ground for belief in any necessary connection of things or events and no reason for the expectation that the sun will rise tomorrow apart from the habit [of mind] due to the regularity of the occurrence heretofore. This regularity, furthermore, is not to be ascribed to or conceived in terms of causality; we have no direct awareness of causality. Causality itself in truth is a human construction, a by-resultant of habit. Why habits should originate with repeated events we need not undertake to consider. What is pre-

[38] Cf. especially Rádl, "Masaryk und Kant," *Festschrift*, II, 157-160.

Philosophical Nature of Criticism 165

eminently important is that the mathematicians have arrived at results on this issue which are fully convincing: e.g., that there are logical considerations on which their conclusions are based and which show the reliabilities of human convictions. Habit may still participate so strongly that it makes my expectation (with respect to the future) invalid. The associations which in each instance facilitate the inference from the past to the future have to be, however, or at least can be, established for the greatest part by means of reflection. Not only can I, in fact, anticipate a future result but I can determine its probability by rules which the penetration of the greatest geniuses in mathematics have ascertained by wearisome mental work.

"These rules have not been established by empirical methods. The fact that a Bernoulli had to reflect 20 years over the proof of his theorems shows distinctly that in determining the laws of probability it is not a matter merely of empiricism or indeed of empirics at all, even in such fashion as Mill declared the axioms of mathematics to be generalizings from experience. Assuredly, the mathematician can, by trying empirically, find many a principle of probability, but subsequently he can justify it through a process of reasoning which is the definitive *establishing* of the empirical hypothesis.

"Induction, in truth, is no such passive mental task as it is portrayed in the thought of Hume and his successors: Mill, Bain, and others. It is no blind intake of experiences forced on one from without, but an active seeking, continual verifying of hypotheses which the creative imagination constantly advances. . . . The frequency of experiences, furthermore, stands in no direct relation to the results produced or the consequences to be anticipated, as would be the case if Hume's view were true." One can generalize mathematically from one single instance.

It was Leibniz, first, who really recognized the significance of the calculus of probability for inductive logic. His wish that some mathematician might undertake the task of determining the specific laws of probability was fulfilled by Bernoulli. The latter in his posthumous work, *Ars Conjectandi* (1713), really showed how a scientific theory of induction must be carried through. Laplace, after Bernoulli, clarified the epistemological significance of the principles of probability; while he in turn was followed by still others who dealt with logical aspects of the issue.

Yet "all of these new works lacked direct reference to Hume. Therein, I may say, they missed the special point [of their study]. Only when, to speak concretely, Laplace's rules and explanations are set in contrast to Hume's scepticism does it become evident what significance Laplace's words definitely have: that the whole of induction and analogy rests on the calculus of probability. Implicitly, Hume's passive theory of induction, as Mill developed it, is basically refuted by . . . the mathematicians, and most notably Laplace. And when one considers the particularly rough formulation of Hume, the works of these mathematicians appear in a still more glowing light. . . . For it is then evident that the axioms of mathematics generally and the calculus of probability in particular are *a priori*" (forms and conditions of knowledge).

Hume himself spoke much, indeed, of probability, but he did not know, quite evidently, the mathematical rules for objective calculus of probabilities. He was, in fact, unable to distinguish probability in the subjective sense from probability which is accurately determined by mathematics; and it is therefore obvious how he could not but attain to his sceptical theory of induction. Had he thought about the extensive usage of mathematics in empirical science, had he had modern mechanics and mathematical physics before him to consider, he would have found it difficult to advance his sceptical view of induction. The very science which he himself declared to be

Philosophical Nature of Criticism 167

fully established could in fact have saved him from his fundamental error.[39]

Masaryk, therefore, pointed the way to the transcending of scepticism through criticism of scepticism itself, the determination like Descartes of what cannot be doubted if thought is to have any function whatsoever, the construction of a system of thinking through critically organized science, and the calculation by exact mathematical logic of degrees of philosophical believability. A realism of dialectic thought as the groundwork of organized science is thus the standpoint of knowledge and enlightened belief, and the way to substantial construction in all phases of thinking and life. Criticism was not fully "critical" to Masaryk until it was solidly creative. Not only, therefore, must philosophic criticism discover bedrock for reflection and life, but it must build firmly step by step and test out all of its art and its science as it proceeds. And here, we find, there emerges a new and honored role for myth, though Masaryk did not call it myth, but, in Goethe's words, *exakte Phantasie*. For criticism, in its higher and its broader sense, both permits and requires "precise imagination." The whole superstructure of coördinated science, and the whole overworld of self-vindicating values, is unfolded through the critically advised imagination. The dynamic integrity of thought, life, and nature is, furthermore, its most essential criterion.

[39] *David Hume's Skepsis und die Wahrscheinlichkeitsrechnung*, pp. 8-15.

Chapter Seven

Constructive Realism: A Philosophy of Values

MASARYK'S THOUGHT ADVANCED, we have elaborated, from Plato via Comte through Kant, surmounting each of these standpoints and emerging as an independent system of conceptions. We must now therefore undertake to think of Masaryk's philosophic outlook in and of itself and to try to characterize his whole philosophic way of thinking—and living—in its most distinctive principle.

The term "Realism" was employed by Masaryk to distinguish his conceptual standpoint, adding the qualification that it was "Critical Realism" in order to demark its scientific and epistemological rigors. Masaryk's philosophy, however, was the meeting point of opposing philosophic outlooks such as Idealism and Realism, Theism and Humanism, Pragmatism and Platonism, Positivism and Rationalism. We must, in consequence, question whether any single term can sufficiently subserve his whole thinking. It might seem indeed that this last phrase, "whole thinking," could really serve that end, since his, as we have found, was a philosophy of inclusive culture. Yet there is no good reason why "whole thinking" is not also *ipso facto* realistic—except indeed that certain anti-"realists" have attempted to pre-empt and do violence to the whole-ist viewpoint, while many an avowed, self-designated "realist" seems to have considered it his responsibility to be philosophically dissociated. We can most incisively, however, approach this issue if we inquire what are the specific objections that have been voiced to Realism as the best descriptive term for Masaryk's philosophy.

Two immediate objections have, in fact, been raised: one by Daniel Essertier of Poitiers, the other by I. A. Bláha of Prague. We shall therefore treat of these.

Consider Essertier's opposition first. He acknowledges that "critical realism" characterized a most important phase of Masaryk's philosophy but not its whole "ensemble." This titular phrase applies definitely to the original or initial phase, which was left behind as soon as Masaryk began to be constructive. The words "critical realism," Essertier maintains, "form the motto with which the young Professor of the University of Prague marched to battle [in the 1880's]; they are not the Alpha and Omega of his thinking." Masaryk "possessed in the adequate measure himself that quality which was rarest around him and the absence of which was the cause of all the trouble, i.e., he had *courage:* courage in the face of ideas, to see things as they are and not to hesitate to ferret out all prejudices and submit them to severest criticism; courage in the face of men, to stand for the right, with one's head high, before the Masters of Vienna and their valets; to risk position, fortune, payment with one's life if necessary, for fidelity to a great ideal." From the moment that Masaryk discerned the lethargy and poison of romanticism in Czech politics and life, he "knew what his philosophy would be: it would be the generator of intellectual and moral courage; it would be a realism, in that sense which opposed reality incessantly not to the ideal but to imagination, the fruit of lax complacence in and for itself. And it would be a critical realism for it would pass through the sieve of an uncompromising reason the malformed conceptions, accepted on all sides, and too favorable to the breeding of sophisms.

"But this critical realism was only a prologue. It was necessary, first, that it should be fully established that apart from truth or in opposition to it nothing was likely to survive. That done, was the task completed? It had only begun.

"The work of Masaryk is not just a critical performance; it desires, above all, to construct. Humanity has need of a faith, an ideal, a reason for living. The task of philosophy is to provide them with this." Ideals are the highest realities. "Critical realism in the respect of its method, the philosophy of M. Masaryk, in so far as a system, seems to us to be, in fact, a constructive idealism." [1]

Here, in truth, we have what in the prevailing view demarked Masaryk from all Realists and linked him, by false contrast, with Plato. Professor Essertier is, nevertheless, confused in conceptions. He mistakes *realistic* social idealism for an idealism which *is* encompassingly idealistic. He confounds realism with things as they are instead of also as they may, in fact, and even must, become. It was just that sort of pseudo-realism among the Austrians and Germans which Masaryk was as much concerned to discredit as he was with the mythical romanticism of the Czechoslovaks. His view was realistic in the inclusive sense that it insisted on fundamental principles and standards as well as facts and situations of the moment. The one had to be taken into account just as much as the other. "A considerable field of activity," he held, "is allotted to ideas and ideals; individuals and nations are to a great extent the creators of their own future, and it has already frequently and correctly been said that in the long run it is the idealists who always win. Yet the victorious ideas and ideals are not born of fantasy and indifference to facts." [2] They must be connected

[1] *Festschrift*, II, 187-189.
[2] *Speech on Tenth Anniversary*, p. 11.

Constructive Realism 171

with and rooted in reality and entail critical exactness in conception. Constructive thinking must in and of itself be realistic.

I. A. Bláha's criticism is more penetrating. He acknowledged that Masaryk called himself a critical realist, and was a realist in the sense of always starting from the facts and proceeding step by step with the horizon open. For Masaryk, moreover, the mind and world of objects (entities, beings, processes, and events) were both real, and neither could be explained epistemologically in terms of the other. Yet Masaryk admitted with Kant that knowing is not by any means a purely passive registering of "objects" but an elaboration of experience: experience actually becomes knowledge only through the intervention of the intellective functions. Knowledge, therefore, means a synergism of the mind and world, and a collaboration, full and conscientious, of the individual with society. Bláha urges "synergism" consequently as a more descriptive term than "realism" for Masaryk's philosophy. Synergism holds, in fact, he urged, not only in reference to Masaryk's epistemology but in all aspects of his thinking. His whole standpoint was that of synergism: epistemologically, sociologically, metaphysically, practically.[3]

There can be little doubt that synergism represents an essential moral and socio-metaphysical moment in Masaryk's philosophical system and that, actually, he was quite sympathetic toward the *Theodicee* of Leibniz.[4] Epistemologically, likewise, Masaryk's system definitely involves a synergism of the critically active mind with its objects, and that itself, in turn, is an achievement which is significantly social. But this is not at all to say that Masaryk's system is unrealistic. It is, in fact, to indicate the contrary: that an intellectually critical relationship of men's minds to objects is essential to knowledge, and that

[3] Herben, Hartl, Bláha, *T. G. Masaryk*, p. 147.
[4] *Versuch einer Concreten Logik*, pp. 281, 302; "Sub Specie Aeternitatis," *New Europe*, Dec. 21, 1916, p. 300.

knowledge is a process of alert discovery. There is no suggestion in the works of Masaryk that human thinking creates or reconstructs the objects of real knowledge in this process of discovery. The problem is to know the facts, and knowledge is clear ascertaining of these facts. Creation enters into building on this world of facts, and that in turn requires discovery, through realistic thought and science, of valid possibilities and definitely effective principles, which are operative in this world of concrete actualities.

Bláha's argument neglects the difference of creation from discovery. The latter likewise perhaps is in a special sense creative, involving insights based on some degree of spontaneity. Yet it is not construction of the objects discovered. Realism stands for recognition of this difference and for the notion of validity in projects and in values. That the world itself is reconstructed just by critical thought and scientific awareness Masaryk did not and could not concede.

Bláha has, however, raised a fundamental question, in that of the respective roles of empiricism and rationalism in critical realism. Masaryk significantly related these two. He found rationalism in itself to be unrealistic, empiricism without rationalism to be unpenetrating. Empirical rationalism or rational empiricism was the substance of realism in its most accurate and defensible conception. Its first principle indeed was to discover and to take account of all the facts to be relevantly considered. A second was to see them in their relationships, each with the others. A third was to conceive these relations in terms of intelligible principles and rationally defensible assumptions. Critically scientific realism, undertook, therefore, to adjust the conflicts and confusions of ideas with reference to each other, while using adequate techniques for determination of their concrete references to objects. It subjoined empiricism in the sense of factually inductive science with rationalism in the sense of sound analyses of thought, critical comparisons of

Constructive Realism 173

ideas, logical syntheses, and deduction of conclusions. Rationalism and empiricism are not therefore basically discrepant or disjoined. They pass into and complete one another, in the process of knowledge and in the defense of its findings. Bláha, like so many others (some at least of whom denominate themselves as "realists"), fails to recognize this fact: that realism must be *rationally* scientific and objective to be wholly realistic.

Realism, as Masaryk explained it, takes the viewpoint of *knowledge* and inclusively scientific culture. "It is a system" as well as a method, a system of things-in-themselves to be known by critical methods and given full credence in whatever spheres they are found—whether in morals, in politics, religion, or as material factors and forces. Realism simply denies that the mind creates the ground work of substantial existence, inasmuch as brute facts are the cues and the clues for both thinking and living. The mind can improve on the past and the present on the basis of facts and of laws that obtain, but it must do so in the light of validities and values and by methods of science and of synthesized culture.[5]

The writer was told more than once in Prague that Masaryk's philosophy could not be adequately understood without explicit reference to Czech culture and that quite particularly *The Czech Question* (1898)—which was not available in English, French, or German—was essential for a comprehension of both Masaryk's philosophy and life. Czech life comprised the direct milieu and the immediate issue for Masaryk. Better than any other work, perhaps, *The Czech Question* represents what realism was to him. Czech social consciousness had been extinguished in the 160 years from the Battle of White Mountain (1620) to the death of centralistic Maria Theresa. Group feeling began only to be revived, by Czech "Awakeners," with

[5] C. J. C. Street, *President Masaryk*, p. 109; Ludwig, *Defender of Democracy*, p. 132; *The Czech Question*, Chap. IV.

the reforms of the philosophical despot Josef II. The question then arose: what should be the status and objectives of the Czechs and Slovaks, distinctive Slavic peoples, amid the Germans, Magyars, Ruthenes, and others in the zone of central European nations?

Masaryk insisted that this was a philosophically realistic issue. The Czechs must discover via scientific history wherein their true genius consists, set for themselves that guiding conception for internal culture and relations with all other nations, and use realistic methods continually. Romantic or Jesuitic methods and conceptions could not serve. Sentiment and chauvinism were far from enough. They lacked solidarity with historic and current facts. Truth is the only sound basis for group, as for personal, life; and truth must be clarified and substantiated through criticism and exact science. The Czechs succeeded notably in history in certain actual circumstances. They failed quite ignobly in others. The issue was to isolate the facts and principles which led to their successes and those similarly conducing to their failures. The simple truth was that national, besides individual, life is a process to be sustained, and indeed reconstructed, continually. Reality *in toto* was undergoing construction. Construction is a first principle of social and cultural living. A whole cultural philosophy was needed for the adequate guidance of national living. But this cannot be created *ex nihilo*. It should take its cues from what already is, and learn from history and thorough science what can be achieved and implemented.

This was Masaryk's insistent emphasis in opposition to both romanticists and to static objectivists. The Czechs had waged an intellectual civil war themselves from the time of Kollár and Šafařík to the "Battle of the Manuscripts," and the sequel encounters. Kollár had viewed all Slavs from his Slovak viewpoint, as dove-like harbingers of good will, in contrast to the war-like Germans. He overlooked the historic fact and influ-

Constructive Realism 175

ence of Žižka with his fighting Hussites, and he also underemphasized the courageous suffering of Chelčický's Czech Brethren. These men were not just sentimentalists; they were determined pacifists who undertook to carry moral and religious culture into every reach of human living—notably through thorough education. Their humanitarianism needed scientific study. Romanticism falsified these truths of history, neglecting the differing realisms of Huss, Chelčický, Comenius, and Žižka.[6]

It was Kollár's time, in fact, which produced the unauthentic Králove Dvur and Zelená Hora manuscripts, ascribing a high level of culture to the Czechs when their German contemporaries, their bodies daubed with dye, still lived in savagery. The testing and rejecting of these manuscripts was incumbent on the Czechs not only for respect of other nations and for self-respect among themselves, but also to insure their present and, still more significantly, their future fundamental interests. An artificial social consciousness, which belied the actual facts and genius of their history and had recourse romantically to chauvinism and to black-mailing of Austrian politicians, permitted of no stable future—if somehow momentary gains might questionably be had. "A lie has short legs," whether in politically social life or in purely individual relations.

With Palacký and Havlíček, and most thoroughly the latter (though Masaryk went beyond both), Masaryk showed that Czech life must be founded on and guided by its own especial history. Czech history was a social process; and social rightness must begin at home. The Czechs could not succeed by either force or intrigue. They were materially and numerically outclassed by their neighbor nations. As witnessed, none the less, by Hussite history, they could carry on with notable success when they based their social life upon morality and a spiritually scientific culture. But, first, they must repair 1487; for in

[6] *Ibid.*, Chap. II.

that year the higher and the lower Czech nobility compacted against the peasants and enslaved them almost from the very start of their newly-found possibilities as Czech Brethren. That was the beginning of the end for Czech historic greatness; for while greater days were still to come, the foundations of their life were undermined, and one more error—the election of a Hapsburg as their king in 1526—served within a century to bring complete defeat. Peasants enslaved, nobility demoralized, the Czechs had neither moral courage nor the wisdom of the former Taborites of Žižka. They were, and had been since 1487, unrealistic, deficient in their comprehension of the facts and even more especially in their sense of human values.

Masaryk's Realism centered ultimately, in fact, in a philosophy of values. He was not technically an axiologist, although a student of Brentano. Masaryk never even undertook to work out explicitly an inclusive view of values. His was, none the less, preeminently a value-philosophy, and Masaryk may yet come to be viewed as a noteworthy contributor to the understanding of values. Indubitably, his work in different value-fields is not without significance. But even more than this, his implicit view that all values are validities of things in their functional relations, and must function in the total scope of interactivity and culture, marks him as the herald of a soundly practicable philosophy of values with the very broadest possibilities in its application.

That values were prime actualities to Masaryk was shown in the evolution of his conception of philosophy. He conceived this to begin with, we have seen, as metaphysics, and metaphysics as the integrated content of all sciences. On second thought, he held that philosophy included logic, as its comprehensive method, with metaphysics as its synthetic picture of reality. Then Masaryk reached a further stage in his *Syllabus of Sociology*. For there he gave a place to ethics beside metaphysics and logic, in philosophy *per se*. He had first held ethics,

Constructive Realism

we have noted, to be but one among the diverse special sciences—with a strongly philosophic flavor, to be sure, but still not actually philosophy for discriminating usage. Now he gave it philosophic parity both with logic and with metaphysics. Not that ethics had become less scientific in his thinking; there must be no relaxing of the scientfic vigil in ethics any more than in any other branch of concrete logic; otherwise there would be scant validity in ethics. Ethics is life-wisdom, the theory of sound human living within the social cosmos. Ethics, therefore, cuts across one's entire knowledge and whole system of conceptions, and is philosophy in life and action—practical philosophy in distinction from metaphysics which is theoretic.[7]

Slight wonder that Masaryk went beyond this stage to the view that ethics is the *noyau* of philosophy and not a secondary or even just equivalent primary phase.[8] For philosophy in the truest meaning of the term concerned the world-conceptions and life-principles which are lived—not those for which men do not stake their lives; the latter are less meaningful despite demands of thought or forthright implications. Philosophers indeed are living while and in philosophizing, and in so far as they commit themselves to their own speculative life-and-world conceptions these are their real philosophies. But dualisms between thought and life bespeak reservations on the part of life and a philosophy or philosophies of life *upon a different metaphysic*. Ethics is philosophy to be lived, without those reservations; and its full formulation is complete philosophy—with logic and a metaphysics which includes and has an adequate regard for life. This is the final goal of criticism or epistemological inquiry: an outlook on the universe which affords a full sense of human and of cosmic values. The needs and

---

[7] Kozák, "Masaryks Stellung zur Metaphysik," *Festschrift*, II, 191, 193-194, 203.
[8] Škrach, "Masaryk et le positivisme français," *Festschrift*, II, 22.

enduringly significant values of life must be provided for in any adequate philosophy, and man's anthropocentric viewpoint requires, in fact, that these be prime determinants of philosophical principles and vision.

It is from this standpoint that we must view Masaryk's assertion that to him "philosophy was, above all, ethics, sociology, politics." Modern philosophy, as Kant indeed showed, "is essentially ethical and humanitarian," aiming at the "foundation of a new morality, at the elaboration of the new democratic political and administrative system, at democratic anthropocracy." Philosophy seeks, in fact, a new, a satisfactory, life.[9] Philosophy resolves, and must undertake to resolve, all questions of reflection, but thereby it resolves, and must aim to resolve, all issues of living. Resolution of the problems of living entails the actual resolution of the questions of reflection, for the real philosophies of men are those in terms of which they live—not those in terms of which they simply claim to think. Philosophy is no mere speculative *game;* it is *thought in life,* at both work and play: as perspective, insighted enterprise, intelligently coordinated action, persistently high-minded and long-sighted life. Philosophy involves living from the viewpoint of the facts of the whole and the long-run—the very contrary of evasion in any or in all issues, of either facts or values. It is putting life upon a total fact-and-value basis. Philosophy first and foremost, therefore, centers in the philosophy of standards and values. This is its end-task, final fruitage and testing.[10]

[9] *The Making of a State,* p. 318; *The Spirit of Russia,* II, 511; *Grundlagen des Marxismus,* p. 515.

[10] Contrast, however, Čapek, *Masaryk on Thought and Life,* p. 10. Here Masaryk reasserts at eighty or later that of "real philosophical sciences there are only two: logic, including epistemology, and metaphysics. . . . For me, philosophy, I mean scientific philosophy, is an attempt to achieve a general conception of the world, inclusive of the mind." The last qualifying clause, however, restores the notion that philosophy must take account of and do justice to feelings and volitions

Values, further, are not just interests or desires, much less purely pleasures or just practicalities. That would be but partial realism in or with regard to values. Values are validities for relationships and functions. Wherever there is any function or fulfillment of a function, the entity or thing which functions is a value of some type for the process which it serves. The tests of human life are tests of human values. This is the realistic view of values. Whatever is a human value fulfills a function in the structure or from the point of view of human life. Values validate themselves. This is what constitutes and distinguishes them as values. Not only do they elicit, but they justify, appraisals and appreciations on the part of men, and may validate themselves without the consciousness at all that they are actual values. We have seen this with regard to Czech history.[11]

VALUES OF ART AND ENJOYMENT

There are different manners and degrees of validation from some mere quasi-functionality to total solidarity with life. We have cited Masaryk's critiques of literature and art and how he refused to accord the aesthetic moment of experience any final independence. It is an experience of human life, whenever it

---

as well as explicit ideas and that the adequacy of theoretic thought to human activity is one of the problems of thought if also a problem of the effective controlling of action. Masaryk said categorically to Čapek: "I deny this dualism: a man is not divided into one half that acts: through action he obtains knowledge, obtaining knowledge is itself work and action—and what a powerful activity . . . !"—*Ibid.*, p. 19.

[11] The issue of value was not, as we have seen, attacked by Masaryk as a single problem but as a series of problems in ethics, sociology, religion, and aesthetics. Herein furthermore is his affinity with recent realists disclosed for these have dealt characteristically with specialized issues and have not undertaken to treat an entire problem at one fell swoop. Masaryk's difference in viewpoint appears in his insistence on the integrity of scientific culture and, more strongly still, on the integrity of human life. His was throughout a constructively sociological interest and effort.

obtains, and must be fitted in so far as valid into all of life. If art fails in this and makes for life's demoralizing or disintegration, it is a disvalue, whether as an art or as the object of any sort of satisfaction. There can be no justified equivocation on that point. That men gain direct satisfactions from a supposedly aesthetic object seems indeed an outright validation, but that they lose energy and quality of life means greater loss than gain by much to life. That aesthetic satisfactions should grow anti-social, coarse, and cheap, decadent and devitalizing, means that one's aesthetic life is not, to say the least, self-sustaining; aesthetic consciousness is out of proper focus, and the aesthetic phase of life is failing in its interactions.

There is a sociology, furthermore, to art, and aesthetic theorists cannot justifiably ignore its sociological elements and functions. Human life, in point of fact, cannot be treated in any, however splendid, isolation. It is a long-run social question. One might maintain in total independence "the right to sin" so long as one "desired" the satisfaction of the sin. There is no logic, it is held, to men's desires, and no basis, therefore, for their criticism. Even health and strength of life may be or may not be desired; and so with life itself. There is a structure, none the less, to life itself, and this is not just passive structure. It functions to assimilate, coördinate, recreate, and quite variously perform. Whatever it can utilize may be a human value, though the process of this utilizing is no mere momentary experience. Human values consist of all that can be *consolidated* into or from the point of view of human life within its social settings. Decadence, suicide, neurosis, revolution, war are symptoms of disvalues: objects which refuse consolidation into or from the point of view of consolidated and consolidating living. The tests of validation entail the evidence of generations—possibly of centuries. Yet that far-reaching consequences unfold themselves in due course of time is witness of effectiveness. Those who pronounce sophistically that they don't

Constructive Realism

know what is right (or valid) are weak members of society: weak in their reflective processes and weak in socially domestic consciousness. And those who claim "the right to sin," if they should wish to do so, are weaker still and more socially defective. " 'The right to be wrong' sounds like a trumpet call, but it is an announcement of weakness." Strength and solidarity with an interacting social, cosmic environment are the tokens of full validations of value.[12]

One might think, unquestionably, that Masaryk had scant appreciation for the values of enjoyment just in and for themselves. And stated in this fashion there is some justice to such thinking, for enjoyment, simply in and of itself, without regard to other values is apt to be a violation of man's own life and that of his society. But enjoyment, none the less, was one of Masaryk's fortresses, and therein is the realism of his philosophy of values particularly apparent. With him, enjoyment was among the greatest of all values.[13] Yet for him enjoyment was concomitant to other values: enjoyment of significant activity and of people and things, enjoyment conditioned by knowledge and breadth of perspective.

Happiness is not to be found, he pointed out with a simple illustration, by seeking it directly. Utilitarians maintained that every person seeks, and deliberately should seek, his own satisfactions. And pessimism à la Schopenhauer was in quest of happiness directly, but came to the conclusion that it was utterly impossible. "I, too, think," Masaryk insisted, "that happiness does not exist, or rather, that it exists no longer when people set about to find it. Whoever seeks for happiness has already lost it. Everybody wishes to be happy; there is no doubt of that. But whoever deliberately seeks happiness at any cost

[12] *The Ideals of Humanity*, Chap. III, cf. especially p. 47. Contrast Rudolph Carnap and others for whom value-problems are not susceptible of critical approaches.
[13] Beneš, Funeral oration, *Masaryk's Path and Legacy*, p. 23.

can no longer find it. This is beautifully expressed in the tale of John the Simple. His two intelligent and educated brothers race after happiness, and yet fail to gain it. John the Simple does not think of happiness, but works and helps his neighbors as best he can, and lo! he is happy; and in the end, he comes to the aid of his unhappy brothers. In this story, our people have given us a moral of great wisdom: that it is useless to seek happiness. The conscious, and even the enlightened, quest for happiness produces unhappiness. Since the Great Revolution, modern man appears lost incessantly in pursuit of happiness, of a lost paradise—in all domains of life, economic and political, besides philosophic and aesthetic. Yet the race for happiness has made no one happy." [14]

Nor ought people to concern themselves specifically to make others happy. This is a mode of sentimentalism, and sentimentalism is egoism. We like to fondle and to pamper children and also even adults, but have no open-eyed affection for those whom we claim to love. What mankind, "our nation, family, party, comrades need from us is work," whereby they themselves shall have the opportunity to live significantly in terms of values other than themselves.[15] This is the psychology of human enjoyments.

The values of enjoyment are functions of objective interests and activities which commend themselves to human life by their solidarity with wholesome living; and this obtains quite definitely for art and all the satisfactions of imagination. Until he became President, Masaryk said, he had lived all his life as far as possible in seclusion, and found great values in the activities and productions of imagination. It is difficult, in fact, to overemphasize the significance of imagination in the life and thought of Masaryk, or the values which he found in art for life. "I need art," he stressed, "to live spiritually. I have not

[14] *Ideals of Humanity*, Chap. V; English ed., pp. 66-67.
[15] *Ibid.*, Chap. IX; English ed., p. 92.

Constructive Realism

been musically trained, although I have played the violin, as every Czech does." "Metaphysical experience I found in art and particularly in poetry." "I live in fiction. I should never have held out without it..." "All my life I have tried to enter into the thought and through it the culture not only of our own and other Slav literatures, but of Greece, Rome, Germany, France, England, America, Italy, Scandinavia, and Spain..." "I have read, far longer than I can remember, the great poets side by side with the philosophers, and perhaps more than they: and of what are called 'the poet thinkers' Goethe interested me no less than Kant—more, even—and so did the other poets from Shakespeare downwards."[16]

Masaryk stood, in point of fact, "at the cradle" of a great deal of "modern Czech activity in poetry, philosophy, art, science, and civilization," as "organizer, inspiring force, critic," "winnower and encouraging influence."[17] That due to love of truth and men he had, as Ludwig has construed, a certain measure of distaste for art, as being properly "the province of the inventor, the actor," and, in that sense, "the liar,"[18] is entirely false. That it has been held that Masaryk was deficient in appreciation of aesthetic form is intelligible indeed in view of his insistent consciousness of art's relatedness to all of life and of the human value in art's content. Art was art of objects, themes, and modes of conscious life. Goethe was Masaryk's first and greatest teacher of aesthetic criticism, and Goethe set his themes in strong and well-informed relief, in spite of all the richness and the beauty of his language.[19] Why should art be

[16] The quotations in this paragraph are a mosaic from the following sources: Čapek, *President Masaryk Tells His Story*, pp. 102, 104, 242, 293; Ludwig, *Defender of Democracy*, p. 160.

[17] F. X. Šalda, "Civilization in Czechoslovakia and the Influence of Western Ideas," *President Masaryk in Paris, Brussels, and London in October, 1923*, p. 30.

[18] Ludwig, *Defender of Democracy*, p. 58.

[19] Werner, *Th. G. Masaryk*, p. 21; cf. Masaryk, "Mein Verhältnis zu Goethe," sonderabdruck *Prager Rundschau*, September, 1931.

empty, superficial? And why should it attempt to falsify instead of beautify and creatively improve reality? In either circumstance, art is open to a fundamental criticism. Experiments with forms are creatively essential but that form should be taken in essential emptiness or isolation or should present decadent content, means but partial or defective art. Life itself presents the drama, "just as Shakespearean drama is life," and all the forms we find for art are forms of content which we project for life. We measure life by too simple a standard. We think much more of how we can increase its length or isolate the satisfactions of the moment than how we can unfold life's depth and outreach, strengthen and refine its interactions.[20]

It is the function of art to create; art is but genius in creative action: the human mind at play with themes of its own feelings, intuitions, insights, and imaginative projections. Art is not confined to poetry or music or to what are known as "arts" even in their broader reference. The whole creative organization of life itself is art; and to try to isolate the special arts from life, except for momentary purposes, is to miss the larger meanings and the interactive functions within art as art. In art's fullest sense, Masaryk himself was consciously an artist. He had undertaken in quite early life to write a novel, and in later years he had proposed a theme to Tolstoy. But in that special sense creative art was not his primary genius—or his limitation. It was his genius to see the place and possibilities of art in all of life, and to understand the significance of science and philosophy for the inclusive art of human living. His was the master art of life in its totality.[21]

The tests of art were tests, accordingly, of life, not merely of enjoyment. Enjoyment was a function surely of the quality of life, and taken in itself would give the lie to aesthetic dilettantisms. Enjoyment, none the less, was not taken in itself

[20] Čapek, *President Masaryk Tells His Story*, pp. 224, 284-285.
[21] Herben, Hartl, Bláha, *T. G. Masaryk*, p. 145.

but as the function of the ego at the moment, while objects which were the occasions of enjoyment were treated in quite mystical abstraction. This indeed was not aesthetic realism, but subjectivism such as in the most subjective of idealisms. Aesthetics ought, contrarily, to be taken in the fullness of its data, their organization and totality of functions.

We shall not undertake to elaborate Masaryk's *Studies of Poetic Works*, two series of which he published, and in which he dealt in the history of aesthetics from Plato to Avenarius and Fechner. The fact of which we must especially take note is that while the forms of art contain great possibilities for articulation and happy enrichment of feelings, and empirical analyses of form need to be critically pursued—its richness and suggestiveness of elements, unified congruity, undercurrents, contrasts, comic features, and whole orchestration—the very principle of unity requires that form and content be integrally proportioned to each other, that art contain intelligible finesse and be humanly enriching.[22]

We have here, rather, to consider Masaryk's emphasis on science in art and on the function of art in social relations. Aesthetics was, in fact, a special source and mode of knowledge, presenting insights and ideas the validity of which was subject to the same criticism as any insights and ideas. True, art was not a matter only of men's thinking, but of their feeling too. Yet logic and feeling did not "exclude each other": they found their harmonizing in what Goethe called *Exakte Phantasie*. The emphasis on feeling in art to exclusion of thinking, was as one-sided and mystifying to life and its meanings as would be an emphasis on pure logic for living. Certain arts indeed appealed more fully to feeling than thought and tended to keep the personality under-balanced and unfree. Poetry, however, bestirred the actualizing of the whole human

[22] Lapschin, "Th. G. Masaryk als Aesthetiker," *Festschrift*, II, 226 ff.

heart and was accordingly, or at least was able to be, art in its higher sense.[23]

Science and poetry, in fact, were essentials of each other. "Goethe was a great poet," and Goethe, Masaryk emphasized, had a scientific training. "The researcher must have imagination, but he works with concepts, whereas Goethe worked with pictorial images. Grillparzer says that the poet must have an exact training but that he must forget it when he begins to write poetry. . . . I know poetry," Masaryk pointed out, "and I am convinced that the scientific investigator and creator must have imagination." [24] "My imagination I exercised deliberately and, thanks to scientific precision, I escaped becoming fantastic." True "philosophy and science demand," in fact, that "men should think, that they should gather wide experience, observing and comparing the present and the past, and verifying their deductions from experience by further experience so that haste may not lead them to fantastic conclusions. In art, as in politics and life, there is a difference between fantastic imaginings and the power of imagination, pure imagination as Goethe called it, for precise imagination is a very necessary means to right and exact thinking. A thinking man, ponderate in action, is he whose power of imagination can take him beyond himself, free him from the circumstances to which custom has bound him—a man who, by feeling and thought, can enter into the lives of other men and other times, immerse himself in the spirit of his race, of Europe, of humanity. Only thus can he create something and become a new man." [25]

There is an especial connection between poetry and politics, and this was one of Masaryk's most notable themes. He made a surprising address in New York, in 1918, on this very subject. In answer there to Paderewski's eulogy of him, Masaryk de-

---

[23] Čapek, *President Masaryk Tells His Story*, pp. 152, 224-225.
[24] Ludwig, *Defender of Democracy*, pp. 132, 160.
[25] Masaryk, *The Making of a State*, pp. 319, 443-444.

Constructive Realism

cided to say little of his own Czech program but to "speak for Paderewski by explaining the relationship of politics to art. ... Incidentally," Masaryk wrote, "I wished also to defend him against those of his own fellow-countrymen who opposed his political leadership because he could 'only play the piano.' Polish literature, particularly the writings of Mickiewicz and Krasiński," enabled Masaryk to illustrate "the bearing of poetry upon politics, and to reveal the artist Paderewski as a true political awakener of his people." [26] "I once published an essay," Masaryk explained, "on the relationship of poetry to politics. My master, Plato, was a politician but also a poet. Goethe said a poet must have an exact imagination. The politician must have the same." [27] "Poetry," in fact, "educates imagination, and in politics more perhaps than anywhere else we need imagination, a vision of the future, a penetration into the souls of others." [28]

Politics is, or at least should be, a science: a science of the social transactions of states. Yet "what are politics in the best sense of the word but the conscious forming of people, the fashioning and transforming of real life," the drama indeed of the organizing of living personalities? "Even in the most delicate political situation we must notice and plan carefully, what, how, and on whom we can count . . ." Our observations have to be as "accurate as mathematics." But the objectives, our aims in terms of human life and values, demand imagination and creative insight; "the conception is an eternal poem." [29]

Here indeed there must be interaction between literature and life, and Masaryk related in *The Making of a State* how in his own work and life this was actually effected. "In political life," he said, "I studied and observed men in the same way as

---

[26] *Ibid.*, pp. 250-251.
[27] Ludwig, *Defender of Democracy*, p. 160.
[28] Šalda, *President Masaryk in Paris, Brussels and London*, p. 101.
[29] Čapek, *President Masaryk Tells His Story*, pp. 224-225.

I study characters in novels or in modern poetry. One must know men, select them and assign to them suitable tasks if one is to organize them politically. At an early stage I acquired the habit of observing the people with whom I had to deal, or who were prominent in public life, as though I intended to write a book about them. I collected all possible data upon friend and foe, and gathered biographical material upon those who played an active political part. Before meeting statesmen and public men, I read their writings or speeches and got as much information as I could about them. This habit really began in childhood. At the age of fourteen, when I was about to become a teacher, Lavater's 'Physiognomy' fell into my hands. I read it eagerly and grasped its importance for teachers. Hence, possibly, my continual study of men—and of myself." [30]

This method, furthermore, Masaryk found highly valuable in analyzing the genius of nations. He applied it throughout to the cultural characters of France, England, Germany, Russia, America, and Bohemia, and projected on the grounds of both science and art not just what was, but what should be the interacting social structures of peoples. Other values were at issue, however, besides those of technology and of aesthetics. Some of these were more urgent and basic: especially truth values and the values of morality. To these, therefore, we must turn.

[30] *The Making of a State*, pp. 319-320.

Chapter Eight

Humanism: Moral Necessities in Values

TRUTH VALUES

AESTHETIC VALUES WERE TO A HIGH DEGREE over-values of men's living, concomitants in fact of due regard for other values which were preliminary and basic. Of these there were two major types: truth values and the values of morality. It was questioned then, however, as Pilate questioned in the first century A.D.: "What is truth?" And, as it is often questioned now, should one view truth as actually a value or even speak of truth at all? Sophisticates talked cautiously of "knowledge" and of working-conceptions. There was no such *thing* as truth, Masaryk's own notable teacher, Brentano, maintained but only other things with special modes of interaction.[1] That "true ideas" may have no counterparts at all in nature was witnessed by the paradox of "nothing":

> It is greater than God,
> The dead eat it,
> But when the living eat it, they die.[2]

---

[1] Criticism of the correspondence theory of truth by Brentano and others.

[2] Oskar Kraus, *Wege und Abwege der Philosophie* (Prague, 1934), p. 114.

Nothing corresponds to our conception of "nothing." Yet *nothing* has produced greater confusion from the days of the Eleatics through those of Hegel and his twentieth-century followers. How could truth exist? Or be itself a value? There were things and people and personal feelings; and values were the objects of interests or feelings: of likes and of loves of man's life. But that feelings should show any solidarity with facts and cultural actualities was not considered necessary for any experience of values or for proper valuations by men's value-consciousness. And that feelings in themselves might show penetration into actuality was not to be confused with or compared with evaluation by processes of thought.

For Masaryk, however, truth was the most basic of all of the values. It bespoke the structure and the functions of existence and governed the whole organization and control of life. Truth might be but human judgment but it was judgment which had "passed through the testing fire of criticism" and had certified to human thoughts that they had solid grounds in actuality.[3] Without *rapport* with real existence no value could maintain or justify itself and life must rend itself on reefs of unknown nature and location. Truth was at once the foundational, directional and organizational value for all other values of life. It certified to every value that it was genuine and it illumined men's quest for new and higher vital values. To "buy the truth and sell her not" was essential to any sort of satisfactory living.

This was the meaning for Masaryk of his whole "logic" of culture and the ground of his insistence on science and epistemological criticism as the bases of faith for each phase of life or of interest. Czech life could not be founded on a lie. No more could Austrian politics, or European culture generally. Each must be based on and actually embody the true and adequate ideas of its culture.[4]

[3] Čapek, *Masaryk on Thought and Life*, pp. 21-22.
[4] *The New Europe*, especially pp. 34-35.

Moral Necessities in Values 191

To live "without Idea," in the sense of a valid life conception gained from thorough knowledge of oneself and of life's facts and values is as difficult of successful outcome as was Russia's entrance into the Japo-Russian and World wars.[5] "Knowledge is power": this, we have seen, was the motto of the club which Masaryk founded in Vienna, 1876. "Truth conquers": that was his motto for his country; and for living throughout. That "nothing is great which is not true" he had emphasized in his first *Curriculum Vitae*.[6] Not ideas only, but clear, true, accurate, full conceptions: these were principles and prime essentialities of life. Ideas of men must correspond, in fact, not only to the elemental characters of existent or subsistent nature, but they must be ordered into systems which validly interpret the relationships and processes of nature. Ideas cannot elaborate themselves. They must be true to actuality not just in their separate units, if this were possible alone, but in their unions with each other.

For Masaryk truth, furthermore, had significant additional values. It was in itself an object of appreciation and attachment, worthy of the devotion of men. It was the main fabric or groundwork of culture, bespeaking ideals and objectives as well as prosaic items of platitudinous and even ignominious fact; and truth unfolded an infinite storehouse of fresh comprehensions that not only gave undying interest to the world of men's habituations but disclosed the amazing horizons and reaches of their habitations.

It is from all these standpoints that men should think of philosophies as modes of living, regardless of whether they purport to be philosophies of life or of non-human nature. This was shown, for instance, in pure psychological empiricism, which led to a philosophy of solipsistic subjectivity and disso-

[5] *The Spirit of Russia*, I, 169; *The Making of a State*, pp. 15-16.
[6] See Chap. I.

ciationism; [7] and by materialism, which entailed a denial of the validity of consciousness and disillusionment about all human values.[8] It was further shown by Vitalism, in the form of the biologic theory of survival of the fittest. "Applied solely to animals at first, this doctrine was extended step by step to society, the history of humanity and to man generally." Discussions arose over the disvalues in artificial selection. In military service and medicine it was found that artificial selection functioned to enfeeble life. "Natural selection, contrarily, is unindulgent with weaklings." These facts "led many unequivocally to declare that the logical consequence of natural selection is the right of the strong to destroy the weak. A completely antihumanistic viewpoint began therefore to spread. The ethic of humanity, it was said, enfeebles mankind physically and mentally. A new kind of *Faustrecht,* based on natural science, was heralded instead. This was proclaimed for both individuals and nations. The idea of selected nations was promulgated, in consequence, not at all in the sense that one speaks of the ancient Hebrews as divinely chosen but of nations naturally selected. Nietzsche in particular made himself famous by the formula which he gleaned from Darwinism: "right belongs to the stronger; might is truth." [9]

MORAL VALUES

It was at this point, in thinking on the biological view of existence, that moral values came clearly on the human scene and constituted at once a special group of both truth and moral values. "It is difficult, in fact, to understand why, if man is—as this [foregoing] doctrine undertakes to urge—a being of

[7] With its sequel in German post-Kantianism especially, and in Russian anarchism.
[8] See above Chap. VI, section on Marxism.
[9] *Ideals of Humanity,* Chap. VI, p. 70. See German edition, 1902, p. 33; also French translation, 1930, pp. 71-72.

nature, the idea and the ethics of 'humanity' should be so completely contra-natural." If an "ethic of humanity" enfeebled men it could not be an actual ethic of "humanity." Men, however, "became frightened and began to ask whether those conclusions logically followed from Darwinism. Some said: it is a mistake to deduce ethical and juridical justification of the right of the stronger from the natural sciences; morality is independent of theory. Theoretically one could accept the struggle for existence, but in practice he should adopt humanitarianism, Christianity. This [Masaryk pointed out] is obviously sophistic. If we are convinced that a struggle for existence rules in all of nature, including society, then Nietzsche and his followers are right." [10] The question is: what does rule in human life and nature to make it most continuously satisfactory and effective? This is a question of the nature and motives of life, and it embraces all that has any consequence at all for life. Ethics is and ought to be the truth of the control of human life for better or for worse, the economics of man's personality in his social environment.

We have found already that ethics was the *noyau* of philosophy to Masaryk: that philosophy most significantly was ethics, as the philosophy distinctively of human life. Masaryk built his work around ethics, in fact, from the beginning. While ramifying into every field and lecturing on epistemology, history of philosophy, and philosophy of history, his major course at Prague was ethics—i.e., ethics and the sociology of history, each of which involved the other. Scepticism was, indeed, his crucial theoretic problem in both philosophy of religion and epistemology; for practical reasons, as we have seen in treating of his work on suicide and social tendencies. But scepticism gave him no especial cause to pause in ethics. The talk of people with regard to relativity in ethics showed a lack of penetration or of power of comprehensive judgment. Evidence was

[10] *Ibid.*

quite readily at hand to show wherein morality consists: that *rightness* is not just a speculative question. Moral rightness is a functional state of human attitudes and life, in its social milieu, else that life is failing in its interchanges and accord.

Masaryk was no non-naturalist in ethics. Morals were, for him, not just purely *mores* or conventions, but just as surely morals were not simply indefinables—much less extramundane impositions. Morals were the qualities of human relations in so far as those were expansive or at least self-sustaining: concerned with what is really sound (and therefore right) in human life if thought of in and for itself, yet not only what is essential for maintaining *personal* morale and psychological integrity but also what is required to keep life satisfactory in and for society. Morality was socio-personal rightness functionally, because structurally, in attitudes and active relations. Was there any special clue, however, to the nature of these attitudes and relations? Or any fundamental trait to rightness which tended to demark moral soundness generally in human dispositions and relations and the absence of which tended definitely to be wrong?

Masaryk found two master-clues to this key-problem. The sceptic Hume, actually, uncovered one; modern history afforded the other. For Hume had "called a halt to his scepticism" when he came to morals and society; [11] and while he did this partly from the standpoint of utility, he found a psychological element in human life which made for moral responsiveness to issues of human well-being. According to both Hume and Kant, Masaryk pointed out, "no precise epistemological foundation has hitherto been provided for natural right." Kant's appeal to reason for imperatives furnished no real sanction for morality; it was too doctrinaire. Yet Hume went back to human feelings and found an inborn principle of social justice and of structural human solidarity, an inner conscious-

[11] *The Spirit of Russia,* I, 210, II, 538.

ness of moral right. "Hume makes all society," Masaryk stated in *Les Problèmes de la Démocratie*, "rest on the concept of humanity."[12]

Mrs. Masaryk had translated Hume's *Principles of Morals* while they were still located in Vienna. Masaryk published this, with a preface by himself and his own index of names and topics. "In Hume," said Masaryk in the preface, "we have the classic model of that method in ethics which he himself designated as empirical. Schopenhauer and many others have accepted this, but no one has fully grasped Hume's method and carried out his modality and type consistently.... From the viewpoint of theory, Hume's refutation of egoism is especially significant and should add not a little to the clarification of the idea. One will, at all events, no longer list Hume as a utilitarian, so long as that ambiguous word, utilitarianism, is not more accurately defined than it has been to date.... His doctrine, finally, is particularly important in that the actual motive of all human conduct is not to be sought in reason but in feeling."

The index of names and topics was designed by Masaryk for his own class use. There, in midst of numerous references and annotations which undertook to compass the essentials of ethics, he stated in the tersest terms the type of feeling which induces and governs morals: "Goodwill = sympathy = humanity; this is the ground principle of morals; no one lacks it, and it is self-justifying."

It is at this point, in fact, that we find Masaryk's closest affinity with his great teacher, Franz Brentano: in the notion of "self-justifying" feelings. That these are sources of our consciousness of values and have no need or possibility of more final validation was Brentano's view.[13] In Masaryk's own living

[12] P. 39.
[13] Elaborated notably in Franz Brentano's *Vom Ursprung der Sittlicher Erkenntnis* (Felix Meiner), Leipzig, 1934.

and efforts we see the concrete force of this position. When men were led by him to forego immediate, hardheaded, national interests in the larger interests of humanity, the sense of moral rightness in his point of view must have functioned in their feelings. It is easy to perceive, indeed, that humane feelings justify themselves to sentiments of people everywhere, when expansive feelings simply by themselves are to be considered. The problem is to bring egoistic attitudes and actions within bounds as human sentiments, and to convince self-centered businessmen that "humanity" is not just a nice sentiment, but that it actually works. This requires the functionally historical approach, and it was from this that Masaryk obtained the second of his master-clues.

In an essay on *Progress, Evolution, and Civilization*, 1877, he had already found humanity to be the basic principle of historical advance.[14] The maximizing of individualities in and on behalf of organized society had, in fact, been advocated as early as the thought and work of Plato. Then came the Christians, teaching universal brotherhood and cosmopolitan conceptions. The Renaissance and Reformation brought modern history to birth with humanism as a conscious movement toward enhancing human life. The increasing trend of European history, especially since the Middle Ages, has been toward more humanity. Freedom! Human rights for human beings! Political and moral fraternity! Away with oppressors! These have been the outcries of suppressed and variously exploited peoples. To these, indeed, aristocrats generally, like the Hungarians, have simply yet characteristically said: "The Slovak is not a man." Great revolutions have, none the less, been carried through. The oppressed have watched their opportunities, and leadership has been rather steadily forthcoming. Increasing culture and extension of responsibilities have paved the way for certain basic social changes. With freedom from sheer

[14] Skrach, "Masaryk et le positivisme français," *Festschrift*, II, 11-13.

servitude, men have claimed both economic and cultural prerogatives. Equality and brotherhood are still, indeed, demands of men today. Release of suppressed energies, the satisfaction of requirements in relationship to other men, the balancing and harmonizing of men's interests: the stabilizing and enlarging of men's lives is, in fact, the central urge and principle of history.[15]

History assuredly is full and complicated, and all who use the proof text method can claim to gainsay any principle or rule by pointing to significant exceptions. That history moves by combinations of both bad and good in a commonly reactionary fashion is conceived to mean that every move is simply bad and that there is no "humanity" at all in history. To say indeed that one state of things is better than another has no convincing force so long as goods and evils are not weighed and net results determined. But those specifically who cannot take a broadly horizontal and also long-run view could not grasp the merits of the human status in one era regardless how improved might be the social circumstances. They could not see that social health can be gradually progressive, despite side-eddies and relapses, and that on the whole the human social patient makes decisive gains. To Masaryk, however, who had the training and ability to take a total view, history had no purely relative significance. It offered disappointing strivings and approximations without doubt; yet these were often central tendencies and currents which anticipated the onward march of men to better, if also more complex, conditions. Reversions and decadence might occur in social as in individual existence, but regressions could be diagnosed and isolated once one knew the past and its defections. Gains and goals could be determined, and principles of enduringly effective and sound life could be brought increasingly to social

[15] Cf. Introduction to the *Ideals of Humanity*, *The New Europe*, *The Making of a State*, and other works.

recognition. Human ills or maladjustments were bound, in fact, to call persistently for righting. The foremost and insistent principle of modern European history has been toward sensitizing human consciences and expanding the range of the values to be obtained and shared.

Should it be supposed that this was generalizing from too wide and actually confused a field, Masaryk had a concrete instance in Czech history. Bohemia ran the course of moral revolution years before the Reformation took its start in Germany. And Bohemia was the first to carry reformation to an essentially spiritual completion. Huss had voiced appeal to the finality of enlightened individual thinking. Žižka ran the anti-human absolutists from Bohemia. Chelčický, only forty years from Huss, organized his Czech Brotherhood on the basis of true social brotherhood and service. Czech brethren carried their activities into all domains of life. Comenius, who was the greatest of them all, established modern education on the grounds of full humanitarian morality, governed by philosophy and science. That was the banner era of the Czechs. They achieved a high level of national culture and success under the leadership of Huss and the Brethren. The Czech "Awakening," furthermore, which started in the eighteenth century—and continued through the nineteenth to the World War in the twentieth century—took its stand again on this humanitarianism of the Brethren, reinforced this time by the whole humanitarian movement of Europe. Development of Czech literature and life, from the days and efforts of Dobrovský (1753–1829), was insistently motivated by this principle. The Czechs had variously lapsed in their obedience to life's imperatives; yet they had none the less discovered and disclosed wherein social health and happiness consists. They succeeded notably, as Palacký asserted, when in the moral right; they failed when they deserted the moral standards of their Reformation. Yet these, they had held and shown, were the principles of sound living in society. This was the acknowledged ground of their restored state life. Had not post-war leadership in other democratic nations been of inadequate grade and variety, Czechoslovakia could very well uphold its standards still today. The force of the dictatorships is indubitably due, in considerable part, to the degree to which they have been not merely appeased but definitely courted.

There is no doubt of both healthy and decadent processes in history. But history offers time to prove results and shows the central course of solid gain. It shows wherein real solidarity and effectiveness consists, when counting long-run costs and final losses. There are no repercussions from stabilizing and enhancing life. Repercussions and reactions come from anti-human impositions on people, whether one imposes them on himself or others. For every such encroachment on human life and individuality, oppressors and oppressed must pay the price, not only in less wholesomely desirable enjoyments and relationships but in destruction of their vital and creative energies. The moral laws of human living are not for long to be gainsaid. They may be partially repudiated, without convincing costs, but that the ills of life become more complicated and less soluble means that men's principles of living are significantly wrong.

Moral rightness is a natural human matter. "There is no other foundation for morality," and therefore for politics, Masaryk wrote in 1917, "than respect and love for one another, whether it be called humanity, philanthropy, altruism, sympathy, equality, or solidarity." [16] Essential harmony and solidarity of both individual and group life are resultants of humanity; for individual and social life are functions of each other. Love, in its realistic form, is this sense of human solidarity.

Humanity, however, Masaryk emphasized, is no abandon-

[16] *The New Europe*, p. 20.

ment of self, *à la* Tolstoy. That would be abandonment as well of those who were particularly dependent on one and of all those goods which needed one's sustained endeavor. Humanity entails the consciously considered caring for oneself, along with an informed concern for others; and not merely for their sakes but because one ought himself to be in the clearest sense a man: a full-orbed instance of humanity, true to manhood in himself and worthy of the effort and attachments of others. Self and society alike require that one uphold humanity, first of all, in and with regard to self. This is, in fact, the primary duty of humanity. Then comes naturally, though no less secondarily, the service of others. Yet even this proceeds on a self-referential basis. Each person has an immediate responsibility for those who form his closest human circle, and differing degrees of human obligation as his circles widen. Humanity cannot wisely or effectually begin upon the outskirts of one's social compass. Humanity must start at the center of one's human world and be mediated out by dispositions kindled at the fire of actual human interest and deliberate helpfulness. To foster visions of humanity without immediate regard for self or personalities whom one has to deal with every day is not actually humanity but sentimentalism subjoined with evasive hardness.[17]

Humanity is no merely or even mainly sentimentalist conception. Humanity involves the actual good of men, with whatever that entails in feelings and in enterprise. Humanity means strengthening and advancing human life by adequate techniques and procedures. Humanity is realism in relationships of life, and realism which is deliberately social and constructive. It is universalistic in standpoint, as expressed in Kant's moral axioms, while yet immediate in action. Moral wrongness is its outright contrary. It frustrates life within and without and complicates men's inter-relations.

[17] *Ideals of Humanity.* Chap. IX, pp. 89 ff.

The term "humanitism," which Masaryk used on numerous occasions, bespoke this sense of humane practicality, and is to be preferred to the sentimentally beclouded word "humanitarianism," on one hand, and the atheistically associated term "humanism," on the other. Humanity, Masaryk indicated, has been undergoing factualizing in the process of historical elaboration, and any phobia of sentimentalism, such as impelled Marx to a wholly mechanistic view of human morality, is definitely unwarranted. The concept of humanity has been subjected to too many rigorously refining onslaughts to be essentially an effervescent viewpoint or motif. Kant's puritanic rationalistic moralism, Beneke's practical hedonism, Feuerbach's humanistic love, Schopenhauer's bitterness and anger, Nietzsche's supermanish hardness, Mill's scientifically positivistic utilitarianism, Spencer's philosophic evolutionism: these are merely some of the crossroads and currents which the ideal of humanity has been compelled to run. Lessing, Herder, Schiller, besides the humanists of France, brought the anthropocratic standpoint to articulation, and succeeding thinkers gave it a clearer, firmer content.[18] Any other moral view defeats itself inevitably. Humanity is the only recourse for human conduct and relations. And whether it defeats itself depends on the degree to which it becomes something much more concrete and effective than any pure sentiment. As William James would have stated, humanity must be hard-headed while also soft-hearted.

It was in his *Ideals of Humanity* that Masaryk developed this conception in most notable detail. He had already treated it in *The Czech Question* and *The Social Question,* as well as other writings. In the *Ideals of Humanity,* however, he appraised the concepts of humanity in seven recent ethical philosophies and explained the human motive which entered into each. Socialism, individualism, utilitarianism, pessimism, evo-

[18] *Grundlagen des Marxismus,* p. 492; cf. *Ideals of Humanity,* Chap. I.

lutionism, positivism, Nietzscheanism, were the views which he considered. We need not treat the detail of those studies. What we must take record of is that Masaryk viewed all of these diverse conceptions as attempts to formulate a valid ethic of humanity within modern culture, and, though each was crucially inadequate, all contributed to the clarifying and the actualizing of a true humanitism within world society. To understand the meaning of humanity—in its strictest and effective sense—we must view it in the light of its hard-fought development. No sentimentalism can do justice to this realism of critically socio-personal thinking and sheer struggle.

Humanity, however, cannot be independent of feeling. There must be definite respect and goodwill in the inner attitudes and dispositions of individuals with reference to each other, and in relation to self. Humanity can no more be effected mechanically, or on purely intellectual bases, than human life can muster spontaneity and appreciation without impulsion from within. Feelings are the primary sources of morals. They may themselves be good or bad, noble or ignoble, expansive or brutal; and human life will tend, in consequence, to be guided by those qualities. Humanity must issue from within as a dynamic and infective motive which gives human values to all social relations and treats each person always as an end—never purely as a means. Masaryk agreed in this first principle with Kant and insisted on the sheer universal moral import of human individuality. Yet though formalities of human duty might save men from overt disaster, they could not themselves enkindle consciousness of human possibilities nor yet devotion to a human group or any of its noble causes. There is no substitute for actual love in human life, though this itself, if not wisely moral, may do much more injury than good. Humanity is a new name for the old love of one's neighbor, without which individual and group life will disintegrate and despoil itself. Modern morality is not to be founded on something which is new. The old universally acknowledged law of love is its first and always foremost principle.[19]

Despite this basis in feeling, however, humanity is reflective in function. Men are too sentimental, even in their rationalities, and sentimentalism is a self-indulgent harrowing of feelings. Humanity requires that feelings be enlightened as well as enkindled, that they be governed by the actual facts and circumstances of people. Men do not know how to have proper regard for themselves, much less love others, wisely. "Artifice and calculation are not love of self. To love thyself means to take care of thyself." Because humanity is founded in feeling, it is not on that account entitled to be blind or stupid; for then it fails to operate as love. Feelings need illumination through knowledge and reflection. Humanity entails "combining the serpent with the dove." This is why men need to educate themselves, gaining broad and philosophic, besides practical, training. Morality today is largely political morality, and human interests can be more and more the sport of politics because politics has become more and more the sport of human life. Yet because men like to be deceived is no reason for deceiving them. Men must educate their political and other feelings in the light of human nature and history, and direct them all in view of current facts and circumstances to valid humane ends. Modern love, in consequence, is largely work.[20]

Humanity is positive foremost of all; not even partially negative. People often take the hatred of another object, such as a foreign nation, to be love of one's own objects and causes; or think that caring for one's nation demands the hatred of all others. Far better and more genuinely effective is it "to learn to love our own nation, our own family, our own party positively—with no background of hate." "A whole new moral

[19] *Ideals of Humanity*, Chap. IX.   [20] *Ibid.*

world will then be opened to us." Mankind, in fact, "is simply a greater or smaller number of people for whom we can do something positive in deeds, not only in words." [21]

Humanity needs actually to be directed to specific objects. "To love one's neighbor," for example, "if that love is to be effective and definite, is to love the person who in point of fact is nearest. To everyone, accordingly, his mother, father, brother, sister, wife, child—is his neighbor. . . . How great is our accord with those who are nearest to us?" How closely do we know and understand them? "We cannot claim to love those much whom we know so little. Our children should be nearest to us of all neighbors. It has long been written: Honor thy father and mother. It is essential to add, I hold: 'Respect the soul of your child.' Think of the future generations! Let love be reciprocated, indeed, but let it not stop with reciprocation!" [22] That would be selfishness, not true humanity.

Love must be directly effective to be actual humanity. Modern love, *in concreto,* is work. "We must do something, work, for our neighbor" and group. But restless, excited, noisy bustling and fussing is not work. Work must be calm and conscious of goals. Work is urged everywhere today, but people do not know the principle or scope of work. They neglect too much the works of inactivity. "They also serve who only stand and wait," said Milton, on his blindness. We need to pause and watch what is occurring, to rest and to reflect on both means and ends. Work itself is but a means, and whether it is effective as a means to worthy or to valid ends depends quite largely on preceding work.[23]

Work basically, moreover, is a matter of small and toilsome tasks which no one likes specifically to do. Neither heroism nor

[21] *Ibid.*, cf. French and German editions; also Čapek, *Masaryk on Thought and Life,* p. 213.
[22] *Ideals of Humanity,* Chap. IX.
[23] *Ibid.*

Moral Necessities in Values

yet martyrdom are entailed in work. Men wish indeed to serve great causes and to effect them by some single *coup d'état*, but great deeds are built on small ones and one must do the petty to achieve the large. There is no definitely constructive work of which this is not true. Achievement is built up, and sound achievement is built by sound performance in all lesser deeds. Honors of leadership, in fact, belong to those who have capacities for getting most small tasks definitely and well done. Chance is the friend of honest, thinking workers; the enemy of those who wish to take their goals by cunning or by storm. Humanity has and is no magic slogan whereby to treat at once all human ills, or to treat any ill once for all completely. Humanity is nothing other than the continual doing of what men need in specific circumstances for maintaining and for maximizing their distinctive possibilities and values.

Strange that men should prefer death to the constructive doing of small and sundry tasks! If they cannot readily be heroes, they conceive of situations in which they may be martyrs to the "cause." Men ought not to prefer death. It is strange indeed that people want to live and yet would rather die than work for life. "As long, in fact, as there are oppressors, there will of course be martyrs," but "so long as there are martyrs there will certainly be persecutors." Humanity demands that people live instead of die for humane causes and give themselves to basic services rather than to martyrdom. Masaryk illustrates this attitude by Marianne in Turgenev's novel, *Virgin Soil*. "She wants to give her life for Russia. She waits constantly for the time to come when the nation will call to her and say, 'Now put your head upon the block.' The moment never comes, so greatly and continuously looked for, but the time does come when Solomin, a practical man, superintendent of a factory, arrives and tells her what it is that is actually at issue. Russia expects no sacrifice of life, he shows. What is essential is that this dirty child should have his hair combed and that these unclean dishes should be washed, and such work." [24]

To work humanely means, in general, to do two types of task: first, to fight evil continuously, everywhere, and in its very germ. Evil is no merely lesser good, in which men might find their joy if they could only rid themselves of thoughts of God or gods. Nor is evil but a lack of human good or goods; at least, not all evils. Evils are direct despoilers and destroyers of men's lives, which sap and inundate their energies and rush them into rottenness or violence. Humanity permits no compromise with evils. Humanity requires a constant and effective fight against all that frustrates or destroys human life.

To work humanely, secondly, means to work for growth and gain in concrete human goods. This does not mean that moral workers are or must be radical, but that they must be persevering and they must be unafraid. "Fear is the mother of deceit and violence. The tyrant and the liar are afraid; he who commits violence is himself a slave." We must have faith in goodness and humanity, and believe that progress can be gradually effected through intelligently constructive work. "He who believes in progress will not be impatient. . . . Yet to conquer evil by good is not so very difficult; the difficulty is to overcome the good by means of the better." Man is not fundamentally bad or evil. Nor is matter evil, the matter of his body and his world. Evil really is an inorganic product of the mind. "This is why we can progress, with the collaboration of all." [25]

Humanity is an ideal, indubitably, toward which men may rather weakly strive, due to wrong conceptions and malfostered motives, stupidities and emotionalized responses. But humanity is an ideal which *works*, prevailingly and constructively, when deliberately applied. "The history of the Czech

[24] *Ibid.*   [25] *Ibid.*

people shows this sufficiently," Masaryk's successor Eduard Beneš, has similarly emphasized.[26] And Masaryk himself never wearied of insisting that the only way by which life can be clearly satisfactory for anyone or any group, or for all society *in toto,* is through methods governed honestly in everything by intelligent humanity. Nations must be trained in attitudes and outlooks, as in scientific procedures, to establish humanity in human society and withstand all efforts to restore long-accepted oppressive orders.

History moves gradually in advancing humanity, protects its flanks and consolidates its gains by intermittent and often uninformed work. History does not stake its faith on simple revolutions or even five-year plans. Yet these may be essential for social construction. Humanity implies and requires a sufficient order. History has in fact to face the conscious and the scheming work of men to circumvent humanity, to secure unwarranted advantages, and to maintain them by the wizardry of force and tricks. If the great battle of the intellectually theoretic sphere has been between mythology and science, its parallel in social practice has been and is between inhumanity of mere politics and force and a humanity which is expressed in consistently humane scientific work. The problem is to crystallize humanity into something other than a half-dumb feeling or merely intermittent force: to make it the enlightened and decisive motive of men's work and play, the always-working principle of life. It has been indeed a massive tendency of the last two centuries of European history; but it needs concretion in the minds of people, with scientifically cultural statesmanship on the part of its leaders. It cannot be abandoned to mysticism or pure pacifist surrender, still less to the makeshift convenience of demagogues and bigots. Humanity must be worked at from every angle incessantly.

[26] Louis Eisenmann, *Un Grand Européen, Édouard Beneš,* p. 58.

These are the principles of realistic ethics, and they are no less national or political because so deliberately human. "If I ask politics to serve mankind," Masaryk stated, "I do not infer that they ought not to be national but just and decent" and intelligently committed to the interests of mankind in the nation. "Humanity does not consist in daydreaming about the whole of mankind but in always acting humanely." "We shall solve our own problem aright," Masaryk told his people, "if we comprehend that the more humane we are the more national we shall be. The relationship between the nation and mankind, between nationality and internationality, between nationalism and humaneness of feeling, is not that mankind as a whole and internationalism and humaneness are something apart from, against or above the nations and nationality, but that nations are the natural organs of mankind." "Between love of one's nation, love of one's country, and humanity there is no conflict.... The community whose troubles I share, the nation to which I am related by speech and culture, are mankind," and one's most immediate group neighbors. The crucial factor, in every case, is whether the principles of one's relationship are those of moral human solidarity and of spiritualized rightness.[27]

These principles "are nothing new. We must not look for new revelations of heaven-knows-what sort if we wish to solve the mysteries and problems of life correctly ... These problems are old and likewise the solutions." What modern men must do is to appropriate old principles to their relationships and living. "Much that you have already heard," Masaryk concluded, "will then acquire new meaning. Thus we shall push forward, comprehending in a new light what we already know and discovering new aspects to old things. Depth of thought

[27] Čapek, *Masaryk on Thought and Life*, pp. 212, 213; cf. *Selections from Czechoslovak Literature and Science, 1935* (Orbis, Prague), pp. 11, 12; *The Making of a State*, p. 435.

and penetration is disclosed in the art of discovering something new in that which we have long known, in what we hear every day, in that to which we have been directed and which we were convinced that we understood perfectly." [28]

[28] *Ideals of Humanity,* Chap. IX.

Chapter Nine

Theistic Humanism: Masaryk's Philosophy of Religion

EVEN MORAL VALUES do not exhaust the major and the most far-reaching fields of human value. There are more far-reaching values still and lesser ones—like the materially component and the purely instrumental—which are no less essential. Religious values, in particular, comprise a more far-reaching, dynamic, and most privileged kind. While moral values are necessities in men's relationships with men, religion is concerned with cosmic loyalties and horizons: the outreach and strength of human life as a universal functionary based on ultimate convictions of its status in reality. Whereas atheistic humanism takes the view that trans-human cosmically religious faith makes for weakness and dependence, Masaryk maintained that it might either make for weakness or for far greater strength. There are different levels of perspective and of human function which vary widely with one's cosmic knowledge and reflection; and to think of any simple antithetic opposition of humanism to theism is to neglect the wide varieties of both.

Two truths, indeed, are certain: (1) "morality is not religion, religion is not ethicality"; (2) "religion constitutes the central and the centralising mental force in the life of the individual and of society. The ethical ideals of mankind are formed by

Masaryk's Philosophy of Religion

religion: religion gives rise to the mental trend, to the life mood of human beings."[1] Religion not only affords the final and effective sanctions of morality but is itself a primary variable in morality's fundamental nature.

To think of morals in disseverance from religion is, in fact, to think of human life out of all relation to men's cosmic faith. Morality assuredly is not religion; religious values are not solely moral. Yet human values can no more be dissociated from men's trans-human outlooks and beliefs than trust in Providence could be dissevered from some disposition to be trustful. Religion is man's feeling for the world and life: a function of his philosophic viewpoints and world theories. Should he be a solipsist in cosmic standpoint and conception, then he himself, as Dostoievski showed, is God. What though is there for that God to do? Such a being puts too great an onus on himself, is too circumscribed. Whence comes revolution and terror![2] Such religion totally invalidates itself, as do others of its forms. Still men can no more avoid a cosmic viewpoint and a cosmic faith than they can forego all thought and feelings for themselves: cosmic faith and self-concern are part and parcel of each other. Man is himself a member of his world, and whatever outlook on that world he holds environs his consideration of himself. The question, therefore, as we saw in Chapter VI, is not whether men should have any religion at all—religion is inevitable—but what kinds of religion people have and whether it is adequate to the creative advancement of life.

The significance of Masaryk's thought and work would in truth be largely missed without consideration of his standpoint in religion. For Masaryk not only was a student of religion from his Leipzig days, honored as D.D. by the Hussite Faculty in Prague—with all the major sources in religion right up to the

[1] *Ideals of Humanity*, Chap. IX; *The Spirit of Russia*, II, 557.
[2] *Ideals of Humanity*, Chap. III, p. 49.

moment in his personal library—but he was notably a philosopher of religion. That his business first of all was politics, and that he always was an unrelenting critic of ecclesiasticism and dogmatic faith does not void this claim. Religion and religions were quite different issues, and religion in its essential character was too utterly significant and far-reaching to be left to the stultifying of ecclesiastical professionals. Religion was in process of true actualizing and advancement. History indeed presents master examples, and Jesus, not Caesar, is the meaning of history, but it was reserved for the future for men to attain that true religion of the spirit which would validate itself alike to honest understanding and morally effective life. Numerous men "like Emerson, Carlyle, Ruskin, Tolstoy, Kierkegaard, and many others . . . all strove and worked for the new religion." [3] Yet this is still seemingly a far-off divine, if urgent, event.

Masaryk's own concern for this development, along with his universality of outlook and life, led Christian von Ehrenfels, in fact, to think of him as the leader of this faith. "All in all," wrote Ehrenfels in *Die Religion zu Zukunft*, "Masaryk is the only man today . . . who could undertake to go before the world as the actualizer of the religion of the future. . . . Not only in power but also in uniqueness of emotional nature, Masaryk appears as the personality destined for the historical demand which comes forward to meet him." [4] And Masaryk has that thoroughness in knowledge, completeness in both moral and philosophical perspective, and sense of the supreme and the eternal, which marks him as the creative exponent of full spirituality in religion.

These were strong words with which to refer to anyone who never claimed to be other than a layman in religion. Yet they were written by a reputable Austrian philosopher, whose own knowledge of Masaryk led him to appeal to and appraise him

[3] "Los von Rom," an address, Boston, 1902.
[4] Pp. 22-25.

Masaryk's Philosophy of Religion 213

in those terms. We quoted, Chapter III, Ehrenfels' analysis of his high regard for Masaryk in spite of Masaryk's part in the breaking up of Austria. "This man alone," he concluded, "in all questions of life and death, can decide and deal with absolute selflessness."[5] Masaryk's was, in point of daily concrete fact, a transcendent perspective and life with an unbiased universality of informed judgment and conception.

Masaryk never envisaged himself, however, as a prophet of religion, and Ehrenfels' public appeal to his leadership brought no prophetic pronouncement. Yet religion held too much by far in human values and disvalues for Masaryk to be but lightly concerned about it. He asserted early and maintained throughout his life that there is but one great question of our time: "the religious question."[6] And this was most immediately a sociological question. In *Suicide as a Social Mass Phenomenon*, 1882, he had already pointed out the need for a new and honestly enlightened faith, transcending sceptical subjectivism as well as sheer credulity.[7] The modern man was nervously exhausted from his life-impasse and knew not where to turn. From philosophy he wanted "an explanation of life, of real life, of the whole of life—he wants to know how to live."[8] From religion he demanded an objective cosmic loyalty, an intelligible faith, and a significant function. There was no hope in any of the common formulations of religion. Christianity ran the gamut from sheer magic and authoritarian mythology to the most modernistic rationalism. Catholicism, on one side, with its dualism and decadence; Protestantism, on the other, with its anarchism and its liberalistic sloppiness: both were Jesuitic, or at least Scholastic, assuming what they wished to

---

[5] *Ibid.*, p. 23.
[6] "Los von Rom"; *Modern Man and Religion; Spirit of Russia;* Čapek, *Masaryk on Thought and Life;* etc.
[7] *Der Selbstmord als Sociale Massenerscheinung der Modernen Civilisation,* pp. 232, 241.
[8] *Modern Man and Religion,* pp. 46-51, 212.

prove by specious argument or demonstration. Liberal protestants, in particular, undertook to rationalize absurdities into comprehensibles and to ameliorate ecclesiasticism while retaining it in principle. The protestant became a rationalist; the catholic a sceptic. Both were sceptics finally: one neurotic and asocialistic; the other erotic and socially a radical. The catholic might find outlet momentarily in aestheticism and symbolic mysteries. The protestant could have no such refuge whereby he might ease the strain upon his heart or head except the pseudo-promises of some fresh authority. Luther set the spirit of the modern protestant. He was too vulgar for a reformer, first of all, and he but replaced one kind of papacy by another.[9]

Religion must be carried to a further stage than obtained in either primary form of Christianity. It must be de-ecclesiasticized, made spiritually pure and effective.[10] It must be a faith, first of all, which is intelligibly basic. We have seen this in the chapter on Criticism. Appeal to revelation and authority beyond the bounds of human comprehension is appeal to ignorance and, actually, to scepticism. Men doubt the very bases of their faith. Revelation and authority, to be authoritative, must show their credentials. Otherwise, men lend themselves to exploitation by their own desires and unquestioned suggestions—not to overlook delusions of others. Religion cannot be at odds with honest wholeness in thinking without discounting its own merits and values. Religion has the means, however,

[9] Ludwig, *Defender of Democracy*, pp. 78-82; cf. *The Spirit of Russia*, II, 500-505.

[10] "The Religious Situation in Austro-Bohemia," an address made in Boston, 1907, in which Masaryk said: "We must unchurch all our life. . . . Religion must be separated from the Church and I am sure from all the churches. . . . We have to overcome Catholicism in our hearts. . . . We need a constructive, a creative religious liberty. We not only must have religion, we must have a higher and more ennobling religion. . . . We want positive progress in religion, we want a religious life which will overcome all the ecclesiastical forms of religion."

Masaryk's Philosophy of Religion

to validate its essential character and values.[11] And therein is the essential scepticism of all its insistently unquestioning devotees apparent, for they betray religion and their own special faiths when they hysterically demand that religion must be kept in opposition to philosophy and science. Religion may and does entail indeed that men have faith in God and good, but not that they should be distrustful of that faith itself, or ignorantly unrealistic about its meaning and basis. Religion can be conviction rather than unthinking faith: conviction with respect to the whole universe and life, their meanings and their values for mankind (and God). How any one can accordingly be true to religion's potentialities and yet persistently be uninformed about the universe and life is the paradox of modern life and issue for the philosopher of religious values.

Masaryk undertook to deal with this issue as an issue in essentials of culture. In the *Concrete Logic* he had given status to religion as a philosophical rather than scientific study; its data seemed too intangible and open to conjecture to provide the groundwork for a special science. And he had already reached the conviction in agreement with Schleiermacher that religion is feeling which attaches to the world of one's interpretation or conception.[12] Religion, therefore, in his view was a function quite distinctly of philosophy. Theologies also (as well as philosophies) were world-theories. But in so far as theologies distinguished themselves from philosophical theories, they were dogmatic and unscientific. In his *Syllabus of*

---

[11] Its very inevitability in some form in men's lives is one phase of religion's validation. Its especial solidarity with a unified cosmic perspective, grounded in scientific yet all-around culture, is a further, fuller means of vindication. The resultant moral and enlightened spirituality of life, in devotion to the highest in the universe, completes the validation of religion. That this is but approximated within any person's thought and life does not alter its significance. Religion justifies itself by its integrality to life and culture and its possibilities for enhancing life immensely, *or destroying it.*

[12] *Versuch einer Concreten Logik*, p. 276.

Sociology (1900), however, Masaryk held that theology could and must be formulated as a science. "Whoever recognizes religion and religious life, along with the intellectual and artistic, as I recognize it," he said, must "acknowledge among the special sciences a special expert study of theology; a scientific study, I repeat. Thereby only can the development of modern theology be conceived; thereby only is the relationship of theology and philosophy, religion and ethics to be explained." Theology has, in fact, he pointed out, three different phases: an abstract or a philosophic phase (philosophy of religion); a concrete or directly scientific phase (embracing different theological inquiries, so far as these are not just parts of history or of other sciences); third, practical or applied theology. All three of these are interwoven and interdependent.[13]

Here indeed we glimpse the prospect of a scientific philosophy of religion, wherein religion could have opportunity to validate itself in relationship to all other aspects of culture. There is, in fact, no more striking witness to Masaryk's cultural realism in religion, as in politics and all socio-personal living, than his surprising interpellation in parliament, 1908, on science, ethics, and free faith. In spite of constant heckling from the benches of clerics, Masaryk took the government to task for an unethical action against Professor Wahrmund of Innsbruck who had published a brochure on science in opposition to the Syllabus of Pope Pius IX and the encyclical *Pascendi Gregis* of Pope Pius X. The government and clerics, Masaryk urged, were using religion for political ends in a servitude to error as well as to Rome. Religious philosophy, he had elsewhere asserted, is also inevitably political philosophy; but the values of religion, he repeatedly urged in this instance, are those of enlightened conviction, not of irrational faith. Religion cannot be placed in opposition to science without destroying its own moral force by producing cleavage in

[13] Kozák, "Masaryk's Stellung zur Metaphysik," *Festschrift*, II, 203.

the minds and lives of its adherents. Art and science can deepen both moral and religious feelings and give them knowledge and reality as the solid grounds of their perspectives and devotion. Opposition to science and morals, in the name of religion, is opposition to truth and to right and the failure of faith to validate itself from two essential standpoints in life. Religion must show its meaning and power not in opposition to all other human values but through its implementing and uplifting of life.[14]

Masaryk has been charged, none the less, with the failure to elaborate a distinctively scientific philosophy of religion. Professor J. B. Kozák, Masaryk's successor at the University of Prague, has even stated that Masaryk seemed unable to define religion. Masaryk's statements of what religion is not, Professor Kozák pointed out, have become proverbial. Religion is not philosophy or science, theology or credulity, morality or ceremonial. In *Modern Man and Religion,* Masaryk had indeed treated the religious philosophies of Hume, Kant, Comte, Spencer, and Augustin Smetana under the respective titles: "Philosophy is Religion," "Religion is Morality," "Religion is Superstition," "Ignorance is Religion," "Creative Love is Religion." Scepticism, criticism, positivism, historicalism, humanism were representative recent philosophic standpoints on religion and reality. They were not merely systems of thought. They were "sources of moods, momentary and permanent," expressions of men's minds and characters. A synthesis of all of them, and notably the latter four, was needed in philosophy. Yet as conceptions of religion none of them was adequate. Nor were all of them together.[15] Religion at its purest and best was other and more than could be gained by any mere combining of these several views. Still, as to his own *sanctissi-*

[14] *Freie Wissenschaftliche und Kirchlich gebundene Weltanschauung und Lebensauffassung.*
[15] *Modern Man and Religion,* pp. 211-212, etc.

mum, Professor Kozák pointed out, "Masaryk in general keeps silence." Professor Kozák augmented, however, that the reason for Masaryk's seeming incapacity to define religion was that religion for Masaryk was not just an intellectual or even an objective matter. Rather, it was a matter pre-eminently of the immediacy of life.[16]

It would have been a sign of superficiality rather than of great insight if Masaryk had been able to give definitions of religion with especial readiness. Yet positive affirmations he did make in significant abundance. "Religion is a feeling for the world and life," a "feeling of security." Religion represents the quest of "new higher vital values." It is the very essence of religious faith to give man cosmic "values and a conviction ... for which proof can be given." Religion, in fact, is "the most important and most profound social force which keeps men in organic union not only with heaven but with their fellowmen." Religion is striving to live in view of ultimates and to envisage all cosmically from the outlook of eternity. It represents man's consciousness of citizenship in the universe.[17]

The phrase *sub specie aeternitatis* which Masaryk carried into politics and sociology expressed the actual standpoint of religion.[18] The specie of eternity was both universal and en-

---

[16] "Masaryk as Philosopher," *The Slavonic Review*, March, 1930, p. 494.

[17] Ludwig, *Defender of Democracy*, pp. 75, 83, 85, 183; Masaryk, *Im Kampf um die Religion*, p. 26; cf. *Festschrift*, II, 127; Žilka, "T. G. Masaryk's im Kampf um die Religion," *Slavische Rundschau*, March, 1935, p. 76: religion is "striving" to solve the problem of eternity.

[18] The phrase, *sub specie aeternitatis*, which emphasizes the religious basis and religious complementing of morality and politics is biblically interpreted in *The Making of a State* (p. 455) where Masaryk quotes II Corinthians 4: "Therefore, seeing we have this Ministry, as we have received mercy, we faint not; but have renounced the hidden things of dishonesty, not walking in craftiness nor handling the word of God deceitfully; but by manifestation of the truth commending ourselves to every man's conscience in the sight of God." *That*, Masaryk maintained, "is the program of the Republic and of Democracy." Cf. also "*Sub Specie Aeternitatis*" in the periodical *The New Europe*, Dec. 21, 1916.

during, involving cosmic consciousness with a sense of final outcomes and consolidarity. We need have no recourse to Bucke's elaboration of historic instances to understand the cosmic viewpoint or perspective as conceived by Masaryk.[19] We know this from his writings. Von Ehrenfels' description of Masaryk's transcendence of himself in thought and action presents the cosmic viewpoint in long-sighted outreach.[20] It meant wholeness of perspective. Stated in its simplest and most practical terms, the standpoint of eternity involved taking cognizance critically yet positively of all the facts and values—human and trans-human—to be relevantly considered in the course of daily life, seeing these in their substantial unity and order in so far as possible, and living objectively in terms of persisting interacting results. Religion, therefore, was a "feeling for the world and life" from the outlook of the long run: a life of whole reason and of whole culture with a sense of citizenship in the whole cosmic order.

Herein lay the arch-value of religion, apart entirely from its value or values in outright worshipful experience.[21] It lifted, or might lift, men from an ego-centered or purely mundane outlook to a cosmic status and placed their work upon the level of the cosmically significant and metaphysical. Religion meant the possibility of a vastly different quality and scope of life for men. Morality itself entailed in some considerable degree the standpoint of the enduring or the permanent, and morality in other ways was intertwined with religion. Moral humanism by its very nature reaches out beyond itself and becomes cosmic. But the sense of cosmic values, whereby morality is made adequately effective, is the special genius of

[19] R. M. Bucke, *Cosmic Consciousness, A Study in the Evolution of the Human Mind*. New York, 1923.

[20] Cf. above statements from von Ehrenfels' open letter quoted in this chapter and first paragraph, Chap. III.

[21] I.e., the obviously distinctive values of religion: experience of relation to an Object worthy of supreme commitment and devotion; of God as Highest Value because supreme Existence.

religion. This might indeed be highly circumscribed, as in solipsism or sheer credulous mythology. But the possibilities of experience and creative achievement through outreach of life, understanding the cosmos, and sense of the eternal and supreme, constituted religion as the source of by far life's greatest values: values which were supra-mundane and transcendently objective. The problem was to achieve that cultural faith which would be not just factually informed, but would grant men also life's true vista of values.[22]

Comenius, Masaryk emphasized, achieved the right conception of religion. Comenius was a synthesis of Chelčický and Huss: Chelčický who foreshadowed Tolstoy's ultra-altruism by more than four centuries,[23] and Huss who preceded Luther by one and went beyond him in the spirit of reform. Comenius gave full content and full implementing to the motives of the Reformation.[24]

Masaryk took his stand, therefore, with both Comenius and Schleiermacher, founders of the modern viewpoint in theology. While starting from Pascal and Hume and denying all recourse to inexplicable authority, Masaryk found the validation of religion in its own intrinsic value, its inevitable integrality with whatever viewpoint or whatever type of culture people have, and its possibilities for a scientifically moral outlook on the

---

[22] Masaryk's writings on religion include in consequence: *The Modern Man and Religion* (1897), discussed in Chapter VI; *In Battle for Religion* (1904), against ecclesiasticism and theocratic politics; "Outline of a Modern Philosophy of Religion" (1905); "Intelligence and Religion" (1907); "Science and the Church" (1908); besides treatments in all his major works and especially those which concerned Czech leadership and history.

[23] Chelčický was the founder of the Czech Brethren, who undertook to base their lives on concrete brotherhood and to carry it into all domains of life. In contrast to the militant Hussite general Žižka, Chelčický was an utter, though constructive, pacifist.

[24] *The Czech Question*, Chap. V.

whole universe with which to orient, consolidate, empower, and maximize life.

Now, there could be no strong objection to this view of religion even on the part of positivists and atheists—far-reaching though it appears. The difficulty starts when one talks of God and immortality, and Masaryk used both these terms freely. True, Professor Hromádka held that there was no marked religious warmth in Masaryk's references to deity. Yet, there Professor Žilka disagreed with Professor Hromádka: Masaryk did not readily express his deepest feelings. Masaryk stood, at all events, avowedly for theism. Religion, specifically, involved a "conviction as to the existence of God and the immortality of the individual, with Hope arising therefrom, and Courage through all the vicissitudes of life." [25] Masaryk never seriously doubted God's existence, though just how God was to be conceived was a different issue. People do not dispense with God just by thinking they are atheists. As Dostoievski pictured it: it was either God or murder. And it was some God of some kind in any circumstance. The question was: is one's God sufficient to His cosmic functions? How shall we think most adequately of deity? This was the primary issue, rather than that of the existence of God.

Theism was an hypothesis, surely, "side by side with the pantheistic and other hypotheses," but theism was the most defensible hypothesis. Scepticism, doubt, was incapable of *work*. Effectiveness at work is governed by a faith in the fundamental values of humanity, in a metaphysics of expansive human good. Belief in final transciency of every human and trans-human value makes for moral lethargy and incompetence. To make the best of things right here and now is not an urgent motive. What matter if one does not really do his best? There is no final loss. The best is then a second and, much more frequently, third best. It lacks the rigor of a categorical

[25] Ludwig, *Defender of Democracy*, p. 85.

imperative. But as a cosmic principle, humanity uncompromisingly requires the sustaining and advancing of men's lives. It sets men a significantly cosmic motive and function; for then enlightened love is the constructive goal of universal nature.[26]

The case for theism was not, however, to be settled in so summary a fashion. It was not a matter simply of what ought to be for human life at best or of that faith which people need to safeguard solidarity and integrity of personality on a less ambitious basis. It was a matter of the most intelligible and most defensible hypothesis in light of all the facts of actuality. Materialistic atheism was epistemologically untenable; it offered no psychology wherewith to enlighten life. Pantheism, furthermore, despite its mystical appeal, was opposed by all intelligible experience. Theism, in some sense, was the lone alternative.[27] The very principles and laws of solidarity and progress were witness of control in universal nature: control which gains its most distinctive form in reflective learning from experience. "A purposeful order in the world is provided by reason; our knowledge itself is teleological." In point of fact, "God himself is reason," a personal reason which is at the same time the principle of the world order. "The purposiveness of the world, of life, of historical happenings, of our knowledge, and of moral endeavour" seemed to Masaryk so strongly on the side of theism that even though it remained an hypothesis instead of an established position it was the one intelligible, besides livable, viewpoint to hold.[28] The sense of forces out beyond oneself, in fact, conjoining and co-urging one to constructive undertakings was a consciousness of Providence. To Masaryk, who thought through and planned all major undertakings of life in substantial detail—on grounds of coördinated science—the consciousness of being taught, prepared, and led

---

[26] *Ibid.*, p. 75; *Ideals of Humanity*, Chap. IX.
[27] Herben, Hartl, Bláha, *T. G. Masaryk*, pp. 155-156.
[28] Čapek, *Masaryk on Thought and Life*, pp. 62-63.

was strangely, or unstrangely, keen. Even all the disappointing and the turbulent events of life paved the way, he found, for his momentous work in and following the War.

"When I think how we went into it unprepared," he said, "and yet really completing a century of the efforts of such men as Dobrovský, Kollár, Palacký, and Havlíček; how isolated we were, we abroad and those at home, and yet with what sureness we fulfilled the mandate of the whole nation; how we set out with naked hands, and how at the end we returned bearing them freedom, the Republic, Slovakia, Ruthenia—it still seems like a dream to me. There you have an example of Providence." [29] The force and the effectiveness of Masaryk's own work presents indeed an instance of a providential blending of events, which has most intelligible import for a progressive, theistic conception of history. True, Masaryk's was no wholly other-worldly guidance, but the control of a trained mind by concretely conjoined eventualities and facts. Yet right here was Masaryk's great power and advantage, inasmuch as his philosophic acceptance of Providence gave him the courage and conviction to oppose wrong in every circumstance and to work with tireless science for human right. "Without belief in Providence," Ludwig quotes Masaryk, "without belief in an ordered universe, I could not live, nor even work for the community. I cannot say exactly by what Power, but I feel that there is a power which drives me onward. The logic of events is construed after the events have happened." [30] That there is a universal logic, none the less, was the presupposition of Masaryk's whole philosophy and above all of his conception of Providence.

Masaryk's theism, accordingly, was no theism of a divine Super-Personality who could be readily described. Yet it did involve a confidence in a consciously humane Spirit as the First

---

[29] Čapek, *President Masaryk Tells His Story*, p. 225.
[30] Ludwig, *Defender of Democracy*, p. 256.

Principle of actuality. Theism meant primarily that the universe was purposive, that it was fundamentally yet definitely favorable to humanity, and that living from the cosmic and eternal point of view is the function and the destiny of man. God was the creative source and directive Purpose of existence, the Providence "Who Cares for the Whole." Leibniz came the closest to the formulation of a positive religious interpretation of reality, but Leibniz was still "more of a scholastic than a psychologist." His monadology was artificial and unrealistic.[31]

Both Masaryk and Leibniz, however, were determinists in their philosophical conceptions. Masaryk, under the influence of his great teacher, Franz Brentano, conceived determinism as a consequence of theism. The progressive, synergistic, law-abiding causal order of existence was itself, we noted, an evidence for theism. And so too was also the contingency of all immediate existence. This last had been appealed to by both Leibniz and Aquinas in their arguments for God; Bolzano and Brentano had been mediators of that view. Masaryk, none the less, had been open from the first to the viewpoint of Plato; and Masaryk believed in an intelligible order as expressed in principles and species. Teleology, in fact, was a presupposition of his constructive realism.[32] His determinism was a theory actually of human freedom, wherein existence was in some measure plastic and could be facilitated or advanced by creative science. One of the most significantly essential of all the means for advancing existence was by aiding men to formulate a more totally and naturally religious conception of all nature and culture and by giving them the truest and most meaningfully valid outlook on existence. This sense not only of meaning but of function would make men more effective agents in the social cosmos. Nor would this violate the principle of causality but rather show that there were higher media of determina-

[31] *Ibid.*, pp. 75, 256.
[32] Cf. Čapek, *Masaryk on Thought and Life*, p. 62.

Masaryk's Philosophy of Religion 225

tion: by means of knowledge, reflection, and organic unities. Philosophy of religion thereby involved, integrated, and completed the whole philosophy of functional human values.

For those who were disposed to think that religion makes for quietism or indifference to the evils which we now have, because of the belief that one already somehow has a self-realizing option on what needs really to be striven for, Masaryk's position offered a distinct alternative. Religion to him was no method of obtaining any actual value without effort. His was a religion of responsibility and work; of coöperative work for concrete goods which lead to lasting values. Religion, he even characterized, "is responsibility." [33] We can put nothing off on the remoteness of eternity, since it is here and now. Nor can we be content with sheer practicalities. We must "weigh everything with exactness" in all that we have for our doing.[34] For we shall either build substantially and cosmically for mankind and God, or we shall add the load of some defective and decadent structure to the moral burden of mankind and human history. There is no place in religiously sound work for products which will not stand the cosmic test of ongoing time and of real humanity.

This is not to say, indeed, that mankind may not wisely try out possibilities for themselves, but that they must take counsel of all history and all future time, and in the aspect of the truly cosmic and eternal, advance the cause of mankind and "humanity." And this is not at all to state that theists are to have no rest nor joy. "The modern man" is really he who "has no peace or rest," for he has thrown off all perspective and thinks and lives in terms of hurried outcomes. For him, however, who views all facts and processes in the aspect of their cosmic principles and values, there is ample time for pride and thoroughness in work, for rest from labors, for recreation as for inspira-

[33] Cf. Kozák, "Masaryks Stellung zur Metaphysik," *Festschrift*, II, 207.
[34] *Ideals of Humanity*, Chap. IX.

tion. He has no need to be nervously excited. What he cannot do today he may do tomorrow. What he cannot do at all another may accomplish. And if neither he nor anyone succeeds in doing it, they can trust in Providence which constrains all finally toward constructive ends and by grace of which humanity sustains and fulfils itself.[35] Religion is man's active sense of cosmic synergism.

A late though rather prosaic summary of Masaryk's conclusions on religion is given by Čapek in *Masaryk on Thought and Life*.[36] There, though needing amplifying in the light of a dozen other sources, we have the confirmation of this preceding analysis. In religion, Masaryk states, "man obtains the deepest sense of his life." "Religion is the orientation of man to the universe, to God, to the world, and to himself. . . . It is not only the understanding of the sense of life as a whole, it is at the same time a state of mind springing from this understanding of life and of the world."[37] And "theism, religion as a whole, after all, is not merely a personal attitude, it is a collective order." Democracy, with its economic and material consequences, he emphasized, is a socio-metaphysical program. It is based on love: "on love and the justice that is the mathematics of love, and on the conviction that we should help in the world toward the realization of the rule of God, toward synergism with the divine will." "True democracy . . . is the realization of the rule of God on earth." "I conceive the state, national life, politics, like the whole of life, in truth *sub specie aeternitatis*."[38]

[35] *Ibid.*
[36] Pp. 83-93 ff.
[37] *Ibid.*, p. 88.
[38] *Ibid.*, pp. 191, 192, 193.

Chapter Ten

Conclusion

IT WOULD BE VENTURESOME to attempt to suggest what shall be Masaryk's status in history. History has mountainous slopes, and a geological standpoint on time. Historians, *per contra*, are freqeuntly fadists, debunking their heroes and whitewashing their villains until roles are reversed. The net, composite result tends often at best to be an insipid, socio-moral neutrality. Slight wonder that human history has such chance for reverses as it has had in the most recent past—a chance scarcely missed at any one point by the condoned aggressors. Two points, none the less, are important for evaluation of Masaryk. To these we thus turn in conclusion.

There is no doubt, first of all, that Masaryk represents a high point in history. The positive values of both the Renaissance and Reformation had their summing up in him, with their limitations largely overcome. The Christian humanizing of culture, on one side, and full cultural complementing of religion, on the other, surmounted inhumanity, superstitious absolutism and subjective relativism respectively. One may go so far, indeed, as to suggest that in Masaryk the Reformation *per se* reached substantial completion and that its impact on social and international life gained unhesitating expression and extension. We may go even further and point out the fact that Masaryk bespoke the crystallizing in Europe as a whole of the humane idealisms of both the American and French revolutions, without their inexperience and one-sided enthusiasms. It was not only, in fact, through the espousal of self-determination for all European nationalities—in which Masaryk was the first great proponent—but also in the socializing, insistent enlightening, and moral implementing of this program, that Masaryk headed up the democratic movement in its broadest social and world aspects. His was a functional view of democracy, we saw in Chapter II, and not in the superficial sense of immediate expedients but from the point of view of full-orbed, self-sustaining results. In this interpretation and articulation of democracy, which Masaryk made effective in the midst of untold opposition (though betrayed finally by the supposedly friendly yet surprisingly uninformed or undiscerning statesmen of the world), it is a fair question whether Masaryk does not stand at one of the highest peaks in socio-personal history.

Certainly there are few with whom to compare him. There is Plato from the more distant past and in a lesser degree there is Socrates. The penetrating conviction and courage of both Masaryk and Socrates relate them distinctively, though the broad socio-cultural program, extensive writing and political effort connect Masaryk more fully with Plato. There is Jan Christian Smuts from the present, a genius of very high rank: lawyer, philosopher, soldier, and statesman. His courage, penetration, sense of international moral principle, and effective efforts relate him in at least a fourfold way with Masaryk. They were united in viewpoint and essentials of program in and after the War. Both were high-minded men of preeminent learning who never compromised on principle and always seemed to comprehend the issues of human right and the tragedy of human wrong. Comparison of these men is not easy. Both have highly notable achievements to their credit, against persisting animus and opposition. To venture, therefore, in brief space to credit one with merits that the other does

Conclusion

not have is a questionable procedure. Yet knowledge of Masaryk and impressions of Smuts suggest that Masaryk was somewhat more systematic, concrete, and full-orbed, while no greater genius.

Masaryk's own genius consisted, in fact, not so much in intellectual brilliance or profundity as in social effectiveness through an amazing capacity for intelligent work. It is not suggested, much less maintained, that he worked out a full, final philosophy, but that he elaborated a viewpoint in extensive detail and that he advanced a method to be used in coping with every sort of problem. That method involved at least three indispensables: inclusive and intensive knowledge, judgment rising from philosophic comprehension based on familiarity with the great conceptual viewpoints of history and their implications, and, thirdly, unflinching work. None of these could be anywhere omitted without substantial likelihood of failure.

It was this method which enabled Masaryk to be consistently and insistently honest in politics, as in all other relations, and to refuse to compromise on principle at any point. The place for compromise lay in the incidentals of projects and in means of attainment—if these did not invalidate the principle. There was no moral nor yet philosophic basis for compromise in first principles or in educated effort. The notion that compromise could be an end in itself, Masaryk exposed as demagogic.[1] Compromise was not itself a first principle of human interactions, but as Jesus rather than Caesar would have said, of the hardness of men's hearts. William James would probably have added to this that it was also, in significant degree, a matter of the softness of their heads. Masaryk was in agreement with both. The principles in the light of which he held compromise might be employed as a *means* to an end were those specifically of the "facts" to be dealt with, on one hand, and of the

[1] Cf. *The Making of a State*, p. 467.

basic socio-moral goods of human individuality on the other. These "realities" come foremost from the start and that reality especially which concerned the actual basic good of the largest number in the long run with the minimum ultimate evils. Masaryk's awareness of issues in the light of these ultimates allowed him no leeway to resort to "expedients" in the hope that all would work out satisfactorily later. Time itself did not solve human problems though it brought opportunity for knowledge, ripened judgment, and work.

Neither in culture nor in work was one entitled, therefore, to attempt makeshifts or short-cuts. These latter would but sacrifice the human values at issue and leave them at the mercy of ignorance, unsubstantiality, and sheer, not more than fifty-fifty, chance. Such methods offered no real solution to men's problems, any more than pure, passive sentimental trust, without actual effort on the parts of people, afforded concrete grounds for hope that inhumanities would heal themselves. Masaryk's was no such slipshod type of democratic culture. His view held to interactive social planning, full-preparedness for all types of eventuality, education of the soundest and most thorough-going type, development of the human capacity for judging, and unmitigated work. This was how he succeeded so well in uniting the ideal and the real. If any such union of the ideal and real has elsewhere been advocated, it has not been more fully or strongly urged.

It is worth pointing out also, at the risk of some repetition, that Masaryk's ideas developed not in armchair detachment from serious problems or difficulties but in difficulties such as central Europe has had in very marked form. At no time in his life, up to sixty-eight, was his status one of vantage either in its ease of life or in its control of social situations. Yet, he could not compromise in standards or objectives without the sacrifice of actual solutions to those very problems with which he was most immediately concerned. So compromise was not entered

Conclusion

into except in method or in sundries of detail. What Masaryk did instead was to compile the full fund of facts, assess them in the light of a background of broad understandings, and to work unequivocally for advancing human individualities. It was, in fact, his ability to bring armchair objectivity and resources to bear on immediate problems, even in heat of a battle, which enabled Masaryk to put issues of method and principle in fair perspective and to keep basic questions of sociopersonal solidarity always in the foreground.

"Concretism" he called his philosophy,[2] thereby defining his functional, all-rounded realism. But Masaryk's concretism never did become disjointed or chaotic. Always, he seems to have had a consciousness of relation and principle; and it is from the standpoint of his "concrete logic," reinforced by his philosophies of criticism and human values, that we must view his "concretism"—rather than as any sort of unmodified pluralistic individualism. The concrete could not be understood, in fact, without ideas which are variously abstract;[3] the real could not be reasonably comprehended out of all relation to some type of ideal. Reality, although concrete, was interwoven and dynamic. Socially, this meant that while individualities are primary, they are interdependent and have a common ground and sphere of activity.

This union of the ideal and real is particularly evident in Masaryk's viewpoint on pacifism. "I am a convinced pacifist," he said in conversation with Čapek.[4] But, he added in *The Making of a State*, "there are several sorts of pacifism—for instance, a pacifism of the naturally weak and timorous, a pacifism of the terrified and sentimental, and a pacifism of speculators. Yet another variety was that of the extreme International Socialists which found vent in their Conference at Zimmerwald

[2] Čapek, *Masaryk on Thought and Life*, pp. 55 ff.
[3] *Versuch einer Concreten Logik*, p. 280.
[4] *President Masaryk Tells His Story*, p. 299.

on September 3, 1915. Very repugnant to me were the pacifists who defended the Germans as though they had been victims of aggression whereas they had long been and then were the bitterest foes of pacifism. I refer, of course, to official Germany which wanted war and waged it. Among the German people themselves, as elsewhere, there always had been pacifist tendencies, some of which survived even during the War."[5] That pacifism meant unpreparedness or non-resistance to evil Masaryk would not concede. This, in fact, was counter to everything which he stood for. He stood and worked for peace, not by holding up one's hands at each threat of international aggression but by elaborating and improving the sociological bases of peace, and by upholding its conditions and values against all aggression. Here again was the union of the ideal and the real without the surrender of one to the other.

The second point to be considered in evaluation of Masaryk is his actual applicability to the issues of the present. One may cite Wickham Steed's Preface to *The Making of a State* to accentuate the sense of eclipse that the past two years seem to have brought to Masaryk. Mr. Steed suggested in 1927 that a generation hence would probably bring Masaryk's pre-eminence as a constructive statesman. A generation has not yet passed, and obviously the world has not gained clear "perspective." What it has gained meanwhile is an almost universal travesty. Yet it is not Masaryk who has been eclipsed, but those whose lack of realism, on one hand, or of idealism, on the other, set the stage for the acting out by Hitler and his lesser compeers of the present debacle. Masaryk throughout was at odds with both types of mistakes made by the Allies: the exacting of a humiliating vengeance; and, conversely, the placating of a Germany recommitted to militarism and unwilling to negotiate any honest agreements. He never succumbed to the disposition to alleviate Germany's responsibility for the War.

[5] *The Making of a State*, pp. 60-61.

Conclusion

Nor did he adopt the view that significant German minorities should never have been included in Czechoslovakia.⁶ These were reactionary rather than informed or intelligent tendencies. He stood, rather, for open diplomacy on the grounds of the "indispensabilities" listed above, and upheld the principle of ultra-fairness to Germans within Bohemia and Moravia and to Germany in her entirety, as a Republic in the first instance and a dictatorship in the second. Mutuality he regarded as the only sound basis for international, as for all social, relations. Had his methods been applied in European relations—and his Foreign Minister, Eduard Beneš, undertook from the first to the last to apply them ⁷—the story would assuredly be very different.

More important still, however, is the fact that there is no hopeful alternative whatever to Masaryk's method. Militarism itself can solve no international tangles. Pacifism, in the simple form of non-resistance to aggression, abets the dictators. Other approaches are, to a notable degree, but combinations and variants of these two modes of procedure. Masaryk's whole philosophy of basically functional, scientific culture may be a strenuous alternative but in its intensively realistic articulation of the valid ideal, without one-sidedness at any point, it presents a course of action which holds hope. If anything like the commitment should go into application of this method that has gone into "pacifism" on one hand and totalitarian militarisms on the other, the difficulties of achieving sound social peace could scarcely loom like sheer impossibilities before us. Without education, however, in such a substantial viewpoint and method, all the "commitment" under heaven will have scant opportunity to avail. The starting point must be with human culture itself in its most basic and all-around sense.

⁶ *The New Europe*, p. 71.
⁷ Cf. Warren, "The Democratic Diplomacy of President Beneš," *Furman Bulletin*, April, 1937.

In this conception of culture, in fact, we have an antidote to two other opposing conceptions. One of these is German, vaunted for its philosophic genius and its scientific absoluteness. In its stress on race, however, which seems intrinsic to its braggadocio, it is more like culture in its bacteriological meaning than like culture in either its educational or sociological references. It is not culture, assuredly, in the inclusive sense for which Masaryk stood. German culture, he discovered, is deep yet radically one-sided; so much so, in fact, as to be pathologically introverted.[8] Nor are its extremisms and disbalances offset by its scientificism which likewise is carried to that dire extremity which neglects almost every human value.

The other view of culture seems most strikingly American. Superficiality and haziness are symptoms of its immaturity, though it too, from its very incapacity to be critically constructive, is one-sided.[9] Haste, experimenting, immediate results, self-interest, and success are likewise guiding motives. A leveling-down process takes precedence over building up the quality of culture. Education for the masses has come to be construed to mean the expunging of linguistic, scientific, and philosophic basics from essentials of culture. Understandings, wealth of background, unadulterated learning appear as extravagances which interfere with the sharing of "experience," than which it appears very uncertain that anything else exists. As for a working day exceeding eight hours, either at home or elsewhere, that would be anti-social and hopelessly undemocratic. Against such miscomprehensions as this, Masaryk's conception of culture holds up the bases of cultural solidarity and progress. It offers wisdom versus ignorance, compromise, and reaction.

Masaryk's view of culture, while inclusive, is pre-eminently sociological. His professorial chair in Prague, in fact, was that

[8] *The Making of a State*, pp. 341 ff.   [9] *Ibid.*, p. 232.

of both philosophy and sociology, and he conceived himself most fully as a sociologist. His sociology was indeed of that ideal type which centers in a whole philosophy of existence and culture. His whole outlook, none the less, was anthropocentric and practical. In deepest earnestness he sought to determine the principles governing men's associations, not just for the sake of producing an abstract body of theory, but in order to have a foundation on which to proceed soundly in dealing with human (notably Czech) problems.[10] And he envisaged no solutions which did not entail basic satisfaction on all sides (after readjustments had had full opportunity to function). Sociology, in consequence, was a scientific, philosophic, historical, aesthetic, international matter and no mere question of isolated community or case efforts. Practicality in these very issues involved the larger and more basic issues of full orientation from the standpoint of whole culture. Otherwise, the sociologist was doing but a portion of his task, and leaving others to relate their work to his without adequately enlightened efforts at coördination.

It was said to the author some months ago that Masaryk seemed to represent the "overripened fruit of liberalism" and to be therefore a spokesman for the past rather than the present. Nothing seems more removed from the facts. He was not afraid to use principles and methods which might appear hoary with age. Much that was old needed reinterpretation rather than discarding. As a spokesman for liberalism Masaryk stood for its adequate fulfillment instead of its rejection; and if his view savors of the simplicity of what is considered passé, it is neither the simplicity of radicalism nor yet that of such current clichés as "activity," "liberalism" meaning sloppiness, or "realism" signifying sordidness and primitivity. Masaryk's denouncing of "individualism" in its Stirnerian and

[10] E. E. Eubank, "T. G. Masaryk: Sociologist," *Social Forces* (March, 1938), pp. 455-462.

Nietzschean senses,[11] and insistence on the moral socializing of all spheres of human relations, is not indeed radical in contrast with Communism; it conserves the principle of individuality which Communism adjures. What socio-moral alternative is there, in fact, to such reinterpretation of the "liberal" social view! Masaryk's liberalism has, in point of fact, been spoken of as socialism. His socialism, he maintained, consisted only in the application of the principle of loving one's neighbor. Yet he extended this to groups, as well as to persons, and demanded, in fact, that this principle become international. To say, therefore, that Masaryk belongs to a decadent liberalism could only have meaning if one were disposed to maintain not just that unmodified individualism is passé but also that individuality itself is not socially (and so morally) basic. Such a contention would amount to acceptance of some type of totalitarianism. But even totalitarian systems drag in individualities, after denouncing them in principle and destroying them in unhesitating fact. Group life, indeed, without individuals to comprise and constitute it and at least one Führer to give it leadership and character, is an unintelligible conception. Group life, in point of fact, requires some means of perpetuating its specific sort of individuality, and this, in turn, depends on the individualities of various "sub-führers." Totalitarianism appears, indeed, to reduce in practice to a gangster kind of individualism.

Masaryk is, in a particularly significant degree, a philosopher-statesman for the present, and the future. It might seem at first thought that Masaryk's Comtean stresses on the evils of mythology were archaic, now at any rate. But if any age in history has been sufficiently free from mythology so that this no longer needed battling, that time is not the present. Not only in the Wagnerian mythology of Hitlerism, which represents a reversion of a ridiculously primitive, if poetic,

---

[11] *Ideals of Humanity*, Chaps. 3, 8.

type;[12] not just in Fascist mythology which turns back to pre-Christian Rome,[13] nor yet in the anthropomorphic imaginings of the Marxists and Bolshevists who created the fiction of the *Will* of the proletariat and took primitivity to be the social ideal while decrying ideology;[14] *but* also among the democracies: in the unrealistic (fictional) appeasement of Chamberlain; wishful unpreparedness of both Britain and France in spite of clear-cut warnings grounded in unmistakable evidence; in the isolationism of supposedly democratic America "prepared" to carry on in a world much more than half-slave, much less than half-free; holding to the view that a general sharing of defense is undemocratic; and sharing with a considerable number of other nations, several of whom have already lost their independence, that "playing safe" is the best course to pursue. In an age fraught with far-reaching disasters and dangers, it is hard to conceive of a more abundant mythology and of less scientific realism than we have had in this era. It is to this age especially that Masaryk's methods apply. Not that Masaryk's work and thought is beyond criticism! It was fragmentary at best, in spite of its volume and the wholeness of his viewpoint. So very much in Masaryk, none the less, is essential to meeting our present predicament, as to our subsequent progress. And it is in extension and completion of his view that society needs to move, rather than in the direction of some other alternative. That his is a philosophy for the future especially is also apparent in its hardworking optimism as in its challenge to human attainment.

It would appear, finally, that in addition to his faith in informed, unrelenting work, society needs his working faith in the essentially positive direction of history. This is admirably portrayed in Dr. Beneš' address at Masaryk's funeral.

---

[12] Otto D. Tolischus, *They Wanted War*, Chap. I.
[13] Ludwig, *Defender of Democracy*, pp. 214 ff.
[14] *Les Problèmes de la Démocratie*, pp. 133-137.

"How," he asked, "can we be other than calm, clear and firm when we look upon the clear and straight path which that life shows us? . . . How beautiful and how exalting is it to see that this great warrior, who never shirked a fight, leaves us in harmony with himself, with his faith in Providence, in harmony with his environment, with his faith in man, faith in the ultimate triumph of man, in the triumph of justice and truth, in the triumph of humanity here amongst us, in Europe and throughout the world!" [15]

[15] *Masaryk's Path and Legacy*, pp. 7, 23.

Bibliography

CHIEF WORKS OF T. G. MASARYK

Chronologically arranged

Der Selbstmord als Sociale Massenerscheinung der Modernen Civilization. Carl Konegen. Vienna, 1881.

David Hume's Skepsis und die Wahrscheinlichkeitsrechnung. Carl Konegen. Vienna, 1884.

Versuch einer Concreten Logik. Carl Konegen. Vienna, 1887.

"Skizze einer sociologischen Analyse der sogenannten Gründberger und Königinhöfer Handschrift." *Archiv für slavische Philologie.* Vienna, 1887.

The Czech Question. (Czech title, *Ceska otazka.* Not translated.) Čas. Praha, 1895.

Karel Havlíćek. Jan Laichter. Praha, 1896.

The Modern Man and Religion. Translated by Ann Bibza and Dr. Václav Beneš. Revised by H. E. Kennedy. Allen & Unwin, Ltd. London, 1938. (First published 1897.)

Die Philosophischen und Sociologischen Grundlagen des Marxismus, Studien zur Socialen Frage. Carl Konegen. Vienna, 1899. (Czech edition 1898.)

"Die wissenschaftliche und philosophische Krise innerhalb des gegenwartigen Marxismus." *Die Zeit.* Praha, 1898.

Palackýs Idee des Böhmischen Volkes. Verlag, JUC. Praha, 1899.

Die Bedeutung des Polnaer Verbrechens für der Ritualaberglauben. H. S. Hermann. Berlin, 1900.

Ideals of Humanity. Translated by W. Preston Warren. Allen & Unwin, Ltd. London, 1938. First published, Čas. Praha, 1902.

"Los von Rom." Address in Boston. Unitarian Historical Society. 1902.

Modern National Philosophy. (Czech title, *Národnostní filosofie doby novější.*) Jičín. Praha, 1905.

Ein Katechetenspiegel. Neuer Frankfurter Verlag. Frankfurt, 1906.

"The Religious Situation in Austro-Bohemia," *Freedom and Fellowship in Religion.* Charles Wendte. Boston, 1907.

Freie Wissenschaftliche und Kirchlich gebundene Weltanschauung und Lebensauffassung. Carl Konegen. Vienna, 1908.

Der Agramer Hochverratsprozess und die Annexion von Bosnien und Herzegovina. Carl Konegen. Vienna, 1909.

Vasič-Forgách-Aehrenthal, Einiges Material zur Characteristik unserer Diplomatie. Čas. Prague, 1911.

The Spirit of Russia, Studies in History, Literature & Philosophy. Translated from the German by Eden and Cedar Paul. 2 vols. Allen and Unwin, Ltd. London, 1919. Originally published in German under the title *Russland und Europa.* Eugen Diederichs. Jena, 1913.

The Problem of Small Nations in the European Crisis. Inaugural lecture, Kings College, London, October, 1915. Council for Study for International Relations. London, 1916.

The Slavs among the Nations. Lecture delivered February 22, 1916, before the Institute of Slav Studies in Paris. Czech National Alliance in Great Britain. London, 1916.

The New Europe. Eyre & Spottiswoode, Ltd. London, 1918.

Sur le Bolschevisme. Sonor. Geneva, 1921.

"The Slavs After the War," *Slavonic Review.* June, 1922.

Les Problèmes de la Démocratie, Essais Politiques et Sociaux. Marcel Rivière. Paris, 1924.

The Making of a State, Memories and Observations, 1914–1918. English version by H. Wickham Steed. Frederick A. Stokes Co., New York, 1927. Allen & Unwin, Ltd. London, 1927.

Speech of T. G. Masaryk, President of the Czechoslovak Republic on the Tenth Anniversary of the Attainment of the Country's Independence, 28th October, 1928. Orbis. Prague, 1928.

"Mein Verhältnis zu Goethe," *Prager Rundschau*. September, 1931.

"Der Grundgedanke der heutigen Ausführung ist: der Weg Zum Glück, Oder aus dem Leben—Für das Leben." Prague, 1932.

SELECTED BIBLIOGRAPHY

Beneš, Eduard. *Masaryk's Path and Legacy*. Funeral oration. Orbis. Prague, 1937.

———. "The Political Activity and Philosophy of T. G. Masaryk." Czechoslovak Foreign Office. English translation (mimeographed) from the Czech published in Prague, 1935.

Brentano, Franz. *Versuch über die Erkenntnis*. Der Philosophischen Bibliothek. Band 194. Felix Meiner. Leipzig, 1925.

Čapek, Karel. *Masaryk on Thought and Life, Conversations with Karel Čapek*. Translated from the Czech by M. and R. Weatherall. Macmillan Co. New York, 1938.

———. *President Masaryk Tells His Story*. Allen and Unwin, Ltd. London, 1934.

———. "T. G. Masaryk, A Modern Type of Universalism," *Central European Observer*, VIII. Prague, 1930.

Ehrenfels, Christian von. *Die Religion der Zukunft*. J. G. Calve'sche Universität-Buchhandlung. Prag, 1929.

Eisenmann, Louis. *Un Grand Européen, Édouard Beneš*. Paul Hartmann, ed. 11 Rue Cujas. Paris, 1934.

Eubank, E. E. "T. G. Masaryk: Sociologist," *Social Forces* (March, 1938), pp. 455-462.

Flint, Robert. *Philosophy as Scientia Scientiarum and a History of Classifications of the Sciences*. William Blackwood and Sons. Edinburgh and London, 1904.

Fournier-Fabre, Émile. *La Vie et L'Oeuvre Politique et Sociale de M. Thomas Garrigue Masaryk*. G. Ficker. Paris, 1927.

Herben, Jan. *Thomas G. Masaryk.* Translated by Elsie Havlasa. Czechoslovak Foreign Office. Prague, 1919.

Herben, Jan; Hartl, Antonín; Bláha, I. A. *T. G. Masaryk: sa Vie, sa Politique, sa Philosophie.* Orbis. Prague, 1923.

Horák, Jiří. "T. G. Masaryk und Die Russische Gedankenwelt," Sonderabdruck, *Prager Rundschau.* Prague, n.d.

Jakowenko, Boris, *Festschrift Th. G. Masaryk zum 80, Geburtstage, 7 März 1930.* Contributors include: E. Rádl, V. Škrach, J. L. Hromádka, J. B. Kozák, N. Losski, K. Krofta, Hans Driesch, I. Lapschin, J. L. Fischer, and a considerable number of others. Friedrich Cohen. Bonn, 1930.

Kozák, J. B. "Masaryk as Philosopher," *Slavonic Review.* London, March, 1930.

Kraus, Oskar. "Die Grundzüge der Welt-und-Lebensauschauung T. G. Masaryks," *Slavische Rundschau.* Jahrgang II, Nr. 3.

———. "T. G. Masaryk und Franz Brentano," *Die Drei Ringe,* Hefte 5, 7, 8. Prag, 1933.

Krofta, Kamil. "Der Geistige Führer Seiner Nation," *Prager Rundschau.* Jahrgang V, Heft I, 1935.

———. "Masaryk's Political Democracy." Czechoslovak Foreign Office. English translation (mimeographed) from the Czech published in Prague, 1935.

Lowrie, Donald. *Masaryk: Nation Builder.* Association Press. New York, 1930.

Ludwig, Emil. *Defender of Democracy, Masaryk of Czechoslovakia.* Robert M. McBride & Co. New York, 1936.

"Masaryk's Philosophy of Life," *Slavonic Review.* London, March, 1930.

Nejedlý, Zdenek. *T. G. Masaryk.* Melantrich. Praha, 1930.

New Europe, The. Periodical. London, 1916-1917.

Nosek, Vladimir. *The Spirit of Bohemia.* Allen and Unwin. London, 1926.

Pitter, Přemysl. *Chelčický, Tolstoi, Masaryk.* Deutschen Gesellschaft für sittliche Erziehung. English translation (mimeographed) from the Czech published in Prague, 1930. German trans. by R. Brandeis, Prague, 1931.

Bibliography

President Masaryk in Paris, Brussels, and London, October, 1923. Czechoslovak Foreign Office. Prague, 1924.

Šalda, F. X. *Masaryk: Staatsmann und Denker.* Symposium on Masaryk. Orbis. Prague, 1930.

Sarolea, Charles. "How Masaryk Converted the Anglo-Saxon World," *Central European Observer.* Prague, March 8, 1935.

———. *President Masaryk and the Spirit of Abraham Lincoln.* Orbis. Prague, 1921.

Seton-Watson, R. W. "President Masaryk," *Contemporary Review.* March, 1930.

Silberstein, I. "L. N. Tolstoy und T. G. Masaryk," *Slavische Rundschau.* Jahrgang VII, Nr. 3. 1935.

Škrach, V. *T. G. Masaryk.* A biographical résumé. Mimeographed.

Steed, H. Wickham. "Thomas Garrigue Masaryk: The Man and the Teacher," *Slavonic Review.* March, 1930.

———. *Through Thirty Years.* William Heinemann. London, 1924.

Stern, Evzen. *Le Socialisme de Masaryk.* L'Eglantine. Bruxelles, 1926.

Street, C. J. C. *President Masaryk.* Geoffrey Bles. London, 1930.

Sychrava, Lev. *T. G. Masaryk, 1850–1930.* Orbis. Prague, 1930.

Utitz, Emil. *Masaryk als Volkserzieher, 1850-1935.* Orbis. Prague, 1935.

Warren, W. P. "The Democratic Diplomacy of President Beneš." *Furman Bulletin,* XIX (April, 1937).

———. "Philosophical Genius and Social Living: T. G. Masaryk's Realistic Synergism," *Furman Bulletin,* January, 1936.

Werner, Arthur. *Th. G. Masaryk: Bild seines Lebens.* Roland Verlag Morawitz. Prague, 1934.

Index

A

Aehrenthal, 23
Aesthetics, mentioned, 115; special scientific status, 125, 127; place in human life, 179-188; history of, 185; source of knowledge, 185. See also Art.
Agram. See Zagreb.
America, democracy of, 32; reaction in, 48; mythology in, 237
American culture, highest, 28 n.; decadence in, 97-98; mentioned, 188; characterized, 234
Anthropomorphism, characteristic, 60; misconceptions of, 143-145; of Marxists, 145, 237; nebulous, 150; in conception of First Cause, 151; replaced by "myth," 155. See also Mythology, Feuerbach, and Comte.
Aristotle, Masaryk's teacher, 13, 68; *Organon* of, 113; mentioned, 120, 122, 157; cited, 153
Army, democratic, 49-50, 101
Art, complement of science, 76, 130-131; source of knowledge, 137, 185; values of, 182-188; and religion, 217
Atheism, accepted by Russians, 150; mythological, 155; humanism and, 210; untenable, 222
Athenaeum, 15
Aquinas, Thomas, 71, 224

Augustine, 156
Austria, annexation of, 2; referred to, 4, 20; chief historian in, 22
Austria-Hungary, decadence of, 18, 19, 20 ff., 23; Zagreb affair and, 20-22; Masaryk's objective for, 23, 83; Masaryk's conclusion on, 24-26, 28, 84; Palacký and, 82
Authority, democratic solution to, 39-40
Avenarius, 185

B

Bacon, Francis, as Masaryk's source, 14, 74; organizer of sciences, 122, 123; mentioned, 126
Bain, A., work of, 122; as source, 126, 131; successor of Hume, 165
"Battle of the Manuscripts," described, 15-16; cited, 105, 116, 174, 175
Beethoven, as true German, 98, 99 n.
Beneke, 201
Beneš, Eduard, quoted, 59, 102, 207, 238; relation to Masaryk, 86-87, 233
Bernoulli, 165, 166
Bismarck, 27, 98 n., 100 n.
Blaha, I. A., quoted, 2; on Masaryk as realist, 171-173

245

Bohemia, national philosophy of, 82-83; mentioned, 188; reformation in, 198; Germans in, 233. See also Czechoslovakia and Czech culture.
Bolshevism, explanation of, 81; anthropomorphic, 237
Bolzano, 224
Brentano, Franz, teacher of Masaryk, 13; Masaryk's relation to, 64-76, 118, 195, 224; axiologist, 176; on truth, 189
Brentano Gesellschaft, established by Masaryk, 65; mentioned, 67
Britain, national philosophy of, 19, 83; motive of, 27; as democracy, 44; reaction in, 48; wishful unpreparedness of, 237. See also English culture.
Bureaucracy, role in democracy, 55-57

C

Carlyle, 212
Carrère, confirms Masaryk's analysis, 96
Catholicism, objectivist, 71; has unified view, 93; liabilities of, 95-96, 213, 214
Chelčický, founder of Czech Brethren, 175, 198; foreshadowed Tolstoy, 220
Comenius, teaching philosophy to children, 55; Masaryk's guide, 73, 74; organizer of sciences, 122, 123; criticised, 123-124; realism of, 175; established modern education, 198; religious philosophy of, 220
Communism, versus democratic socialism, 54; early communism, 146 n.; anti-individualistic, 236
Compromise, place for, 206, 229-231
Comte, Auguste, religious view of, 10, 217; Masaryk's relation to, 13, 68, 69, 73, 74, 113, 114, 118, 168; mentioned, 94, 105, 127, 131; fetishism of, 96; conduces to militarism, 101; keynote of, 117-118; on system of sciences, 122, 124-125; appraisal of, 125-126, 151, 157-159; and mythology, 143-144, 145, 152; contra criticism, 139; cited, 154; atheism of, 155; surpassed, 163
Concrete logic, as integration of all sciences, 106-107, 108; value of, 108; advancement of, 123; relation to abstract logic, 133
Concretism, 231
Criticism, determinant of democracy, 37, 39; Feuerbach's, 98; Masaryk's, 136-137; artistic, 137-138, 184; of criticisms, 138; versus positivism, 138-139, 144; socialistic, 139, 140 ff.; issue of, 140, 177; urgency of, 149; rejected by Russians, 150; science dependent on, 157; epochal importance of, 159-160; as religious, 160, 162, 217; constructive, 167. See also epistemology.
Culture, philosophical problem of, 104, 111, 117, 119; system in, 107, 112; as problem of life, 111, 114; moral and spiritual, 173; Masaryk's philosophy of, 233-235. See also American culture, Czech culture, English culture, French culture, and German culture.
Curriculum Vitae, for Masaryk's doctorate, 5-13, 73, 191; for dozenture, 13
Czech Awakeners, referred to, 65; as sources, 81-84; cited, 173-174, 198
Czech Brethren, referred to, 65, 175; possibilities as, 176; cultural efforts of, 198
Czech culture, level of, 15, 198; loss of, 46; advancing of, 83; and realism, 173-176; Masaryk's influence on, 183

Index 247

Czech history, referred to, 16, 20; study of, 82; foremost era of, 82; cited on realism, 174-176; cited on humanity, 198-199, 206-207

Czech humanism, 70, 83, 198-199, 206-207

Czechoslovakia, annexation of, 2; bases of, 25, 28, 198; as democracy, 44; defence of, 45-46; origin of, 49

Czech question, The, a world issue, 20, 24, 31

Czech reformation, 146, 198

Czech University of Prague, 16, 105

D

Darwinism, philosophical issue, 11-12; influence on Nietzsche, 99 n., 100 n., 192; element in Marxism, 148; accepted in Russia, 150; conclusions from, 193

Decadence, as cultural problem, 94-102, 104, 180, 199; element in Marxism, 148; mentioned, 197

Demagogy, distinguished, 34, 34 n.; mythological, 37; combined with bureaucracy, 55-57; and compromise, 229

Democracy, as faith of all, 26; cited, 28; objective, 29; and morality, 32, 35, 41, 53; functionally scientific, 32, 35, 37-38; essentials of, 34-35, 36; paradoxical, 36, 41 ff.; as a philosophy, 39-41, 61, 157, 178, 226; leadership of, 41-42, 57-58; protection of, 43 ff.; military possibilities of, 47-50, 101; industrialism and, 50-55; and culture, 52, 55-58; and socialism, 52-55; logic of, 61

Descartes, mentioned, 105, 127; validated consciousness, 126; cited, 167

Determinism, mentioned, 69; Masaryk's and Brentano's, 70-71, 224

Dewey, John, comparison with, 109-110; close relation to, 119

Diplomacy, constructive, 3, 28, 233; not admitted to, 4; recent, 109

Dobrovský, Czech authority, 15 n.; "Awakener," 82; humanitarian, 198; efforts completed, 223

Dostoievski, formula of, 72, 221; mentioned, 76; Masaryk's relation to, 79-81; cited, 211; unpublished volume on, 120 n.

E

Education, in Austro-Bohemia and Moravia, 11; function of university, 16, 105; requisites in, 36, 233; essential of trusteeship, 41; issue for democracy, 55-58; Catholic, 95; in America, 234

Ehrenfels, Christian von, quoted, 63, 212-213; cited, 219

Emerson, 212

Empiricism, chaos of, 27; regard for, 68; *reductio ad absurdum*, 110; in critical realism, 172-173; as mode of life, 191-192

Engels, errors of, 140-148; negative and eclectic, 147-148

England. See Britain.

English culture, most humane, 28 n.; mentioned, 188

Epistemology, special status of, 124, 126, 127; basic to living, 139-140, 149; Russian lack of, 150; an achievement of, 159; relation to religion, 162-163; Masaryk's, 171. See also Criticism.

Essertier, Daniel, on Masaryk's "realism," 169-170

Ethics, and democracy, 39; Masaryk's and Brentano's, 69-70, 74; basis of, 70, 134, 193-199; philosophical status of, 75, 121, 131, 176-178; Tolstoy's, 78; and religion, 210-211, 219. See also Morality, and Humanism.

Evolutionism, 103, 201-202

F

Fechner, as source, 127; in aesthetics, 185
Feuerbach, and Kant, 27; materialism of, 81; critic of Prussianism, 98; Marxist source, 99 n.; influence on Russians, 102, 150; positivism of, 139; and anthropomorphism, 143-144, 154; humanism of, 144, 145, 155, 201
Fichte, 93
Flint, Robert, quoted, 126-127, 130, 131
Frame of reference. *See* System of reference.
France, national philosophy of, 19, 83; motive of, 27; democracy of, 32; mentioned, 188, 201; unpreparedness of, 237
French culture, decadence of, 94-97
Friedjung episode, 22
Funck-Brentano, 94
Functionalism. *See* Functional Realism.
Functional realism, Masaryk's, 88, 89, 109

G

Garborg, 93, 162
Gebauer, 15, 15 n.
Geisteswissenschaften, status of, 106, 126, 127-128; Engels' view of, 143
George of Podebrady, King, 13 n., 14
German culture, source of war, 26-28; decadence of, 98-102; characterized, 98, 234; true Germans, 98; expressionism preeminently German, 100; mentioned, 188
Germany, national philosophy of, 19, 82-83; mentioned, 25; responsibility of, 232; ultra-fairness to, 233
God, proof of, 71-72; essential of religion, 221, 223-224. *See also* Theism.
Goethe, mentioned, 76, 85, 101; Masaryk's relation to, 76-77, 183; contrasted with Dostoievski, 79; and German culture, 98 n.; cited, 161, 167, 185, 186, 187
Government, possibilities in, 33-35; and scientific philosophy, 41; ultimate determiners of, 42; and education, 58
Grillparzer, 186

H

Hapsburgs, 25, 28, 30, 176
Harms, 122
Hartmann, von, 154, 158
Havlíček, on politics, 19; as Czech Awakener, 82-84; accord with, 175; efforts completed, 223
Hegel, transcendental solipsism of, 27; influence of, 93, 150; as synthesis, 98 n.-99 n.; mentioned, 101, 190; and philosophy of history, 158
Herder, 201
Hierarchy, value of, 36, 128
Hilsner case, 83, 116
Historians, 227
Historical materialism, indefensible, 142, 145-146, 147
History, direction of, 31, 33, 238-239; philosophy of, 74, 121, 158; solidarity of, 110, 207, 227; science in, 121, 128; Engels' view of, 143; moral meaning of, 196-199, 206-207; religious meaning of, 212
Hitler, 2, 44, 48, 232
Hitlerism, 2, 27, 44, 45, 236
Horák, J., 79, 120 n.
Hromádka, Professor, 221
Humanism, Masaryk's and Brentano's, 70; element in Masaryk's philosophy, 168; varieties of,

Index

210; source of a mood, 217; cosmic, 219
Humanitarianism, 45
Humanitism, Masaryk's humanism, 70, 201
Humanity, scientific, 31; democratic, 35, 39; motive of modern philosophy, 38; spirit of, 54, 103, 192, 193, 204; effectiveness of, 196, 206, 239; basis of morals, 199; and nationalism, 208
Humboldt, 11
Hume, David, relation to, 13, 68-69, 70, 220; import of, 117, 140, 161, 163; mentioned, 127, 147; antidote for, 158, 162, 163, 164-167; and mythology, 144, 145, 159-160; Kant's failure to surmount, 164; and ethics, 194-195; religious view of, 217
Hungarian, 26, 30. *See also* Austria-Hungary.
Huss, John, as source, 14, 83; no economic explanation of, 146; realism of, 175; as reformer, 198, 220
Husserl, Edmund, Masaryk's influence on, 65-66 n.; Brentano's influence on, 76

I

Idealism, in America, 97, 98; German, 101; in Masaryk's philosophy, 168, 170; lack of, 232
Ideology, in human life, 2, 29, 31, 44, 103, 104, 108, 110, 147; analysis needed, 105; and Marxism, 142, 145, 148; mentioned, 237
Immortality, 221
Individualism, relation to nationalism and internationality, 52; and socialism, 53; meanings of, 53-55, 100 n., 103, 115, 201-202, 235, 236; implicated by scepticism, 89; and objectivity, 149

Individuality, direction of progress, 33; as principle, 38, 46, 53, 54, 236; basic resource, 42, 202, 236; of nations, 47, 52; and industrialism, 50-55; of workers, 53; vs. objectivity, 149; universal import of, 202; interdependence of, 231
Industrialism, and democracy, 50-53; attacked in America, 97
Internationalism, harmony with nationalism, 52, 208

J

Jakowenko, Boris, 81
James, William, cited, 201, 229
Jungmann, 82
Justice, vs. violence, 28; "arithmetic of love", 35, 226; motive of democracy, 38; travesty of, 83

K

Kant, Immanuel, rationalism of, 27, 201; mentioned, 32, 101, 127, 147; Masaryk's relation to, 73, 75, 113, 139, 168, 183; subjectivism of, 93, 98 n., 100 n., 115; Brentano's appraisal of, 68, 69; as true German, 98, 99 n.; historic status of, 139, 140, 158-164; and mythology, 143, 144-145, 154, 158; cited, 194; universalism of, 200, 202; religious view of, 217
Kierkegaard, 212
Kollár, 82, 83, 174-175, 223
Kozák, J. B., 112, 217, 218
Krasiński, 187
Kraus, Oskar, 65 n., 67-68, 69, 74, 118-119

L

Lagarde, 98, 99 n.
Lamprecht, confirms Masaryk's analysis, 100 n.

Laplace, 166
Lavater, 12. See also Physiognomy.
League of Nations, 1, 13 n., 49
Leibniz, mentioned, 71, 127; as true German, 98, 99 n.-100 n.; informed vision of, 152; religious interpreter of reality, 155, 224; and probability, 165-166; Masaryk's sympathy with, 171
Lessing, 11, 98, 201
Liberalism, element in Marxism, 148; Masaryk's, 235-236
Lincoln, 28, 33
Literature, complement of science, 76; primary key to human nature, 81, 137; Masaryk's range in, 183; interaction with life, 187-188. See also Art, and Poetry.
Logic, types of, 12, 64, 110, 111, 117, 119, 133, 190, 223; and democracy, 38; Masaryk's, 118, 119; philosophical status of, 124, 125, 127, 132, 133-134, 176, 177, 178 n.; and feeling, 185. See also Concrete Logic.
Ludwig, Emil, 1, 182, 223
Luther, 146, 214, 220

M

Marty, Anton, 67
Marx, Karl, Prussian influence on, 99 n.; anti-individualism of, 115; Masaryk's criticism of, 140-148; cited, 154; mechanistic morality of, 201
Marxism, cultural reaction, 102; elements of, 148; crisis in, 148; positive intent of, 148-149; anthropomorphism of, 237
Masaryk, Charlotte Garrigue, 65, 84-86, 195
Masaryk, Thomas G., statesman, 1, 3, 76, 236-238; death, 2, 132; motif, 3, 135; autobiography, 5-13; interests, 9-10, 11, 12, 13, 15, 75; teachers of, 13, 74 n.; summary of adult career, 13-14; supreme crisis of life, 24; historic achievements, 30-31, 227; writings, 83; philosopher of history, 109; systematic philosopher, 112-113; genius of, 118, 229; as artist, 184, 187-188; philosopher of religion, 212; sociologist, 234-235
Materialism, Masaryk's early study of, 12; undemocratic, 102; as mode of living, 192; untenable, 140-141, 222; accepted by Russians, 150. See also Historical Materialism.
Mathematics, as basic science, 109; Masaryk's discussion of, 131; and scepticism, 164-167
Meinong, 76
Metaphysics, and democracy, 39, 61; Brentano's, 74; and practicality, 75, 89-90, 135; as worldview, 92, 102, 107; and science, 107, 119; revolt from, 108; relation to ethics, 132, 177; philosophy as, 176, 178 n.; and art, 183; of expanding good, 221
Method of Masaryk, 229
Mickiewicz, 187
Militarism, Prussian, 27-28, 100-102; as problem of democracy, 42-50; and suicide, 99 ff.; defensive, not constructive, 233
Mill, J. S., Masaryk's relation to, 10, 13, 68; cited, 125, 201; mentioned, 127; on the sciences, 129, 139, 165; Marx's relation to, 141-142; on induction, 166
Modern philosophy, characterized, 38-39, 178; special issue of, 140, 162
Morality, highest stage of, 50; and metaphysics, 61; foundation of, 199; political, 203; relation to religion, 210-211, 219. See also Ethics, and Humanity.
Mottoes of Masaryk, 3, 13, 13 n., 14, 86, 191
Mutualism, mutualistic Europe, 1; mutualist culture, 42; democracy mutualistic, 34, 43

Mutuality, vs. dictatorships, 2; essential of democracy, 33; in liberty, 41; spiritual, 42; in culture, 47; basic for human relations, 233

Mythology, democracy's liability to, 58; metaphysical, 89; transcending of, 93, 158; leads to aberrations, 105; in all phases of living, 115, 236-237; of Czechs, Austrians, and Russians, 116; analyses of, 118, 150-157; historic relation to science, 120, 154; positive role of, 145, 167; function of imagination, 153-154; mentioned, 207, 220; authoritarian, 213. See also Anthropomorphism.

Mythopoiesis, versus scientific thought, 139, 155

N

Naše Doba, 83, 85

Nationalism, 52, 208

Nationalist philosophy of modern times, 19, 183-184

Nationality, Masaryk's early view of, 10 n.; a democratic trend, 33; sociological concept of, 83; philosophies of, 88; relation to internationality, 208; self-determination and, 228

National Socialism, German, mechanistic, 2; relation to Pan-Germanism, 98. See also German Culture and Pan-Germanism.

Nejedlý, Z., 65 n.-66 n.

Neurosis, as social malady, 80-81; symptom of disvalues, 104-130. See also Psychosis.

New Europe, 23-24, 26, 28, 31

Nietzsche, and Kant, 27; capricious individualism of, 53, 115; and Darwinism, 99 n., 100 n.; cited, 103, 193, 202; formula of, 192; hardness of, 201

P

Pacifism, limitations of, 43, 44-45, 231-232, 233; mentioned, 77; of Czech Brethren, 175. See also Peace.

Paderewski, 186-187

Palacký, Francis, on Austria, 4; Masaryk's relation to, 82, 84, 175; organizer of sciences, 122; cited, 198; efforts completed, 223

Pan-Germanism, antithesis of democracy, 26-28; in recent German culture, 45, 98-102; and French "decadence," 95

Parliamentarianism, 18-19, 34

Pascal, 127, 161, 220

Peace, makers of, 30; principles of, 46-47; mentioned, 49; Masaryk's approach to, 232. See also Pacifism.

Pessimism, cited, 103; human motive of, 181, 201-202

Philosophy, no purely theoretic matter, 16-17; national philosophies, 19; socio-personal function, 38-39, 103, 110-111; relation to science, 39, 119-121, 134; of history, 74, 121, 158; primary business of, 76, 105-107, 108, 121-122; as criticism, 138; primitive philosophy, 152. See also Modern Philosophy.

Physiognomy, Lavater's, 7, 8, 188

Plato, Masaryk's relation to, 4, 13, 55, 67, 68, 70, 73, 104-105, 168, 170, 224, 228; on government, 35; on equality and hierarchy, 36; individualism of, 41, 196; mentioned, 85, 122, 157; Comte's community with, 113-114; quasi-mythological, 154; example cited, 155; in aesthetics, 185; as politician, 187

Poetry, 183, 185, 186-188. See also Art, and Literature.

Poland, 2, 19, 82-83

Politics, crucial role of, 15, 19, 20, 31; Masaryk in, 17-18; extant nature, 18-19; "unpolitical politics," 19, 82; *sub specie aeternitatis*, 60-61, 218, 226; as philosophy, 75, 88, 121, 178; and suicides, 91; relation to science, 114, 134; and poetry, 186-188

Positivism, Masaryk's, 68, 151, 168; surrendered to fetishism, 96; mentioned, 101; cited, 103; Comte's, 118; untenable, 139-140; in Marxism, 141, 143-144, 148; humane motive of, 201-202; source of a mood, 217

Practicality, and philosophy, 89, 129, 179 n.; technical issue, 129-130

Pragmatism, Masaryk's, 88, 168; makeshift, 89; assailed in America, 97

Press, role in democracy, 37, 58-59

Probability, 164-167

Propaganda, Masaryk's principles of, 59

Protestantism, liabilities of, 93, 213-214; realistic, 96

Psychology, 12, 125-126

Psychosis, and suicide, 94; and militarism, 99-102

R

Rationalism, in Masaryk's philosophy, 104, 168; in critical realism, 172-173; modernistic, 213

Realism, political, 17-18, 19-20, 40-41, 48; Masaryk's philosophy as, 79, 168-172; dialectic, 167; summarized, 173; illustrated, 173-176; and values, 176 ff., 181; aesthetic, 185; moral, 200-202; religious, 216; as concretism, 231; mentioned, 232, 237. *See also* Functional Realism.

Reformation, motives of, 196, 220; in Bohemia, 198; carried on by Masaryk, 227

Religion, and philosophy, 61, 160-161, 211, 225; and science, 114, 131-132, 217; morals and ecclesiasticism, 116 n.; Marxism and, 142; values of, 161-162, 210 ff., 219-220, 226; of the future, 212 ff.; sociological question, 213; validation of, 214-215 n., 220-221; cultural realism in, 216-217; specific affirmations on, 218; as citizenship, 218, 224, 226; writings on, 220 n. *See also* Morality.

Revolution, problem of, 80; Russian revolutionism, 81; justified, 84; sources of, 94, 96, 104, 180, 228; World War as, 110; Great Revolution, 182

Romanticism, 95-97, 169, 170, 175

Rousseau, 32, 101

Ruskin, 212

Russell, Bertrand, 115, 115 n.-116 n.

Russia, culture of, 19, 84, 102, 188; mentioned, 75; Dostoievski as interpreter of, 79, 80-81; Masaryk and, 138-139, 149; philosophical analysis of, 149-150, 158

S

Šafařík, 82, 174

Scepticism, and metaphysics, 89; problem of, 93, 214, 215, 217, 221; surmounting of, 150-151, 158, 164-167; methodological importance, 159; Hume's, 159-160; and ethics, 193-194

Schelling, 150

Schiller, 98, 201

Schleiermacher, 215, 220

Schopenhauer, pessimism of, 92, 181; quasi-mythological, 154, 158; empiricist, 195; bitterness of, 201

Science, Masaryk's early interest in, 11, 13; democratic, 37; relation to philosophy, 39, 119-121, 134; and practicality, 75, 129-131; limits of, 93-94; mathematics basic, 109; issue of the

unity of, 110, 114, 122; meaning of, 116-117; Masaryk's system of, 127-132; Marx's and Engels' view of, 141-143; relation to religion, 155, 160-161, 162-163, 217; and poetry, 186-188; mentioned, 207
Serbia, 22, 23
Shakespeare, 85, 183, 184
Slavs, 94, 99 n.
Smetana, Augustin, 217
Smetana, Bedřich, 85
Smuts, Jan Christian, 1, 228-229
Socialism, relation to democracy, 52-55; Masaryk's, 54, 236; cited, 103, 201-202; reactionary, 115, 140 ff.
Sociology, Masaryk and, 13, 179 n.; deterministic, 70; as philosophy, 75, 121, 178, 234-235; science of effectiveness in living, 79, 134; of Funck-Brentano, 94; as abstract science, 128; of art, 180; *sub specie aeternitatis*, 218
Socrates, Masaryk compared with, 31, 64, 228; Socratic criticism, 159
Solipsism, 100 n., 220
Spencer, 127, 201, 217
States, distinguished from nations, 52; cosmic function of, 61
Steed, Wickham, 17 n.-18 n., 40, 232
Stirner, carried Kant to conclusion, 27; capricious individualism of, 53, 115
Stocks, J. L., 33, 34 n.
Stumpf, 76
Sub specie aeternitatis, standpoint of social wellbeing, 29, 60-61, 226; standpoint of religion, 218, 218 n.
Suicide, as social problem, 80, 90-94; function of perspective, 104, 180
Synergism, essential to social advance, 61; in Masaryk's philosophy, 171; religion as the sense of, 226

System of reference, Masaryk's, 113, 132

T

Teleology, accepted by Masaryk, 71; essential to best living, 72; evidence for, 222-223; as meaning of Theism, 224
Theism, mentioned, 69; in Masaryk's philosophy, 71-73, 168; contrasting forms of, 152, 155, 210; case for, 221-225; a social outlook, 226
Theocracy, as dictatorship, 34; non-progressive, 36; unscientific, 37; undemocratic, 39; of superman, 99 n.
Theology, vs. philosophy, 38; mentioned, 73; Pan-German, 98; relation to mythology, 120, 156-157, 160-161; as a science, 132, 215-216; Marxism and, 142; modern viewpoint in, 220
Tolstoy, Masaryk's relation to, 45, 77-78, 184; mentioned, 76; mystic altruist, 79, 200; and religion, 212; anteceded by four centuries, 220
Truth, 189-192
Turgenev, 205

U

United States, as democracy, 44
United States of Europe, 1, 25-26
Utilitarianism, influence on Masaryk, 70; makeshift, 89; cited, 103; motive of, 181, 201-202; ambiguous, 195

V

Values, realism and, 176 ff.; of art and enjoyment, 179-188; truth values, 189 ff.; moral, 192 ff., 210; religious, 210 ff., 219-220

Vasitch, 21-22
Versailles, 3, 29
Vitalism, 192-193

W

Wahrmund, Professor, 216
War, a function of perspective, 44, 94, 104, 180; not the worst evil, 46-47; relation to suicide, 91; modern, 101
Whitehead, A. N., 89, 109-110, 113-114
White Mountain, Battle of, 30, 111, 173

Wilson, Woodrow, 1
World War, supreme crisis of Masaryk's life, 24; meaning of, 26, 29-30, 110
Wundt, Wilhelm, Masaryk's relation to, 13, 127, 131; system builder, 112, 122

Z

Zagreb Trial, 20-22
Zilka, Professor, 221
Zimmerman, 13, 67, 73, 74
Žižka, 175, 176, 198
Zola, 96, 148

www.ingramcontent.com/pod-product-compliance
Lightning Source LLC
Chambersburg PA
CBHW021121300426
44113CB00006B/240